A Marriage in Startled Air

CRUX
THE GEORGIA SERIES IN LITERARY NONFICTION

A Marriage in Startled Air

a memoir

Patricia Foster

The University of Georgia Press
Athens

Published by the University of Georgia Press
Athens, Georgia 30602
www.ugapress.org

Designed by Melissa Buchanan
Set in Garamond Premier Pro
Printed and bound by Sheridan Books

The paper in this book meets the guidelines for permanence and durability of the Committee on Production Guidelines for Book Longevity of the Council on Library Resources.

Printed in the United States of America
26 27 28 29 30 P 5 4 3 2 1

EU Authorized Representative
Easy Access System Europe—Mustamäe tee 50, 10621 Tallinn, Estonia,
gpsr.requests@easproject.com

Library of Congress Control Number: 2026009834
ISBN: 9780820377025 (paperback: alk paper)
ISBN: 9780820377032 (ebook)
ISBN: 9780820377049 (PDF)

Contents

A Marriage in Startled Air

Prologue

LATE AT NIGHT WHEN I couldn't sleep, I opened the double garage doors at the back of the studio and stared into darkness, a smear of black, a glimmer of stars. Refried beans, chili peppers, and exhaust fumes flooded the alley that separated our studio from the small stucco bungalows crowding the streets just off Lincoln Boulevard. The year was 1980 in Los Angeles. Even after midnight I could hear the roar of cars, the screech of brakes, the warning scream of a siren, but tonight the sounds felt muted, elsewhere. I turned on music, closing my eyes before pulling myself up onto the trapeze we'd hung from the twenty-two-foot ceiling, the metal bar silvery blue in the dark, sharply cool, and sleek beneath my legs, the chain jangling, then firm in my hands. In the darkness, I swung in a slow, easy rhythm, swaying, my shoulders and head sweeping back, my legs swimming through air as David Bowie's "Ground Control to Major Tooooomm" floated around me, his voice so hypnotic I knew I too was "stepping . . . far above the world." In the steamy dark, I breathed easily, soothed from whatever troubled me as I swung out into the night, leaving the ordinary world behind.

I *was* far above the world.

At least the world I'd known for most of my life in small-town Alabama—my parents' world of financial security and safe sober choices, of pretty things and professional ambition, of a 1950s middle-class reality of marriage, mortgage, and children. I lived now with my boyfriend, David, in this warehouse-style garage attached to the back of a real estate company that faced Lincoln Boulevard, a street full of check-cashing joints, copy shops, adult bookstores, and fried chicken take-outs. David and I were artists and we called the garage—with no hint of irony—"the studio," though it was just a large skeletal room fitted with metal worktables on a concrete floor, the few amenities—a shower, a refrigerator, a hotplate—in an attached smaller room, carpeted and defined by a drafting table. In the large room, a ladder led up to our cramped sleeping loft. To complicate matters, we shared a tiny bathroom with a real estate company, a.k.a. the Money King and his wife.

I'd left the ordinary world when I moved into this studio, but I'd cracked that door three years earlier when I packed up my Alabama life and began an MFA in art at UCLA. Art, to my family, was admirable, but suspicious, a distracting detour from law and medicine and teaching. And yet art claimed me, changed me, led me to this studio with David.

Time to leave that capsule if you dare.

I closed my eyes, dipping my legs and pumping bare feet to swing higher, higher, ascending, up, up, the air cooler, almost clean, as I flew through empty space, back and forth, opening my eyes only to glimpse the shiny chains swallowed by a haze of darkness, the ceiling a smudge of grey. It had been hot and muggy all day and I wanted to get to that place, my place "far above the world," a place where I could be quiet and still. It was hard for me. My body soaked up tension and wore it deep inside, a grip of fear, iron clasps at my wrists, shackles binding my thoughts. When I heard a person's anger, I flinched, a tightening of the thigh, a sucking in of breath; if someone yelled, my brain clouded, began to throb. *Easy,* I thought, letting the night air fill my lungs, run its softness through my hair.

Easy. Easy. Easy.

Twenty minutes later, I climbed the ladder to the loft and sank down beside David on the blue futon. When I slipped under the sheet, he turned toward me, his body warm and heavy with sleep. Usually, he stayed up late, obsessively working on a project—painting, designing an ad, a brochure, cutting glass, always a halo of energy—but today he'd finished an installation for one of his Hollywood clients and surprised us both by crashing at 9 p.m. I snuggled in close.

LOVE CAN BEGIN ANYWHERE—the back seat of a car, the middle of a hike, in a cracked vinyl booth at the local pancake house—but it took root in my body the day we hung the trapeze. That morning, I gazed up at the high ceilings and said wistfully, "I've always wanted a trapeze. It would be like flying."

David brightened at the idea. Before I had a chance to really think about it—*to worry*—we were at the hardware store buying a thirty-six-inch stainless steel bar, lengths of chain, eye hooks, and grab bolts. "I can put it up this afternoon," he said. I don't remember him putting it up. What I remember is coming into the studio from an errand and there it was: in the hazy light from the open garage doors it hung sleek, almost luminous in all that empty space. I'd been eating a blueberry muffin and quickly wiped my sticky fingers on my shorts, placed both hands on the bar, and swung myself up. Thrilled, I hovered four feet over the concrete floor. "Push me," I said and felt the first swoosh of air. But with each swing there was a sharp, grating noise, as if huge metal teeth were scraping against each other. I climbed down immediately. "Whoa. That scares me."

David stared up at his handiwork. "Be back later."

He returned with lengths of sliced rubber from a bicycle tire. At his graphics table, he cut these into tiny strands, then placed our wobbly A-frame ladder beside the trapeze so that if he climbed to the top, he could reach the hooks. As I watched him ascend high into the air above our concrete floor, it reminded me of a man balancing on a narrow catwalk in a TV drama while the audience watched, mesmerized, their fear smothered by curiosity at a feat demanding skill and bravado. But this wasn't TV. This was crazy. Insane. Reckless. "Come *down*!" I begged. "You can't do this. We need two people. We need a sturdier ladder."

"Nonsense." Already he was fiddling with the tiny strips of rubber tubing.

"*Please*." I stared at his big feet planted solidly on the next to top rung. The ladder swayed sometimes when you touched it. I knew because we used this same ladder to climb six feet into the loft each night. "This is scaring me."

"Don't distract me." His voice resonated with certainty, the authority of a working-class guy from Massachusetts. When he decided to do something, he did it.

I gazed at a grayish red patch on the concrete where one of us had spilled paint last week, thinking *this is where he will fall*, then I walked quickly into the smaller, adjoining room and began cutting up broccoli and zucchini and red peppers for our supper. I couldn't bear to watch. I couldn't bear to see what might happen. Consequences. Disaster. My brain fretted, the shackles tightening as I heard creaks and sighs from the other room. Though furious at David for not listening to me, for being foolhardy and cocky, for giving *me* the shakes, as I sliced the veggies, my body felt intimately connected to his, my mind curving into a private space that wrapped around him as if I alone could protect him, keeping him whole while he balanced on the ladder, coiling the tiny rubber strips around the eye hooks and chains, determined to please me. I didn't question this assumption. When the water in the steamer began to boil, I heard the clatter of something hard hit the floor. "Dammit!" he yelled. I flinched, then relaxed. His voice. He was okay. When I stepped toward the door, light soaked the room, the trapeze shimmering. *I love you*, I thought.

ARE CERTAIN MOMENTS PRESCIENT? Did I know that protection and desire, risk and fear, art and play would be the bonds that bound us together? Was this transaction somehow mystically sealed: *I'll try to protect him, and he'll try to give me joy?* For a long time, I didn't think of myself as someone who could keep another person safe, as someone a lover might endanger himself to please, as someone who could climb past the ordinary world and fly. But for a small moment, a sliver of time, I wanted that. To slip free into an unknown world.

As David wrapped the hooks in rubber, removing the squeak from the trapeze's chain, I had no idea of the deeper reasons why he might need protection, and I doubt he understood how much I needed joy. We *sensed* each other more than *knew* each other, having talked mostly about art and philosophy, religion, and movies rather than family history and childhood trauma, arguing about the merits of Vito Acconci and Emmet Gowan, Brueghel and Christo and Joseph Beuys, instead of sibling rivalry and alcoholism, physical abuse and foster care.

"DONE!" DAVID CALLED FROM the other room. I heard the clang of the ladder closing, the scrape of it as he dragged it across the floor to its station as makeshift stairs to the loft.

I turned off the vegetables and rushed into the big room where David had opened both garage doors so that the trapeze glittered in the hard afternoon light. *A thing of beauty*. He'd also pushed the two worktables to the side and swept the floor clean with the big push broom.

"Climb up."

I swung myself up, nudged off each shoe, wiggling my toes, and tightened my grip. "Give me a push." I felt the clean, even pressure of his hands on my back, the low soothing hum of the street, the swish of the chains. And then I was swinging through the air, deliriously happy, racing toward the rest of my life, a sensation of both gaining and relinquishing control.

IN MARCH 2012, THIRTY-TWO years later, we're sitting in a treatment room in the General Surgery Department of the University of Iowa Hospitals and Clinics in Iowa City, Iowa, a pathology report resting in our laps, a drone of words we can't understand.

I gaze at the white walls, hear the zing of an elevator, and try to swallow the metallic taste in my mouth. As if I've become a split-self,

I see my younger self in the small room of the studio, slicing up zucchini while David slowly climbs an unsteady ladder to fix the trapeze, little whorls of dust flying from the heels of his shoes as he lifts each foot, the ladder swaying, then steadying as he moves higher and higher into the danger zone, into thin, dusky light.

I close my eyes.

David's hand tightens on my thigh as the surgeon says, "Eccrine porocarcinoma, cancer of the sweat glands. . . . It's very rare."

I open my eyes, turning to him.

This time I have to look.

WHAT I WANT TO tell you is the story of a marriage, the story of my husband and me, two people acutely aware of our fragile selves but bound to each other and our creative lives. With the diagnosis of David's cancer, the life we once lived is over. That is, as we go through the scary, unpredictable process of illness and recovery, what's been hidden and masked in us will emerge, deepening and complicating our marriage and opening the door to David's buried past in Worcester, Massachusetts. Here, we will discover a place of violence and startled air, a place of secrets and trauma, abandonment, and pain, but also a place of revelation and insight that will awaken us to a new world.

PART I

The Hidden World

2012

Chapter 1

IT'S BARELY NOON BUT David and I lie in our double bed, holding hands. We've been home from the hospital for thirty minutes. "I think I'm feeling one of every emotion," David says, staring at the ceiling, his expression both quizzical and surprised. "They're all inside me at the same time." Because we're nervous, we burst out laughing and turn to each other.

"Ah, Master of Omniscience," I say.

"I mean, I never felt like I had an expiration date."

"2040," I say, keeping my voice light. "Mine's 2041. I'm giving myself an extra year."

"2013," he says.

"Don't say that." We're no longer laughing, the world suddenly unblinking as I lean my head closer to his. We're fully clothed and sprawled across our bed, the covers pushed to the bottom, bunched against our feet. "Listen, we just don't *know* enough. We'll meet with the oncological surgeon next week, then do research and try to figure this out," I say, as if cancer is logical, as if it has manners and will act with civility, "Please" and "Thank you" and "So sorry, I can't stay long," though I too am terrified.

I pull the covers up over us, then squeeze David's hand, wishing we could sleep. Beside me, David is quiet, his eyes wide open.

"2040," I repeat, my voice barely a whisper. "We'll be old."

WHY COULDN'T WE GET the ordinary? I fret as I wander aimlessly around our neighborhood late in the afternoon, cutting through a neighbor's backyard, watching a cat lick its paws in an open doorway. Because I don't know what to do with myself for days after David's diagnosis, I stare into the windows of houses on College Street, hoping to capture familiar moments of other people's lives: people sitting at their desks, drinking coffee, hunched over their computers, couples eating together, laughing, talking, or ignoring each other. Occasionally, I see a man and a woman in their kitchen, one drifting back and forth, talking, the other stationary, perhaps slicing onions or scraping carrots, the peels mounting in that tumbled pile on the cutting board. Always, I wonder how they met and if they're happy. Do they secretly question whether they've found the right partner, someone to love and desire and trust? Does she silently study her partner, waking early in the morning and watching him sleep, his face half-buried in the pillow, one pale hand splayed across the sheet? Does he notice the way she purses her lips and shifts slightly, not quite pleased with what she sees in the mirror? What about those very first moments of desire, the beginning of everything: the flushed heat of pleasure, the apprehensions, the delusions, the foolish expectations?

The beginning.

Always back to the beginning.

David and I first made love on two striped beach towels on the floor of my Westwood apartment near UCLA. We could have made love on the bare floor, on cinder blocks, on gravel, on grass, our feet laced up in mountain boots, but those two towels had been my bed for several months after I hurt my back carrying video equipment to and from the Art Department. I remember the look and smell of those towels thirty-six years later: pink and blue and white striped, faded from frequent washings, the kind of towels I took to the beach every summer as a kid when my brother, sister, and I rushed into the Gulf of Mexico, then wrapped them around our wet shoulders as we trudged behind my mother to the car.

I remember the towels.

And yet the first time David called to ask me out—I'd met him casually at the Rose Café three months earlier to look at studio space—I couldn't remember a single detail about him, as if he'd been wiped clean from my memory. No face. No smile. No freckles. No thicket of brown hair. No body image. On the phone, he said his name and that we'd met before. His voice was low, nasal, with something teasing behind it. He wanted me to go out to a jazz club in Malibu.

"Tonight," he said.

I glanced at the clock. It was past 2:00. Though I couldn't remember who he was, I felt insulted to be called so late on a Friday afternoon. I'd give him three minutes, then hang up.

"Really, we *have* met," he continued, sensing my uncertainty. "Met *twice*, in fact. First at the Rose Café"—his voice softened—"and then I saw you at the Fox Venice Theater, well, I guess, a couple of months ago, but you had a . . . later date."

In an instant, he was real: dark hair, pale blue eyes, a man thick-shouldered but slight. He was the guy I thought of as split in two: first so quiet and still and shy at the Rose Café and later at the Fox Venice Theater high-spirited and ironic.

"So, I was thinking we might—"

"Can't," I said. "Gotta finish my video on penance. Sadly, sorrowfully, sickly, I'm stuck on self-abasement. There's a bunch of flagellation I've got planned for tonight."

He laughed so easily, so spontaneously, I smiled. I heard happiness in his voice. And surprise. "Well, all right then," he said. "But you know . . . degradation"—he laughed—"I'm fully prepped there."

My body relaxed as if fresh air had blown into the room. And with no obligation now between us, we talked easily, flirting, interrupting each other with jokes, making hash out of penance, which really was the focus of my video project at UCLA.

We agreed to go out the following night, a Saturday.

GOING OUT FELT LIKE an escapade, an escape. Why not? We talked easily, bantering and arguing about art and politics, agreeing not to agree about anything, but often buzzed about the same artists—Joseph Cornell and Dwayne Michaels, the early Robert Motherwell, Emmet Gowan, Dubuffet, Klee—and dead sick of Claus Oldenburg and Andy Warhol and all the minimalist painters. One night we drove up to Malibu to listen to a new jazz band; another day we loaded art supplies—Roplex and paint and dyes—into my hatchback from a store somewhere in the ugly, tangled streets of Culver City. We got lost in the hills near Ventura, the air thick and grainy with mist and smog. And then, well, then we slept together on my beach towels and began to make art together and became entwined in a way that thrilled and confused me because we were both engaged in the art of disappearance.

David was disappearing from the working-class slums of Worcester, Massachusetts, from an abusive, alcoholic household and economic ruin, all contributing to an inner turbulence that slowed his ascension to a place of security and professional independence. I didn't know that then; to me everything about him suggested boldness and risk, the ability to act on intuition, to make quick decisions and live on the edge. I was disappearing from a small Alabama town and a wobbly self that vacillated between rebellion from my family's demand for success and acquiescence to its terms. I bounced between career subversion and an earnest pursuit of professional goals, between loyalty and resistance, sacrifice and demand. Los Angeles, of course, had always thrived as an escape hatch, a make-yourself-up kind of place, transient and theatrical and commercial, a place where you tossed your past away to jump-start a future. And yet sometimes, very late at night, it was hard for me to feel the ground beneath my feet, to listen to the dry swish of palms, to hear the heartbeat of happiness.

What was love anyway?

Was it a sinking deep into vulnerability and not drowning?

Was it a war of wills?

Was it a search for tenderness, a quiet attentiveness, or a voracious, hungry exchange?

Was it even possible?

WHAT SEEMS ODD TO me now is that David and I met at a time when neither of us wanted a relationship. If "timing is all," as common wisdom attests, then we should have been doomed. Eight months before we met, David had moved to Los Angeles from Santa Cruz with his partner of six years. He'd left what he considered an ideal life of good friends, a start-up graphics company, and temperate weather to be part of the noisy, crowded, animal buzz of L.A. It was his girlfriend who'd wanted to come to "make money," hoping they could do design work for a new magazine called *Wet*, a magazine of gourmet bathing (the idea of special oils and soaps and slippery tubs made me laugh) where she had friends on the editorial masthead. Though he'd resisted at first, once pushed, David liked reinventing himself, was hardwired to think on his feet, to wake up with a swirl of ideas spinning in his head. He liked to scramble for attention and was exceptionally good at it, never seeming to crash-land or falter, always able—even if it meant staying up all night—to meet a deadline. "The L.A. magic worked for about three months," he told me later, but after the first issue of *Wet*, instead of the two of them blazing a new economic path, "big breaks in the big city," his girlfriend left him for another designer. Since the contacts at the magazine had all been hers, David had to find a place to live and work. Fast.

I imagine him walking to the ocean near Venice Beach, not even bothering to take off his shoes, but moving doggedly toward the water's edge, staring sullenly into the glare of the sun while sand filled the inside of his heels, seeping into his socks and rubbing against his ankles as he wondered what in hell he'd do. He'd loved her. He still loved her. He couldn't quite believe any of it: how he'd been dumped, how he was here in this stupid city without a car (he'd let her have it, hoping...), here without friends except for those of his ex-girlfriend. For two nights, he stayed with an artist he'd briefly met, and then serendipitously bumped into a designer he'd known years before in Santa Cruz, a man who designed and built leaded glass windows and doors for L.A. clients. For a month, David put away his graphic design tools, helped the man with his commissions, and slept in the designer's studio until he had enough money for his own.

It was George, a.k.a. the Money King (our future landlord), who rescued him. One afternoon, the Money King came into the glass studio and asked David to design and build a glass trophy case. When the case was finished, the Money King liked it so much, he offered David the "garage" (our studio) behind his real estate office as a place to live. "Used to warehouse boxes of bed sheets. Now, it can house you."

As for me, I'd just had a ridiculous, obsessive affair with a moody, ambitious painter at UCLA, a man separated—but not yet divorced—from a wife, who still lived in Pennsylvania. Though our initial connection was electric (see me as a dizzy, heart-strung teenager), after three months I began to wake up in his studio in downtown L.A., the windows papered over with dull, beige butcher's block, most of his paintings turned so that they exposed only the frame, the floor damp and cold, the water in the shower always lukewarm, and wonder *what in hell am I doing here?* The painter would either be engrossed in his painting, three half-empty cups of coffee on the floor beside him, or off to teach a class. I'd get my things together to leave for my classes, but when I stepped into those dirty, downtown streets, I felt not happiness but desperate loneliness. What was I doing here in L.A.? In this man's studio? In his bed? It was a relief to head into the snarl of freeway traffic. The next month I quit answering his calls, pausing when I heard the phone ring, then getting busy myself.

I think now that David and I might have pursued our individual disappearing acts if we hadn't surprised each other by using art as a way of flirting and showing off, a competitive daring to see who could trump the other in silliness, outrageousness, or pure, snarky perversion. We began with hood-ornament art. *Very* L.A. As we drove the freeway and the surface streets of Westwood and Brentwood, we scoffed as we passed Mercedes and Alfa Romeros, Rolls Royces and occasional Bentleys, the hood ornament always a brand announcement. "3:00," I'd say. "Two Mercedes." They were parked side by side, gleaming in their moneyed brightness. "Noon. Maserati." One Saturday I found a cha-cha-cha statue at a flea market that seemed to perfectly mock the Flying Lady atop a Rolls Royce. I grabbed it, wrote a poem to tuck between the statue's arms, and left it on the hood of David's secondhand Volvo. *There*. The next day he altered the statue, adding a plastic halo and a rhinestone cross, remnants of his Catholic school education, then rewrote the poem, making it an absurdist dadaist tract, and left it on the hood of my three-year-old Honda. I made red polka-dot bikini pants, bent the halo into a flip-up hat, added doll sunglasses, hung voodoo beads from the cross, and X-ed out the entire poem in red lipstick. *Bam!* Back on his car in the dead of night. It was all about overnight transformation, anything to surprise the other. We took photographs of ourselves, decorated and desecrated them, made them campy and crude, used them as placemats, left them beneath the other's pillow, folded them up in the coffee filters, in the pocket of a bathrobe, called them "Lagniappe" and "False Dialectic" and "Trash Happy" and "Odalisque" and "Medusa Girl" or whatever struck our fancy. It revved up the energy, kept us both on edge, waiting . . . what would the other do? How can I best him?

Art. In many ways it was art that had begun to change me, grabbing me by the collar and turning my head fast in a new direction. In my past, only success and professional certainty had been applauded, with ambition tied to credentials and public praise and financial rewards. "Make more A+'s," my father used to say, smiling at us as he signed our report cards. "Do something important and get your picture in the paper." But the UCLA Art Department in the late 1970s was a place where no one applauded certainty, where pain and perplexity were "in," where doubt and chaos reigned as queen and king. One of my MFA professors, Chris Burden, shot himself in the arm to explore the nature of self-inflicted pain, insatiably obsessed after being operated on without anesthesia as a teenager following a motor-scooter crash. Vito Acconci lay under the floor of the museum and masturbated while art patrons walked around the museum emptied of all paintings and sculpture, drinking wine, eating cheese, and gossiping, his way of ironizing the fickle world of art. My photography professor produced a "Painted Women" series: hand-colored black-and-white photographs of women in corsets and camisoles, their bodies exposed, their faces moody and lyrical, sometimes imperial or sad or frightened. The point, I began to understand, was to grab hold of your obsessions—even your flaws and failures—and let them take you for a ride. You didn't direct them; they directed you. Here, no one gave a hoot about my family's demand for success. Or at least not success defined in traditional terms, achieved in predictable ways using familiar tools, made for middle-class consumption. Here, it was much better to be outrageous, to fail gloriously, as the Romantics had insisted, to think in terms of paradox and contradiction, to gaze closely at the hidden, untold story tucked in the shadows.

By the time I met David I'd already begun to strip away my Southern restraint, had begun to push myself into making art that was autobiographical, conceptual, defiant, driven as much by a search for identity as a pursuit of aesthetics. Art, I understood, was no longer just about beauty. It demanded thinking.

BECAUSE DAVID AND I spent so much time making art or making love or driving to art shows or to get supplies, we seldom spent loose time together, down time, moments where unease or sadness or anxiety might grab hold, where the weight of worry could fester and thicken the air. Maybe that was why I began to wonder as I left the art studio at UCLA and drove to meet David if he ever felt the deep melancholy I associated with my own life, the life beneath the skin. To me, it was the thing you had to keep in touch with to be alone. Covertly, I began to watch him, waiting as if for a signal, a lapse. One day as we were driving to Malibu on a sudden lark to see how the ocean looked in late afternoon, to watch the gulls soaring above the cliffs and the gradual shift of evening light, I glanced at his face in the quiet car and knew instantly that everything I'd seen before had been protection, camouflage, survival. In that one moment his face—without seeming to really change—looked exposed, shattered, his eyes deepening, his skin flushing, then darkening as if charged by some hard memory, some feeling that had washed up onto the periphery of the windshield in a tiny spot that only he could see. He didn't move a muscle. He sped up a little. Then he turned to me and as quickly, his face looked normal, familiar, curious. He smiled.

But now I knew.

Many years later, I'd realize that rather than sadness, what David felt was a deep anguish, a rage so buried it was almost impenetrable, his feelings stuffed and shoved like odd bits of memory into some hidden vortex of the self, perhaps the inevitable reality of adults who've been abused and punished and silenced in childhood. But I didn't know this back then. I didn't know about his multiple moves in foster care as a young child, about his stepfather's beatings and his mother's denials, about the embarrassment of poverty and alcoholism, of cheap clothes and bad housing. I didn't know about his skipping school, his obsession with art, his lighting fires in the kitchen sink. The revelation of this repressed life would eventually erupt not in sadness but in an exhale of suicidal thoughts, a "black dog" of melancholy that surprised us both in our fifties.

I never thought of myself as sad, and yet I wore sorrow like an inner skin, something I lived with, a hidden resource of feeling like the lining of a coat. *It was always there.* I remembered walking as a girl down a narrow, paved stretch of road in Magnolia Springs, Alabama, the huge oaks sheltering the street, their heavy branches like arms embracing while thin streams of light shivered through the leaves. It was mesmerizing, beautiful. I could walk down that road in complete silence, idling toward the banks of the slow-moving river. Walking I felt more alone, more complete, more stripped of self than at any other time. And sometimes, sadder.

And yet what I reveled in with David during our early courtship wasn't sadness or sorrow. It was play. Whimsical, impulsive, theatrical, joyous play.

For me, it was a drug.

Did I want more? Was it possible to feel so visible there was no need to disappear? Or was disappearance so intuitive to me it would always be a part of my life?

I didn't know.

Chapter 2

WHAT WILL NOT DISAPPEAR is that nest of malignant cells, which began—as so many things do—with something small and benign and embarrassing. Because David is rarely sick and seldom sees a doctor, he approaches the body with nonchalance, a predictable blandness. *Mind-on-a-stick*, I call him, as if the body is a snarky interloper to his mental desires. Unlike me, he's been blessed with good health, a resilient immune system, a robust biology.

Until the cyst.

That stupid cyst.

That goddamned cyst.

IN OCTOBER 2011, AN internist suggested outpatient surgery for what he diagnosed as a pilonidal cyst, a creepy knot of hair and skin that had been growing for the past few months high on David's left buttocks. Hating a fuss, David put it off. We'd just returned from Australia, where I'd taught for two weeks in Melbourne and Wollongong, and now he had work to do, photographs to take, websites to design, while I was insanely busy teaching MFA students at the University of Iowa. And yet by February, the cyst's growth had dangerously thickened, becoming so embarrassing David had no choice but to infantilize it, calling it "my tail," as if it were a vestigial remnant, harmless and comic.

"Bumped into your tail last night," I said as I poured water into the kettle for tea one February morning. We were in the kitchen, in our pajamas and still sleepy, going through our morning routine. "You turned over and it rubbed against my hip." I got out my favorite cup.

"You leave my tail alone."

"But it's getting hard." Concern rose in my voice.

David gave me a mock-lascivious look. "Hey, don't try to sexualize my tail." And then he poured coffee beans into the machine and brewed an espresso.

I rolled my eyes, keeping the uneasiness at bay. Nothing to worry about.

But we worried. A few days later, David lay on the examining table at the Family Care Center at the University of Iowa Clinics while a doctor with close-cropped white hair and stooped shoulders put on blue plastic gloves. He pulled them on slowly, almost ritualistically, and I wanted to say, *Hurry up!* because David looked anxious lying on his stomach, his pants around his knees, his buttocks exposed. I stared. The cyst was huge. How had that happened? I couldn't take my eyes away: it was a hard round mass the color of bruised fruit. It didn't look like a tail at all. It looked like a mangled peach embedded in his skin.

"It may be only a sebaceous cyst," the doctor said as he massaged the lump. "Probably filled with a thick fluid that will look like toothpaste. You will need a surgeon to remove it."

I was barely listening. I stared at my husband's worried face, his pale blue eyes holding mine. And at that moment I felt as deeply married to him as in the heat of feverish sex.

TO OUR RELIEF, THE surgery went much better than expected: Dr. P, the general surgeon, removed the entire cyst (it was so large, he feared it would require two surgeries and a three to six-month healing) and sewed up the incision. *"Loosely,"* he emphasized to me in the conference room. I thought of basting threads, those long, even, white stitches that had held together the bodice of my wedding dress—an elegant sheath—for a first fitting. At the dressmaker's, I'd lifted my arms carefully as she pulled it over my head. Temporary. Fragile. That's the way I thought of David's wound: skin lightly basted together, a provisional closing. *Don't take a deep breath.*

That evening, as David slept in the recliner in his study, empty pudding cartons and popsicle wrappers cluttering the little table beside him, I gazed out the window at the fir trees flocked with new snow, the flakes soft and heavy in the wind. I felt both relieved and incredibly tired, a mental fatigue, a dismal flatness I couldn't seem to shake. We'd been up since 4:30 a.m., the surgery at 7:00. All afternoon, David had been irritable and in pain, wanting things instantly and simultaneously wanting to be left alone.

"Don't!" he kept saying. "Don't touch me! Don't try to help me," when I put my hand under his arm as he tried to get out of the recliner.

I pulled away, hurt and confused.

Now I understand that such irritability is often the aftermath of surgery and what I experienced was a caretaker's exhaustion—the vigilance of doing service and being available at all hours—but that afternoon my skin flashed hot with anger, then cooled to sympathy and concern. The evening might have settled into an easier recovery if I hadn't checked my email. For two days I'd ignored my students' work at the university, but while David slept, I went through a pile of messages, only to be crushed by the final email: only one MFA student had chosen me to direct her thesis. My heart paused, then beat like a fist. Always, I'd had four, sometimes five students out of twelve asking me to direct, and though I dutifully complained about the work, I expected the validation. Now I got a Diet Coke from the fridge, a stack of crackers. Fortified, I read the email again, as if I'd misunderstood, my breath quickening. But there it was in black and white.

Absurdly, I became a wounded animal pawing deeper underground. *The Eating Yourself Place*, David and I called it. A quick hit of self-loathing that could degenerate into bad behavior. *You dumbass fucker.* It was the way I'd begun to talk to myself in the last year, as if by growing older, I was empowered to bully myself. I *knew* exhaustion fueled my insecurity, *knew* this was not a catastrophe, merely the ebb and flow of teaching, and yet I wanted to be soothed, to be told, "Oh, honey, don't worry. It's okay. You're a terrific teacher." But the one person who reassured me was lying upstairs in a recliner on pain meds, eight hours out of surgery. I ate another cracker as I stared into the snow's glittering darkness, then stepped onto the deck, shivering in the cold, anxious, dismayed.

AN HOUR LATER I opened David's study door and watched him sleep, his reclining body wrapped in a soft red blanket, a pillow clutched in his lap, his mouth slightly open. 8:00 p.m. He rarely slept more than two hours even with Vicodin, so I decided to wake him at 10:00. He'd asked me earlier to watch Jon Stewart with him.

At 10:00 I climbed the stairs: I just needed to *tell* about the "one" student, to relieve the pressure, to force the anxious words into someone else's brain, gain sympathy, and move on. When I opened the door, David was still asleep, his head slumped onto his shoulder, hands dangling, his earphones plugged into the TV, some show moving toward its denouement. *Let him sleep. He's really tired.* I turned away. Then turned back. I wanted company. I *needed* him. Just for a little while. Just to . . . "David," I called softly. I didn't want to startle him. When he didn't move, I called again. Nothing. *Go back downstairs,* I told myself, turning toward the door, only to feel a sudden squeeze of shame. Very lightly, I touched his arm.

To my surprise, he jerked awake, eyes flashing alarm, his breathing fast and shallow, his body lurching painfully sideways, a move that made him groan. He yanked off his earphones, grimacing. "Why did you *do* that? What's *wrong* with you?" Cold fury throbbed in his voice.

The force of his anger startled me. Though I'd seen it once or twice, it would be another two years before we discovered David had undiagnosed PTSD. Tonight, I had no clue.

"Oh, I'm sorry. I didn't mean—" Because what I was doing?

"Sorry," I tried again. "Jon Stewart," I said lamely. "You said you wanted me to watch Jon Stewart with you." Now I was back in the world of patient and caretaker. A sweep of guilt pushed against my anxiety. He was sick. I was being childish. "Go back to sleep," I said, leaving quickly, going downstairs.

I tried to concentrate on the reading I had to do for my graduate class even as resentment blurred the pages. *What was happening to me?* It seemed as if my life had turned into a dead end, a sick husband, a flailing career, my own health plagued by persistent sinus infections and mysterious fatigue. For the past ten years, my career had been dominant, the financial backbone of our lives, but lately I felt defeated and tired, an emotional emptiness, my spirit as insensate as a numbed limb. Some nights I had to drink three Diet Cokes just to critique papers. Some nights even that wasn't enough. I'd begun to dread the morning flurry of emails, the constant request for recommendations and extra conferences, for updated CVs and grant deadlines, the scholarship files and faculty evaluations. Now I sat at the table, the book folded in my lap, my eyes closed.

AT 11:30 P.M., WHEN I climbed the stairs to check on David, I was surprised to find him awake, sitting on the sofa instead of the recliner. I hoped he had calmed down. I hoped I could too.

"Do you want to watch Jon Stewart?" he asked. His voice sounded strained. Dark circles rimmed his eyes.

"Sure." I tried to be casual. I didn't look at him. I peeled away the last tiny twist of a fingernail. Though I felt hurt, I knew I couldn't explain what had happened and my current vulnerability. I sat in the recliner, waiting.

"Don't ever wake me up that way," David said in a querulous voice.

My face flushed with heat. I should have remembered this was the aftermath of surgery, remembered how often he said, *You are my everything!*, calling me his *Real Gong Girl* (because of my workshop at the

University of Wollongong in Australia), how each night he fondly, ritualistically rubbed my feet, wanting to soothe me. But I didn't. "You had a severe startle response," I said, then showed him how he'd glared at me, eyes bugged, teeth barred, my own face a contortion of fury. Just making that face, my own resentment unfolded: he could be difficult; we could be difficult together—our moods mercurial, our desires thwarted, our authority frittered away. His scolding pricked my vanity, thwarting my good sense. "After you're better, we've got to straighten things out," I continued, using my own fretful voice. "We can't keep acting this way, being angry with each other." Even as I spoke, I sensed my bad timing. I was waving a red flag, implying a larger problem—the way most arguments start.

Between us there was the slightest pause. And in that pause a sudden ugly pressure swept the room, a ripple of fear swimming in the air as it often does before dishes are thrown, insults hurled, tears shed. I could feel it, that dip in my stomach, a visceral collision.

"Don't You Dare Threaten Me," David shouted, his face sweaty and flushed. "Don't you *dare* do something so dismissive at a time like this." Despite his wound, he sprang to his feet and stood, towering above me, his face glowering, so angry it frightened me. It was a face I hadn't seen in years, the face of a cornered man. "Don't you *ever* do it," he hissed. *"Do you hear? Do you hear?"*

I shrank back, startled, though anger curled inside me too. "I'm only talking about us *talking*." I didn't know what had happened, what we were doing. My brain felt slow, confused. Did David think I was threatening him, threatening to betray him, to leave him, to make him vulnerable while he was sick? No! No! That seemed so utterly absurd, I couldn't grasp it, didn't know how to say this is crazy, we're being crazy.

Now I know that being sick and helpless stirs up old nightmares, awakens buried traumas. Much later, I'll understand the psychological horror beneath David's startle response—the abandonment and physical abuse he suffered as a child, the beatings, the bullying, the sharp pain of his stepfather's boot on his hand to make him cry—but sitting in the recliner that night I felt only stupid and stunned as I remembered the doctor's words, *"loosely stitched."* I saw skin ripped, thread yanked, a gaping hole exposing a red, raw wound.

"Please," I began.

But David stomped into our bedroom and slammed the door, the sound shuddering throughout the house. Now I sat alone in the darkness, staring at the snow-laden trees, mere shadows against the windows. I felt shattered and weak and ridiculous. There was absolute silence. Stillness. I didn't feel like me. Whatever was me had vanished. The one good result of the surgery—the large incision could be sewn up—we may have destroyed in ten hours. *What had I done? What had we done?* Only now was I deeply frightened, frightened by my own anger and the insecurity that had fueled it, frightened by how quickly our anger had escalated, by what damage we might have caused, frightened by how little control either of us seemed to have.

Once downstairs, I didn't know what do to until I glanced at the cabinet above the refrigerator. Cognac. Because I'm slightly allergic to liquor, I never drink, but tonight I opened the cabinet, grabbed the bottle of Courvoisier and took two long, thirsty swallows, longing to be drunk, deliriously drunk, so drunk I could unmake the world I inhabited.

I didn't understand my husband.

I didn't understand my students.

I didn't understand myself.

I took another long swallow. As the cognac loosened the tension, I began to cry.

THAT NIGHT I REALIZED—AS I had at other difficult times—that David and I could destroy each other, that our deep insecurities could erode our affection and trust, exaggerating our differences, making us into miserable, mean-spirited rivals. *We are not these people*, or not *only* these people. We were in the *Eating Yourself Place.*

Our marriage was in that place. I didn't know how we'd gotten here, how the stress and disappointments of the last year (David's insomnia and work demands, my sinus infections and writing worries) had loosened us from each other, but I knew that our patience and compassion were being tested by illness, by the difficulties of growing older. We were the baby boom generation, and we never expected to grow old, to feel so diminished and dependent and still need to make a living. "Jesus, get your calm on," David and I used to joke when we'd see someone freaking out at the mall. But there was no calm inside me. I took another big sip of cognac, staring out into the darkness. It was all fucked up.

I DON'T KNOW HOW long I sat there. I knew I'd been foolish, my behavior motivated by defeat and doubt. When I walked upstairs, I quietly opened the door to our bedroom, the glow from the streetlights illuminating the end of the bed where David lay on his back with his earbuds in, his eyes closed. Thank goodness. He seemed okay, though I couldn't see his wound. When I came around to his side, he opened his eyes, his gaze guarded, apprehensive.

We looked at each other in silence. When I touched the sheet, he took out an earbud.

"I'm sorry," I said, leaning over him. "I'm so sorry. This isn't a good way to end our night. I don't want you to hurt more. I want you to get well." I sat at the end of the bed. Not close. We weren't ready to be close. I felt awful: repugnant, distant, hurt. And yet we began to talk, not about the argument, but about small things: what he'd said to the nurses about the TV show "House," how funny he'd looked in the presurgical plastic cap, how I'd forgotten to ask Dr. P about the details of the cyst. I even smiled. And then I remembered I had his wedding ring in an envelope in my purse.

"Bring it to me," he said softly. "And bring some lotion so I can put it back on."

When I returned, I smoothed Clinique on his ring finger, touching it gently, easing the lotion across the knuckle, caressing his skin, then watched as he slipped on the ring. A reprieve.

His face relaxed.

I bent slowly and kissed his hand.

TWO WEEKS LATER, A nurse came into the treatment room where we sat under bright, institutional lights. I barely noticed her, marveling at how—after that awful night—David and I had begun patching up what had pulled us so far apart. As if something vital had snapped and required a slow, gentle mending, each night I tried to carefully dress his wound, warming my hands in hot water before I touched his skin, then removing the tape and gauze slowly, asking how he felt, where he hurt; once the new bandage was in place, we sat close on the white couch—*couch time*, we called it—the blinds pulled, the lights dim. We held hands and talked about our day.

Now I watched him: he sat awkwardly in the seat, hunched and uncomfortable, his dark jacket hiked up on one side, his gray pants sagging. At times like this I swear I can feel his skin breathe, can hear the tick of his thoughts. I know the exact swirl of cowlicks at the crown of his head, the way his hair windmills to the right even when he's facing me. I know he's wearing blue underwear, the one superstition he affirms. I know he's worried and sweating and mentally distancing himself from this room, this clinic, this hospital. His neurons are flashing angles, lines, shadows . . . *click*, the dry green hardness of a cabinet door . . . *click*, the wrinkled dent of a magazine cover . . . *click*, the curved thickness of a passing shoe. He's an artist and thinks in images, puns, the juxtaposition of ideas.

He glanced at me. The stitches held. The wound healed. We were lucky.

"Will Dr. P be here?" David asked, hoping the surgeon would keep up a light banter, telling us the statistics of this monster cyst—its size and shape and color. To tease him, we'd planned to ask for the "cyst in a jar" to put on the counter. We needed to make it irreverent, a farce now that it was over and done with.

"Dr. P's in surgery," the nurse said, "so I'll be removing your stitches." This nurse seemed remote, even bored, perfunctorily taking off the bandage in one clean motion. "You're healing well," she said, then clipped the stitches with surgical scissors.

I flashed David the victory sign as she placed a small gauze pad over the scar attached by a single piece of tape. "You can pull your pants up now." She hadn't yet smiled.

Well, that's that. I picked up my purse from the floor, ready to leave. Maybe we'd drive out Rapid Creek Road, gazing at the black oaks and sugar maples, watching how the winter snow had melted except for pockets lingering on the shadow sides of barns, the air smelling of tree root and dirt.

"I guess I'm not going to know what was in it, what it was," David said, his voice light.

The nurse, her back to us, was writing in David's chart on the computer. Now she turned and stared at him for the first time, her gaze flat, impersonal. "Well, in fact, we just got the pathologist report. It was cancer."

A frozen stillness. I didn't move. David hands were clenched in his lap.

"What do you mean?" he asked.

"It was a malignant tumor," she said and handed him the pathology report.

I moved to the chair beside David, and we both stared at the single sheet of paper as if it was written in Mandarin or Urdu, languages we couldn't possibly understand. Somewhere outside I heard the rolling of a cart. It squeaked, then stopped, then started again, a distant clacking, as I leaned in closer, trying to read.

Chapter 3

IN ONE OF DAVID'S paintings, two blindfolded mannequins draped in white gauze stand at the doorway to a bedroom. Their noses, lips, and ears look deeply human, their bald heads perfectly sculpted. Inside the room, a curtain lifts in the breeze as light floods the floor, but the blindfolded mannequins are paused, frozen in place, not yet able to move. Each time I look at this painting, I feel both intimacy and unease, a sense of anticipation and foreboding. *Something will happen.*

A week after we get the pathology report I think of these fragile-looking mannequins and the luminous room a few steps away as I stare at the patients in the oncology waiting room, their bald heads warmed by knit caps and woolen scarves, their bodies paused. For the first time, it occurs to me that the figures in the painting might not be mannequins at all.

Beside me, David fills out forms: *Current Medical History, Family Health History*. I'm so distracted by my thoughts I'm not paying much attention as David finishes the first one, but when he pulls up the second, a list of relatives in a single column, I glance at it, curious, focused.

Mother
Father
Mother's Mother
Mother's Father
Father's Mother
Father's Father
Sister(s)
Brother(s)

It's a standard list followed by a column that defines them as living (L), deceased (D), unknown (U), then a line for their medical conditions (premature heart disease, diabetes, TB, mellitus, stroke, cancer of any type, prostate, breast, ovarian, etc.).

I watch as David marks "D" after Mother, Mother's Father, and Brother. For all the other family members he marks "U."

I'm both surprised and not surprised at what he doesn't know, what I don't know. David has never known his father, neither the man nor the name, and thus, one-half of his genetic inheritance is missing. The rest is not just hidden away but murky, slippery, secretive. He has no idea about his own childhood diseases, his family's illnesses, or the cause of their deaths. He knows nothing about their eloquence or strong emotions, their ecstatic or ruined moments. Did they have high blood pressure, Alzheimer's, celiac disease? Did they dance in the moonlight or cry shamelessly at sentimental movies or hit the morphine button in a hospital bed? And yet today, for the first time, it occurs to me that what he doesn't know—his biological heredity—might hurt him.

"Didn't your mother have diabetes?" I ask.

"I think so." David yawns and marks that column.

"What did she die of?"

He shakes his head. She's been dead for twelve years.

I knew by age four that I'd been born with erythroblastosis, a word I loved to perform for adults, certain of getting attention, knew by age ten that my family was prone to allergies and heart disease and that our Irish forebears, particularly the men, had a "weakness" for booze. In adulthood, I knew that my father's mother died of a heart attack, my father's father of peritonitis, my mother's mother of a stroke, and my mother's father of a heart attack. I knew at what age and in what city they had died.

David barely looks at the unmarked form, but I can't quit staring. Blank. Blank. Blank. Blank. Blank. An unknown history. True, we often call ourselves "the orphans," a playful term of self-creation, as if we can toss literal inheritance to the wind and will ourselves into being, but today, I wonder about reality, about the blindfolds we've been wearing. David's past has always felt tucked away, smudged in darkness. Instead of the typical happy or anguished childhood memories, he created a cover story, abridged and simplified, a sort of benign traffic jam. "Born in an obscure village, raised in another obscure village," he'd quip at parties. But even to me, his history barely fills several Post-it notes on the fridge. While I watch patients rise as they're called and disappear with a nurse behind the closed door, I think about what I know: David was born in Worcester, Massachusetts, in 1948 to an Italian American mother and put in foster care sometime after he turned three. He lived in foster care in Sturbridge, Massachusetts, for several years—"a nice place," he always said, "with lots of places to roam"—then returned to live with his mother and stepfather in Worcester in 1955. I know he hated his alcoholic stepfather, a brawny ex-marine construction worker, know his mother was often depressed and he had to take care of his two younger half-brothers.

One afternoon, talking about our childhoods and what we did in the summers, David told me, "When I was nine, after I'd been back with my mother and stepfather for a year, I went one day to play with other kids at the public fountain blocks from my house." Here, he plunged in, water spilling across his shoulders, cascading down his back onto his skinny thighs as he darted in and out of the crashing jets with the other boys, slapping sprays of water at each other, jumping and shouting and turning like dervishes. He said he loved it, loved the rolling, shrieking, crashing delight of play, loved sitting breathless in a tight ball beneath the spray, loved the swallowing and spitting of cold water. "I loved it so much I forgot about time and stayed longer than the two hours my mother allowed." When he got home, she was ironing her husband's shirts, her eyes squinty, her thick hair pinned back, cigarette smoke in the air. "You see the time," she said, her face a raw scowl. "You *stayed* too long. You . . . you coulda been *hurt*. Somebody coulda snatched you or run you down with their car . . ." She grabbed his arm. "We were just playing, and I didn't—" he wanted to explain how he'd met a new friend, a boy who laughed and scrunched up his face before he sprinted back into the spurting water, but before he could get out the words, his mother smacked him on the head with a clothes hanger, then slashed it across his face, stinging his cheeks, his ears, welting his lips.

I remember being stunned. How could I tell him about walking with a gang of girls to the neighborhood pool every day, diving and swimming and chasing each other in the cool, chlorinated water, then coming home to dry off on the patio and eat ice cream sandwiches my mother brought from the kitchen?

As I watch David complete the form, I think: How can I know so little and so much about you? How can both things be true? The you I know is sometimes so vague you're like an inked letter left out in the rain, blurred and indecipherable, and other times so clear and crisp, you're like a hair caught under a microscope.

Later, I'll realize that a child shuttled into foster care, into a troubled home—especially an inventive, imaginative child—might learn to divulge as little as possible, finding excitement and solace outside the family where nothing need be revealed, where what isn't known need not dissuade. To not know, to repress, can also be an act of agency. Or, at least, survival.

One night as David and I were watching *Olive Kitteridge* on Netflix, David put the TV on pause in the heart of the story after the son told his parents he wouldn't be coming back to Maine. "After I left for San Francisco," he said into the silence, "I forgot all about my family."

"Really?" I was stunned. The room was dark, his face muted by shadows. "You didn't think about them at all?"

"Nope." He shrugged.

"God, I was the opposite." As much as I sometimes wanted to forget my family, they were always there, just beneath my skin. "Did you think about anyone back in Massachusetts, or was it simply wiped out?"

"Aunt Adeline," he said quickly, and then his gaze flicked back to the screen. "I always remembered her." His foster mother, the woman he called "aunt" to make her familial rather than institutional.

So, there was deep attachment and maybe love. I glanced at the TV, the image blurred, though I could see Olive Kitteridge's face, her eyes narrowed, her face contorted, furious and simultaneously horrified. I loved Olive Kitteridge.

"When I was a kid in foster care," David continued, "I had a hiding place where I could sneak behind the wall in the bathroom linen closet in Aunt Adeline's house."

"Behind the wall?" I was curious. "How is that possible?"

David described a raw, unfinished space between the shelves and the tub and how once he'd climbed over the tangle of plumbing pipes there was just enough room to squeeze in and hide. "No one knew where I was, though I was right in the center of the house, two doors down from the kitchen. I'd hear Aunt Adeline calling me, '*Da-vid, Da-vid.*'" He gazed at the blurry screen, then down at his lap. "I could hide there for thirty minutes. My secret."

In my mind, I could see him, a skinny, freckled five-year-old crouched on a square no bigger than a pizza box, his bony legs still, his mind flickering in the dim light. Maybe he silently prayed for a water pistol, a flamboyant red one to surprise Buzzy, the neighbor kid with the superior flat top, hoping to ambush him in the woods. Maybe he just listened to the hum of the pipes. Regardless, he was hidden away. In the heart of the house.

"I could hear Aunt Adeline calling me, but she never found my secret place. I guess she didn't know about hiding."

"Or maybe she had her own secret place, and you never found hers," I teased.

"Some people don't need to hide."

Everybody hides, I wanted to say. *Count on it!* Instead, I said, "I bet Aunt Adeline was worried . . . I mean, how scary can it be when you can't find your kid. Olive Kitteridge would have gotten it out of you, made you confess."

"I always came out," David said, as if that resolved everything.

NOW I STARE INTO the small treatment rooms as we follow the nurse down the hallway and think: *Mysteries. Secrets. Uncertainties. Hiding.* This too is the conceit of cancer.

Chapter 4

WHEN THE SURGEON ARRIVES, a tall, masterful-looking man with a shaved, sculpted head and a crisp, lavender shirt and dark tie beneath his white coat, I'm caught off-guard: he could be a CEO in a TV series, a lawyer in a board room, a principal coming to caution us. For a moment, I feel small, outclassed, but this is merely my shameless ego. *Get a grip!* I force myself to sit up straighter, to look purposeful while the surgeon focuses intently on David, who, to my surprise, slumps in his seat, the front of his shirt straining against his stomach, a fold of pale skin pushing against two buttons. For the first time I notice that David's wearing his Merrill slip-on shoes with dark socks, the shoes he wears around the house, but never to work, and as suddenly I feel ashamed, as if he's not playing the game, not putting his best self forward, not getting us a good grade, as if this is a formal test with winners and losers.

"I'm Dr. M," the surgeon says, his voice confident, kind. "Your oncological surgeon."

While Dr. M examines David, occasionally asking him questions, my husband—who usually charms doctors and nurses with his easy wit—is monosyllabic. "This kind of cancer," he says when referring to the tumor, and I realize he doesn't know the name of the disease, that while I've been prepping, he's been repressing, unknowing as much as possible, trying to push the cancer out the door. "*Get lost.*" After the formal examination, Dr. M explains the surgery in laymen's terms: "You have a tumor. In two weeks, we're going to excise the margins of the tumor, stain the tissue, and biopsy the sentinel lymph nodes."

For a moment we say nothing, silenced by those spoken words. The doctor looks directly at me, a probing, assessing gaze, and I ask our prepared questions: the length of the surgery, the possible complications of David's sleep apnea for anesthesiology, the pathology report. "And will we know the subtype—infiltrative, pushing, or pagetoid?" I ask, trying to show off. As we talk, David's face looks ashen, his eyes thick with fatigue. He didn't get a shower.

"Do you have anything *you* want to ask?" Dr. M turns to David. But David only stares at the floor, his head down like one of the wasted old men in the waiting room.

"He's frightened," I say impulsively. "He didn't sleep last night.

The doctor, who sits on a stool with rollers, scoots right up to David, so close their legs are almost touching, and to my surprise, he puts both hands on David's knees. "I know you're frightened and that's understandable. You have cancer. Many of my patients are going to die because they have inoperable cancer of the liver or the pancreas, but your cancer is operable. Do you understand?"

In that moment, David becomes his devoted patient. (So much so that three months later, at a future visit, David, with the darkest sense of humor, will draw a hangman's noose on the doctor's blackboard to test his thoroughness. "Let's just see if he notices." And of course, they'll both laugh at the prank.)

IT IS BARELY NOON and we're sitting at our kitchen table. "I'm sorry," David says as if this cancer is his fault.

"Never say that." I take his hand, knowing too well the shame and guilt of illness, as if you're responsible for your trickster body. "You didn't do anything wrong. You'll have surgery, *that's all*." But I also worry. I don't believe in miracle cures, in the power of persuasion, or even putting an optimistic spin on things. What I believe is that I can keep David safe. At least until the surgery, I can push aside the abyss, stand sentinel at the door, and usher him into a clean, well-lighted room, even if that room will be an operating theater. The doctors will do their part—the intricate part—but behind them there will be me, watching and waiting, a vigilant watchdog.

Only later will I understand it's how I perceive safety that is part of the problem. All week I've been edgy and tired and slightly distracted, as if there's a cobwebby substance spread over my psyche that inhibits all my conflicting emotions. All I seem able to do is worry about mundane things: I must find a futon sofa for David to lie on in his study after the surgery (this concern will prove a humorous testament to my naiveté), must buy pajamas for the hospital (ditto!), and must decide what to do with my class the day of his surgery (a substitute, of course, but who will have read this particular Sebald?). Safety, in my mind, means preparedness, as if we're getting ready for an assault: eating healthy foods, walking every day, protecting David's newly healed wound after the first surgery, getting plenty of sleep, doing research. And yet sitting across from him, all I feel is fatigue. I want only to sleep for twelve hours . . . for an entire weekend. To sleep and dream myself into a better place. Then, I can start to worry in earnest. Then, I'll have more energy and will know which sofa to buy.

Chapter 5

SPRING BECKONS: THE SURPRISE of sunny skies and unusually warm temperatures, the ground still bare but the trees less frail, less solemn. It's mid-March 2012. In other years it would be a time of optimism and whimsy, of cracking open the windows for a night breeze, but now it's two weeks before David's scheduled surgery. We're past the freak-out, how-could-this-happen-to-us stage and tossed into a vague, waiting limbo. Nothing and everything matters. We're putting one foot in front of the other, just like the cliché of dreaded expectations.

Until, well, the arrival of the flies. They're noisy black flies that dip and swirl, circling our kitchen, buzzing from the refrigerator to the lamp to the table in a manic frenzy before zeroing in on a salad plate, a curtain, the rim of a glass. I've never seen flies so big, so furry, as if they're not flies at all but miniature airborne cats.

One night I'm at my desk, reading a grad student's thesis, trying to concentrate though I'm sleepy and still have scholarship files to review. I yawn just as a fly swoops past my head and lands on the white window blinds above my desk, restlessly flitting about before settling in like a landlord inspecting the premises. I watch as the fly does its vibratory dance on that tiny patch of real estate, the fourteenth blind up (I count), near the braided ladder cords. Of course, I'm distracted. I'm easily distracted these days (bring on the flies!), but eventually, I get the flyswatter, an old, tattered thing that lies between the stove and the dishwasher, often tossed haphazardly onto the floor. With one quick swat, I kill the fly and feel such pleasure in doing so I close my eyes. *There!*

It's not until the next night that I tell David about the flies. When I arrive home from the university at 9:30 p.m. after teaching my graduate class, I rush to the upstairs bathroom to pee and call out to David who's in his studio working, his door open. I'm talking loudly, telling him about the class discussion on literary artifice, how artifice can distance the reader because of that subtle line between stylishness and intimacy and "blah, blah, blah," I say. As if I've signaled them, the flies begin circling, two, no three, whizzing full speed across the room, flying right at me stranded on the toilet, then back to the mirror to the door to the window, chasing each other in some strategic game of tag. I scream.

"What?" David calls.

"Com'ere. Please. *Hurry.*"

By now, I've pulled up my pants and I'm standing by the window, watching the air show when David appears. "*Look* at them." They're doing zigzag flights across the room, practice races with pure, raw energy, the kind I no longer have.

"I'll get them," he says matter-of-factly. "Go out and close the door."

I nod, happy to do just that. Once in the hall, I hold my breath, the same way I did at age twenty-five when Max von Sydow was trapped in Linda Blair's bedroom with the demon. Ridiculous!

"Got'um," he says, holding the flyswatter and smiling at me. He reaches out to touch me.

"Wash your hands," I say, though this sounds annoying.

He snorts. "I *did.*" And then he pulls me to him, the flyswatter still in his right hand. As I put my arms around his neck, I try to ignore the flyswatter, though in my mind I still see it: the webbed red plastic, warped and smudged with fly viscera and dust and tangled strands of hair, and the slightly bent handle, sticky from lying by the stove on the kitchen floor. We never replace things like this, keeping the same disheveled brooms and mops and flyswatters for years. I don't know why. Finally relaxing, I close my eyes and lean into him, relieved to feel him, the bulk of him, even if we're both fully clothed.

That night as I lie in bed, drowsily pulling up the sheets while

David stands at the foot of our bed saying good night, a fly zooms nonchalantly past as if on reconnaissance. I sit up. "Jesus, I can't believe it!" But, in truth, I think we have flies because last week we ceremoniously cooked a leg of lamb and accidentally smoked up the downstairs, then flung open the front and back doors to create a cross-breeze. At least, there are no bats!

"NOTICE ANYTHING DIFFERENT?" DAVID asks the next morning while he's standing at the counter, fixing coffee. I glance around the kitchen, noting that the sink is clear of dishes, my red tea kettle sparkling on the stove, the coffee made. I keep turning around. There are no new pictures on the fridge, nothing written on the white board where we sometimes leave our coded messages: *A Real Gong Girl* is still there along with *Call Plumber* and *Dentist* with a cheesy drawing of clenched teeth. No secret messages. No sexual innuendos. Because I'm not a morning person and need two hours of blah-time and plenty of tea to wake up, I shake my head.

He points to the flyswatter. "See, I put it on a hook."

I laugh. "Brilliant." There it is. "Our flyswatter's been given a legitimate home."

ODDLY, DURING THE NEXT week, the flies cease to be a surprise. Now they're just an annoyance. I can talk on the phone to my ninety-year-old mother while tracking a fly, waiting until the exact moment it lands, then *whack*! There's even a feeling of pride when I kill three in one morning in my study, flushing them down the toilet and getting on with it, finishing up a critique, Save, Exit, *whack*!, got one in the doorway.

On Wednesday we're due back at the university hospital, a sprawling cityscape of wings and floors and alphabetically designated elevators. We've been told that after surgery, David's wound site will be too large to close in the traditional way and will require plastic surgery. To me, plastic surgery is as enigmatic as the moon: distant and unknowable, something I associate with facelifts and breast implants and cosmetic enhancements rather than cancer surgery.

After we're shown into one of those functional, anonymous exam rooms, the surgeon, Dr. C, arrives in scrubs and a navy blue operating cap decorated with red Chinese letters, beneath which his Asian face is elegant, his dark eyes focused. We try to be alert and cheerful because we don't know how to behave. We want to say, *Do the best for us. We're nice people. We're important,* though in so many ways we know we aren't. When Dr. C, who speaks quietly and with formal manners, asks my husband to tell him about the progression of his cancer, David immediately digresses, making associative remarks about watching *House* on TV, joking that maybe his cancer is a Trojan horse, some sneaky trick that only fictional doctors like House can solve. He's nervous and this banter is his way of loosening up and calming down—a style that works well with the nurses—but Dr. C looks puzzled, then impatient. Seeing this, I pick up the thread, telling him what I know about this rare cancer as if I am an expert instead of a neophyte. When Dr. C begins directing his questions to me, I watch David's body change: he straightens in the chair, his face tightening, his smile fading. "Have the lymph nodes in the groin been checked?" Dr. C asks me, but at that moment, David leans toward him, his face directly in the doctor's line of sight, his body language saying, *I am the patient.* Surprised by this physical intervention, Dr. C nods and begins talking to my husband. I sit back, relieved.

Once the exam begins, I watch as if my task is to monitor Dr. C while he monitors David: he studies the wound site—lightly tracing his hands across my husband's left upper buttocks—as if it's a structural problem (I'll understand later that, of course, it is), then uses a miniature metal ruler and plastic marker to draw a precise, very symmetrical design—two arrowheads joined by a thin connecting line. It's as if he's an engineer drawing a dam, but instead of water, it is blood flow he must balance and preserve.

"WELL, THAT SUCKED," DAVID mutters as we're leaving the hospital, emerging into a bright sunny day, both of us tired, dropped into dead space, unnerved by the unknown. I'm starving. I could eat two almond croissants or four chicken tacos. And yet once at home, I need distraction more than food, so I head to my study with a book to critique for tomorrow night's class. David goes upstairs for a nap. An hour later, as I stand in the kitchen making a cup of tea, I watch two flies flirting above the sink like casual visitors, here for a little while—"Just hanging... and then we'll be off." No bother. I kill them routinely. Swat! Swat! And then I place the flyswatter back on its hook, a little bubble of pride I cede to my husband. All afternoon I stay at my desk reading, but as evening comes, I turn from my book to stare into my backyard, remembering Dr. C bending over David, drawing that intricate design on his butt for a procedure I don't understand. Not a skin graph but a perforator-plus flap, something that requires microsurgery, which means cutting and shifting, actually "rotating" the existing skin, and reconnecting the tiniest of blood vessels, the width of a hair. I gaze out the window where the katsura tree is a dark silhouette, a burst of black branches with knobby buds drawn against the night.

THAT NIGHT I'M CIRCLING a critique of the book I'll be teaching—writing questions, then scratching them out—going around and around like those flies. Because it was unusually hot today, an anomaly at this time of year in Iowa, we turned on the AC, as if it was early May instead of March when there's usually a wreckage of dirty snow. When I go into the bathroom next to my study, I do the radar gaze for flies—nothing—then look quickly in the mirror at the gray streak in my bangs. *Where did that come from*? I'm leaning into the mirror to study myself closer—*ah, you little virtuoso of worry, look what you've done!*—when a strange, musty odor wafts through the floor vent beneath the window. It's a small rectangular vent but the lever is oddly bent, refusing to close so I quickly cover it with a folded towel because I'm hyperallergic to mold, so sensitive I often have to take prednisone. *No more, no more, I can't take anymore*, I think even though I'm not the one who will have my body cut open, the one who may have a difficult recovery. I'm merely getting gray hair. Still, I need to tell David: he'll know how to close the twisted vent and make it right so that I'll be well enough to keep him safe.

In twenty minutes, he calmly takes off the cover and forces the vent closed. "There," he says, smiling. "Done," and then he turns off the AC. "For tonight."

THE NEXT MORNING THE house is quiet, filled with the magic of morning, a faint yellow light to the sky, the twitter of finches on the porch. I like this time alone. Before I sit at my desk to finish the scholarship files, I open my study door and step outside to smell the air, to see the leaves beginning to unfurl on the lilac trees and the knobby shoots of new ferns. I wish I could stay here, prolong the moment, resist the day, but reluctantly I go back inside. David's been staying up late for the last few nights, squeamish about his impending surgery and worried about being unable to work during the recovery. We don't quite know what recovery will mean, though both doctors have said he can't return to work for six weeks. He's semiretired and works only freelance, but he's always been an artist with diverse projects of his own. For the last year he's been obsessed with photography and digital imaging, and when I kissed him before bed last night, he was downloading new photographs.

At 10:30 a.m., I'm reviewing another group of applicants when David comes downstairs dressed in what, after the first surgery, we call "the comfys"—black, baggy pants with elasticized waists and big, loose shirts. His hair is mussed, his glasses off. He's fixing coffee and saying something about last night, how he should have left me a note.

I'm not paying much attention. I'm trying to rename a file and save it, partially distracted by the realization that I'll have to work faster in order to get my review in by midday. "What do you mean?" I ask, not looking up.

"About last night," he says. "I was sitting at my desk when it dawned on me what that smell was."

"That smell from the vent in my bathroom, that moldy smell?"

Holding his cup of coffee, David comes to the door of my study. "Yeah, the smell couldn't have been *in* the vent. It had to be in the crawl space."

I turn to look at him. His eyes are squinty, almost glazed, as if he's still half-asleep. He looks the way I look when I've had an allergy attack, but he has my attention now if only because I feel dread when I think about the crawl space, a raw dirt area reached through a half-door in the basement, a place where I can only imagine snakes hibernate and mice—even rats—congregate with impunity in winter.

"So, at 2:00 a.m. I went into the crawl space and had a look around." He yawns as if distracted. "I didn't get to bed until almost 5:00 . . . that's why I'm still sleepy."

"Wait. You went—?" I'm trying to understand. I shift in my seat, facing him as he takes another sip of his coffee.

"I'm trying to *tell* you. I went down into the crawl space and poked around. The stench was unbearable. I knew I was right. I had to find it."

"You went down . . ."

"Yeah, I did, and behind some of the insulation, there was this decomposing carcass that must have been a raccoon, really gross, this—"

Now he has my full attention. I've forgotten all about the files I'm supposed to critique, about the peace of early morning, about deadlines and the second cup of tea I've been craving. "You did *what*?"

"I'm telling you, I put the carcass in a trash bag and took it outside, and then—" he smiles "—I took a long shower. I just let the water run over me. Thirty minutes. I mean it was that bad. A maggoty old raccoon." He looks at me now like the kid who's found the last, difficult puzzle piece hidden between the sofa and the rug. "And thus, the flies . . . because there are two small openings in the crawl space door, I had to cover up with duct tape."

Now I'm standing up, but for a moment I can't speak. I'd like to say I'm thoughtful and curious, that I understand the urgency he felt, that I know he did this for me, that he wanted to rid our house of that terrible smell, to keep whatever was musty away from his allergic wife, to make me healthier, happier, and pleased with what he's done. Instead, I'm furious, a fury like a gust of madness, a turning, twisting anger crawling all over my body because David's gone down into the darkness . . . but it's the wrong darkness. It's all wrong. "Are you *crazy*?" I say, my face flushed. "You're a man about to have surgery for a malignant tumor and at 2:00 a.m. you decide to go into the crawl space alone and search for a dead animal. Do you have any idea how insane that is?"

His eyes, no longer glazed, are narrowed, the skin around them tightened. He stares sullenly at me. "I wore gloves. I was completely covered." He breathes out heavily. "And I left my shoes in the basement and washed my clothes immediately afterwards."

"But what"—I'm sputtering now—"if something *had* gone wrong. I don't know . . . what if there'd been a rat in the crawl space and it bit your lip or took a nip at your ear? What if there'd been snakes waking up since it's like eighty-two degrees suddenly, and they're seeing Mr. Curious messing in their space? What would you have done at 2:00 in the morning, you know, when everybody else is sleeping?" I haven't realized I'm shouting until the last sentence.

Now he's yelling too. "But it *didn't* happen. Nothing happened. I *fixed* it."

All I can think about is that moment in *The Girl with the Dragon Tattoo* when Lizbeth Salander says to herself before she's about to do something wild and impulsive, "Consequences . . . consider the consequences." Only later, much later, will I consider my own impulsive anger and the consequences of needing so desperately to keep him safe. "But something could have happened. It really could have. You were just lucky."

"Stop scolding me," he says, his voice deadly quiet. "Just stop. I thought you'd be happy." He's turning away from me now. "I thought you'd be glad that I solved the problem."

But what I see is Dr. C drawing delicate lines across his butt with a purple marker, lines that look vaguely archeological, lines that in ten days will be intricate, surgical stitches covering more microscopic surgical stitches attaching one tiny blood vessel to another. "You have no idea what can happen," I say. Only as I say the words am I aware that I've changed the verb tense.

He doesn't notice. Indignant, he walks away from me through the living room, and I listen to his footsteps as he climbs the stairs.

There's no more time. I have student conferences, a faculty meeting, then a doctor's appointment. Quickly, I gather up my things. As I leave the house, I hear him calling the Animal Control Hotline, but now, suddenly spent, I simply close the front door.

HOURS LATER I'M DRIVING home from my doctor's appointment, aware that David and I have avoided each other all day, our cell phones on mute. When I come to the top of a small hill, I see our college town laid out before me, students in T-shirts instead of coats and down vests walking across the bridge over the Iowa River, the trees opening up with leaves, a dark, furtive green in the shade, the sun's light sparkling on the river. I'm paused at a stoplight, my foot on the brake. *I love you more than the trees, the clouds, the sky* comes to me unbidden, a current pushing toward shore. And then, *I don't know why it's so hard*. I've always thought that David and I were intuitively linked, tied by an inner kinship that bound us more than the reckoning of blood. Sometimes I believe it's because we understand the difficulty of our childhood angst, the secret fear of being crushed rivaled only by an inexplicable surge of joy, the sudden buoyancy of art. Everything circles around this bond. And yet there are days when everything goes awry, our choices conflicted as we hurry past each other. Some days I don't know what to do.

After I park in front of our house, I sit for a moment, idly rubbing my right leg. It aches from an old fall and from sitting so much of the day. As I press my hand to my thigh, I remember how tenderly David stroked my feet last night, how his hands, thick, worker's hands with their wide palms and stubby fingers (not "artist's hands," we joke), touched them delicately, easily, while I closed my eyes, letting sleep pull me toward unconsciousness.

I take a deep breath.

Thirty minutes later, we're both in the kitchen making dinner, neither of us talking. My worry has gradually subsided; I wonder if I'm going to be paralyzed by risk and danger, becoming *that* kind of person, some priestess of restraint. I know this territory well, the passivity, the deferment, the holding in of air. I grew up with worriers, survivors of bad times, parents who pushed aside the casual thrill of risk to imagine only tragedy: a drowning, a fall, a car wreck, a snake in the grass. "Don't climb on those monkey bars," my father yelled out the back door as we scrambled toward the neighbor's yard. "Don't you know you can break your neck!" Physical risk carried within it the shadow of a shroud. Danger lurked everywhere. Better to be safe. Better to be careful. Better to stay indoors, to study and prepare, to watch and wait, vigilant, inert. And hadn't I married David, in part, because he was the opposite? Impulsive. Curious. Willful. Restless. He followed his instincts, even when those instincts sent him reeling into trouble, tumbling to earth. In truth, he rarely imagined trouble. Everything seemed possible to him, as if he lacked the skeptical gene. A maddening quality.

I pick up the knife and get busy chopping onions and yellow peppers and then add a dollop of butter to the rice. David is quiet as he seasons the chicken. Tentatively, still not looking at him, I tell him about the doctor I saw today, how encouraging and thoughtful she was. I wait. He tells me about a call from his friend in New York, the one he calls "My General" in jest because the friend grew up during the juntas in Argentina. Then he glances quickly at me. "I took another shower," he says. "Just in case." For the first time we make eye contact. Neither of us directly mentions the crawl space though later tonight I'll see the clothes he wore drying in the dryer. Instead, I recount a story my mother told me about her great-grandson, Emory. He's in second grade and when she picked him up from school, he said quite seriously, "Jason has a girlfriend. I didn't think you could have a girlfriend until fourth grade." Mother said he seemed genuinely puzzled by this betrayal of the rules until she assured him he'd have plenty of girlfriends when he was ready. We smile at this over dinner, laughing about how at age eight, the rules seem inviolable.

"Sometimes I feel like I'm back there right now," I say. "You know, trying to follow the damn rules, trying to get it right."

"Not *you*?" David's eyes are bright. He's wearing, I notice, a blue shirt, not one of the "comfys," as if he's dressed up for me.

"Oh, hush." But I can feel the tension easing, and to my surprise, what's been buried all day rises within me: some part of me believed that now—yes, with a diagnosis of cancer!—I could bring him over to my side, the part of me I've been trying to shed all my life. If only I could instill him with caution, I'd be released from worry, and he'd be stuck with the job. I smile. "How can I possibly follow the rules when I live with a subversive who hogs the rice?"

He nods and passes the bowl to me. "I know," he says, not quite releasing it. And for a moment our eyes hold.

THAT NIGHT I'M BACK at my desk. More essays to read, critiques to write, and emails to answer. I yawn. I need more tea. Getting up from my desk, I pause and look around, checking out the windows and the blinds, the edge of the picture frame, the lampshade where sometimes they like to gather even when the light is off. I stand very still. I don't want to alert them. I've learned to be sneaky. A master at killing. A secret assassin. A woman on a mission.

But there are no flies.

Chapter 6

ON TUESDAY, THE DAY of David's surgery, I wear the lucky dress. Though it was too expensive, last summer I had to have it. I stood in the boutique's dressing room, its softness folded in my arms. Didn't I have presentations in Melbourne and Wollongong in September, two places in Australia I'd never been, meeting with people I didn't yet know? Didn't I have a keynote address at a literary conference in Alabama in the fall? And didn't I need to look good, or if not good, at least decently professional? Quietly, I slid the credit card across the counter, feeling the press of guilt while telling myself I deserved a little extravagance. It had been a crappy year.

The truth is, every time I've worn the dress disaster has been averted: instead of being a shy, scared chicken of a girl, I seem to cross a divide and become poised and confident.

And so the night before David's surgery, I slid the dove-green dress out of my closet, bent the hanger and hung it from the closet door, then stood back, assessing: even on the crooked hanger, the dress looked sleek and smart, cut to fit snugly around the hips and waist, the neckline high above a draped bodice, the skirt short, a good three inches above the knee, much shorter than the dresses I'd worn in the past. It looked stylish, sophisticated. It was like wearing air. Though a part of me thought, *My god, what kind of nutcase believes a pretty dress has talismanic power on the day of her husband's surgery*, another part of me thought, *Why not?* Perhaps desire is not so different from a delicate blue vein: you can't help but want to trace it.

I'M NOT CRAZY, I TELL myself as I slip the dress over my head at 7 a.m. I know I'm wearing the dress only to make me feel better, to help me pretend I'm confident and in control when everything today will depend on the expertise of others: oncologists, surgeons, anesthetists, nurses, residents, aides. I could be wearing curlers and my old plaid pajamas, the collar frayed, the pants hem unraveling. If I were practical, I'd be in dark blue sweatpants and a sweatshirt, something impervious to stains or wrinkles or spills, something I could sleep in if necessary, curled up on one of those two-seater couches in the surgical waiting room. Instead, I think of my mother on the day of my father's open-heart surgery in Birmingham, Alabama, in 1978: she dressed in a beige linen suit accessorized with tiny gold earrings and alligator high heels, as if just sitting in the waiting room or attending him in recovery was the public presentation of a private ritual, a continuation of their life together, the doctor and the doctor's wife, proper and respectable and dressed, ready to go.

But I'm not my mother, I keep telling myself. I've spent the better part of my adulthood casting aside the props of Southern culture, most particularly the propriety of dress ("Do you want people to think you're an *orphan*?" my mother would chide when I refused to dress up). I've insisted on jeans and tank tops, sandals and tennis shoes, choosing utilitarian coats with functional hoods and cotton pajamas or else outlandish clothes like the long black dress I once wore in Memphis, Spanish moss draped like a shawl over my shoulders. But today I look at myself in the mirror, a stark, appraising look: *I am just like my mother*. I want whatever favors may come my way, favors of a pretty dress, of clean hair and a quick smile, favors that have nothing to do with ethical and emotional maturity but simply with first impressions. I want not to be slighted by doctors and nurses and by those who often do the most damage: administrative personnel. Today I want everything I can get.

"Let's go," my husband calls from downstairs, his insistence surprising because he's infamous for being thirty minutes late to everything. Quickly, I gather my things, turning for a fast glance at myself over my right shoulder. *Good butt*, I think. By 8:05 a.m. we're ushered into a small beige room at the university hospital, a surgical holding tank with two chairs and a built-in desk where nurses do intake and prepping. His surgery is scheduled for 10:00.

"Nice," I say, gazing around, pretending interest.

"But not nice enough for two nights," David says, trying for irony though his voice sounds strained. He hunches in his seat, his face grim, his eyes nervous, flitting about. "You look pretty," he says suddenly, glancing at my dress, then at my face. The skin beneath his eyes looks shadowed and puffy, as if he didn't get enough sleep. He takes my hand, squeezing it a little too tightly and then letting it go. He's wearing a long-sleeved gray shirt buttoned to the throat, a choice he agonized over this morning. Though it's not one of his favorites, it was the only clean shirt that looked right with his dark gray pants. I wanted to say, "Don't worry. It won't matter," but of course he has his own private theories about luck. I touch the sleeve of his shirt in a familiar way, as if I'm picking off lint, grooming him, fussing over him, two people getting ready for a party where they'll eat stuffed mushrooms and drink flutes of champagne.

I've just placed a hand on his thigh when the nurse pops in. "Your surgery's been rescheduled for noon," she says brightly, as if we've been bumped to the front of the line instead of delayed for two long hours.

"Noon?" I ask, uncertain. "*Lunch time*?"

I want the doctors to be fresh, caffeinated, hyperalert, ready to tackle the world, to stomp through Tokyo. If they eat before his surgery, won't they be sleepy, their food still digesting, their metabolisms slowed by peristalsis just as they cut into my husband's body? For a moment I see him lying flat out and chloroformed while the doctors stand above him, yawning.

Then again, not eating might be worse, the doctors tired and cranky, their blood sugars fluctuating, their minds distracted, their hands more apt to make mistakes.

"Noon," the nurse says again with that upbeat lilt to her voice as if she's offering a prize.

"Noon." My husband smiles like a man who's been given a reprieve.

But how can I know if this delay will turn out to be good luck or bad? How can I judge the implications of chance, the eccentricities of probability? Though the rescheduling seems to relax my husband, who calmly puts in his earbuds and turns on his iPod, the delay makes me anxious and fidgety. I need to move. I mutter something about finding a restroom and wander down the hall, where I see, through half-open doors, only men in hospital Johnnies. Maybe the women with cancer are on another floor. Then I step into the restroom.

Only here, in the privacy of the stall, in this antiseptic, anonymous space, do I begin to relax. *Okay*, I say, sighing, wadding up toilet paper and then tossing it away. *Okay. There's nothing you can do.* As I wash my hands, I glance at myself in the mirror, examining my skin, staring at the pores on my nose—a faint line of blackheads circling one side—at the smudge of eyeliner beneath one eye. I step back, surprised to see how good my dress looks. I step back a little more, standing up straighter to get a better angle: I love the casual drape of fabric across the bodice, the tucked fit at the waist, the long, close-fitting sleeves. And then I can't seem to help myself; I do the other thing I always do: I put both hands flat against my abdomen and suck in my breath while pressing in, my stomach so flat and smooth I can feel the sharp jut of my hipbones, an almost sexual pleasure. I even close my eyes like a woman in the realm of the erotic. When I release my hands, the soft swell of my stomach pooches back out . . . as it always does ("Why do you *do* that?" David once asked, as if I'd performed a perverse adolescent ritual; "I don't know," I said, suddenly self-conscious. "I've always done it.").

DURING THE NEXT HOUR, I flip through a stack of notes on Marguerite Duras for the graduate class I'm teaching though numbness envelopes me like a musty smell. Even the air feels stale, prebreathed. Waiting has attenuated my emotions, made me slow and tenuous, dull around the edges. I press my front teeth against my bottom lip, rolling the skin back and forth, enjoying the possibility of pain, something I can control while letting my thoughts drift. *I don't know what love is right now*, I think as I shift in the molded, plastic chair. I glance at David, his face tilted away from the door, his body stilled, concentrated, the white cords of his iPod looping into his pocket. He seems elusive, *here but not here*, though I know he's frightened, needing to escape into the novel he's listening to. And I know this too: we're both pulled tightly inside ourselves, aware of "you" and "me" and the space in-between. Though we can and do reach around that space, it often feels inviolable until one of us, for no reason at all, erases it—as easily as wiping chalk from a blackboard—surprising ourselves, laughing and falling into the romance of us, only us. Watching him, I remember when I woke alone in an apartment in a small fishing village by the sea while teaching in France years ago, knowing I should wait five hours before calling David in Iowa but didn't. I remember sitting down at the breakfast table across from him last week, half asleep, my glasses on, my tea steeping, my napkin crumpled, an ordinary day. "Don't you want to fix the eggs?" he smiled, lifting his eyes to me, because he liked the way I cooked them. And as simple as that, the space between us dissolved. *Love is just being here*, I think. *Waiting. Watching him breathe. And then not watching. And then watching again.*

To distract myself, I gaze at the medical equipment, an X-ray light box and some strange white, angular protuberance that looks sterile and invasive. Where does it go? Down the throat? Up the bum? The creepiness of it reminds me that whatever happens today will be dramatic, will change everything, and yet I can't wrap my mind around what that will be. Will the lymph nodes be involved? Will excising the margins cause complications—blood loss, tissue damage, something I can't even imagine? Will the plastic surgeon be able to connect hundreds of tiny blood vessels?

How, I wonder, do people prepare for this kind of thing? For weeks, we've been hovering above it, trying to relax, trying to find a center, a language, a way to respond.

I'M GRATEFUL WHEN WE'RE finally interrupted by a nurse asking my husband to change into his hospital gown, but it's the arrival of the gurney that shatters my thoughts. It looks like every gurney I've ever seen on TV—a rolling tray-like bed pushed slowly, almost casually, down the hall by a young, robust orderly—and oddly, it's this uber-image that makes it real. No sooner is David placed face down on the gurney than he looks vulnerable and helpless, now a patient, a body. Within minutes, Dr. C, the plastic surgeon, arrives to test the blood flow in my husband's lower back and buttocks with a Doppler anemometer. After a quick handshake, Dr. C begins touching and stretching my husband's skin, drawing fine lines across the left butt cheek, using a small metal ruler and magic marker, and explaining to his research fellow why he's bisecting X and then halving Y as he writes notes on the chart. When introduced to doctors with equipment, I feel an instant servility, an outsider in the presence of a club to which I have no rights, a club of hierarchy and expertise and control. I have to remind myself that I have a brain. I listen hard, but I'm distracted by Dr. C's expression. He looks slightly irritable, perturbed because after the first few beeps the Doppler machine quits working and has to be replaced. I want to think of him as a fairy godfather, someone with magical powers (worthy of my subordination), but the truth is, I don't understand what he's saying to the resident, and my god, what if the equipment doesn't work? When I tune back in, I'm aware that the design he's drawing on my husband's butt looks quite different than the one he drew for us in his office, the one I assumed he'd use.

"Are you changing the procedure?" I ask frowning.

He looks at me and nods, then returns to his notes, making calculations, already engaged, I realize, in the surgery. "It's better," he announces, staring directly at me.

I want to say, "Just wait a minute. Explain." But I know that his calculations are crucial, that there's no more time for discussion, assessment, or reconsideration. Though I understand theoretically how he'll close the wound, I realize that I did all my research on the rare cancer rather than on the plastic surgery procedure. How could I have been so stupid?

Even as I'm thinking this, two male nurses arrive to wheel my husband away. He squeezes my hand, a quick, tentative grasp; he's already theirs. The last thing I see is the swirl of his unruly cowlicks, the upper curve of an ear. And then I'm alone in the pre-op room, a tiny fish at the bottom of the aquarium, swimming through murky water. I don't know where to go, only to keep swimming.

"You'll want to wait in the surgical waiting room on the third floor," an attendant says, gently touching my elbow.

WHEN I ENTER THE waiting room, I'm surprised that it's full of Midwestern farmers with sun-roughened skin and clean, faded dungarees and older, bespectacled women knitting or absently watching TV. The room is crowded, and I feel ridiculous, as if decked out in a party dress, one shoulder bared, long earrings dangling. Alone, I feel like a show-off, a vain, frivolous woman, all my worry tucked inside the folds of a pretty dress. My family lives one thousand miles away; my friends and neighbors are all at work. I stand for a moment in the doorway, wishing to be a part of a group, wishing to see a friendly face. A few people glance up, staring at me, neither dismissive nor curious, but no one signals intimacy or even the illusion of friendliness. And why should they? We're all tense and tired. Still, I feel a twinge of rejection. I want to say, "I don't usually dress like this. Every day I sit at my computer wearing black sweatpants and tennis shoes and whatever sweater I can find." Like most writers, I'm invisible much of the time—creating characters and mining memory—but in this waiting room, I stand here conspicuous and incomprehensible, the perennial outsider, the kid in sixth grade with glasses and braces and no bra. No one is going to gather me into their fold.

I imagine only my mother's nod of approval. It's probably no surprise that I come from a family that believes one's professional status is defined by dress, that "pretty things" can provide protection in an indifferent world. An admission of insecurity, I realize now, though I've grown up inside that illusive dream. In truth, the women in my family would spend their last thousand dollars on new shoes and a party dress rather than soffits for the roof or termite control for a crumbling foundation.

I spy a seat in the back of the room across from four men in jeans and plaid shirts, who look about my age, their skin weathered, their faces open, eyes narrowed like men who have spent their days squinting at the sun. Later they'll tell me they are brothers, here for their father's surgery for cancer of the larynx and thyroid. "He's a horse," one of the men says, smiling with pride. "He's already had cancer of the prostate, a heart attack, a pacemaker, and two stents." They look confident, assured that their father, this undefeatable man, will come through, rallying for a breakfast of oatmeal and coffee in the morning.

FOR HOURS, I WATCH other people rise from their seats when the receptionist calls their names, see them step into the side room where I know they're meeting with the surgeon. I don't move. I don't watch the clock. I don't let myself. I feel anxious, but it's the kind of numbing anxiety that leaves me blank and detached, my knees and fingers tight, my bladder full. Once, years ago, a doctor friend of my father's let me scrub up and watch a hip replacement surgery in a small community hospital in my hometown. My father had always wanted me to be a doctor, and perhaps I was trying to please him, to be a willing student, to assume that in that sterile operating room I might see beneath the surface of things. And yet what I remember is blood spilling and pooling onto the instruments, leaking into sterile gauze, the doctor's gloved hands using implements that seemed related only to a carpenter's toolbox. I stood for hours unmoving, tensed in fear as the patient lay like a blunt object on the table, indecent, unknowing. Afterward, I never said a word about it. I never asked to see anything more—nor did I sign up for chemistry—but I was barely twenty and imagined such physical indignities could happen only to others. Now when I think of my husband in the operating room, I stroke my dress, smoothing out my skirt, using my index finger as if I'm ironing the material. I dust the folds in front as if there might be crumbs clinging to the fabric. I sit up straighter. I fluff out my hair.

When the brothers are called, I smile and wish them good luck. "He's a tough one," the one nearest me says, nodding. "Hope things go well for you."

"Thank you." I keep smiling.

After the third hour, when I'm finally called, I try to keep myself from running to that small room where I've seen everyone else go. I arrive before the surgeon and sit, hoping to compose myself. Because I feel empty and tired, I try to imagine myself as someone to whom the doctor will want to give good news. I'll make him see this instantly and he'll have no choice but to comply. I'm sitting on a stool with rollers. Impulsively, I spin around, a giddy release, but Dr. M arrives in the middle of my spin and a blush creeps up my neck, flushing across my face. I have no idea what I'm doing.

"The surgery went well," he says, leaning against the table, his eyes on me. "The area we had to excise was a little more ragged than I'd expected, but Dr. C can work with that." He tells me the quick-frozen samples looked good and have been sent to the lab for further analysis. "We'll know in about five days." I like his New York assertiveness, the noisy intensity of his eyes, his balding head. "It will take about two more hours for Dr. C. to finish."

"What?" I thought the entire surgery was complete, that my husband was in recovery and would be coming soon to the oncology ward. Instead, the most delicate part—the intricate microsurgery—is just beginning. I sink back into darkness, groggy, still, relieved now that a substitute will be teaching my 5–8 p.m. class.

I have little memory of the next two and a half hours. Normally I'm a nail bitter, a foot-tapper, a leg swinger, a shifting, jiggling woman in constant motion, but I'm in a fugue state when I'm called back to the conference room to meet the plastic surgeon. It's 5:30 p.m., nine and a half hours since we arrived. For what seems a long moment, Dr. C sits silently across from me, neither of us speaking. His face is symmetrical and fine-featured, but I can't read his expression, can't see behind his medical composure. "It went well," he says finally. "I was able to close the wound successfully. But it's delicate. *Very* fragile." He pauses, then says carefully, "Your husband won't be able to lie on his back or left side . . . or sit for the next six weeks."

"You mean he can *only* lie on his right side?"

He nods gravely. "The reconnected blood vessels need time to heal. Even the slightest pressure can compromise the site. In a few days, he'll be able to stand up and walk, but we won't get him up for two days."

As he speaks, I'm trying to free my mind from its hiding place. I think about how open-heart surgery patients are forced to stand and walk the very next day to avoid blood clots. Do I need to worry about blood clots? But more than that, I want to ask how my husband will be able to do this, how he'll go to the bathroom, how he'll eat breakfast and dinner and get back and forth to the hospital for follow-up appointments, and yet I can't seem to force out the words. Instead, I gaze at the floor, then at my dress in its lovely folds over my thighs, and though it shames me to admit it, I wonder if the doctor thinks I look nice, and if my looking nice can't make things better, can't modify the results, make the bad parts go away, make him think harder about his expectations for my husband's recovery.

"We'll need to keep him here for five days," he continues. "I've ordered a special bed, one that won't compromise the wound if he should turn, but it won't arrive until tomorrow." Then he hesitates, not quite looking at me. "I think he'll have to go to a residential care facility from here. He'll need to go where they'll be able to take care of him."

With these words, the luck of the dress vanishes, slips from my grasp like a deep swooning desire. *My husband will die in a nursing home.* I see him strapped to a bed, unable to leave, unable to work, unable to talk to me when he wakes in the middle of the night, barely able to move. He's terrified of confinement. I imagine him sinking deeper and deeper into depression, his mind trapped by a broken body, disordered by boredom, by institutional restrictions, by his own resistance, by the timeless surface of night and day. Staring at the doctor, I'm aware that I have no healing powers, no natural grace or sense of sacrifice, no belief in balance or blessings. I look beyond him to the dull, glowing light of the hallway and see myself: exhausted and sleepless and wearing my old blue nightgown, the elastic gone loose in the sleeves. I'm trying to help my husband rise from a prone position without damaging the wound, both of us frustrated and cursing as I stumble beneath his weight, trying to steady him as I grip the back of a chair. Can I care for him at home when I can neither lift nor support him, when I have a full-time job and an illness myself? It's not death I'm afraid of now but something in me, a tightening just beneath my skin, a helplessness I don't want to know.

For the first time today, I recognize a territory beyond fear, a ragged, messy place with no firm bedposts, no safe, cool floors, a place where I'll have to feel my way alone in the dark. For the first time today, I don't know what to do.

"He'll need a special bed," the doctor goes on. "He'll need to be frequently monitored so that he doesn't turn in his sleep . . . *even* with a special bed. If he turns for as much as five minutes, his surgery can be compromised." He leans closer, his voice gentle but firm. "Do you understand?"

I'VE BEEN TOLD TO wait in the oncology lounge, but when I see the gurney emerge from the elevator, my husband more of a heap in a hospital gown placed on its right side than my recognizable husband, I move instinctively close, lightly touching his hair. He's just out of recovery, his face pasty, his eyes closed, IVs trailing from his arms. He looks frail, blunted, morphed into a patient. The nurses, or what I assume to be nurses, are busy getting this new group of patients settled into rooms. Charts are handed between them. Papers rustle. Two other gurneys are parked behind my husband's; the nurses are reading orders and checking IVs, though a few wait beside the beds. I know I should be quiet and inconspicuous, and yet I can't stop myself from saying that my husband has just had a tumor removed from his lower back, had microsurgery to close it and can't have any pressure on the wound. "Don't worry," the man I assume to be a male nurse says. "We'll turn him from right side to left side every few hours. We'll keep him off of his back." Then he turns away, saying something to another nurse.

For a moment I can't breathe. How can it be that the first words I hear on this ward are so crucially wrong. "No," I say quickly. "Dr. C said he can only lie on his *right* side." The man turns back to me. He looks skeptical. "We haven't received the orders yet."

"Can I talk to you a minute?" I ask, as calmly as I can. He follows me into the family lounge, which to my relief is now empty. I straighten. I make my voice confident and clear as I tell him about Dr. C's insistence that my husband have no pressure on the wound, either lying on his back or on his left side because the perforator-plus flap is a repair that takes up much of his left buttocks.

"I work with Dr. C," he says casually. "I'm sure it will be in the orders." And then he holds out his hand. "I'm Dr. X, the resident on the floor."

I take his hand lightly. "I'm Dr. Foster," I say, knowing a doctorate in literature is irrelevant to this situation. But I want my words to matter. After all, he doesn't know what kind of doctor I am. And for the first time today I'm glad to be wearing the lucky dress, glad to have a PhD. The resident looks at me attentively and nods.

But maybe I'm remembering it this way only to reassure myself. Maybe he merely looked at me and thought, *So what?*, then turned back to the ward where two new patients had just arrived from recovery, patients soon to be in pain, patients for whom he'd be responsible.

And yet it's now, in this moment, beneath the harsh fluorescent lights and the musical ping of a closing elevator door, that a decision wings its way through my body. I see my husband five days from now when he's been released from the hospital, at home, lying in our living room, his hospital bed fit just beneath the windows, sunlight alternately shadowing and illuminating his form. If I move the chairs and table, push the lamp and the small bookcase to another corner of the room, I can place the bed so that I can see it from my study, can get to it quickly, can get to him. I see him raising his head, calling out for me. I see myself rising. I don't know how I'll do this, but for the first time I know that I can.

BY 11:00 P.M., MY HUSBAND is finally sleeping, his ordinary hospital bed barricaded with pillows behind his shoulders and upper back, the morphine button slipped from his hand. The nurse, so young she looks like a college freshman, is careful and competent, already an ally. Because there is a shortage of rooms, my husband has been put temporarily in a double room with one of those draped curtains dividing the space. Behind the curtains, I hear a man loudly groaning. "I don't want it all stuck up inside me," he says as he grunts, the squeak of the bed shifting as he tries to get up. On our side, a single chair is pushed up against the wall on my husband's right side, a chair that's in my way but I'm not allowed to move. Earlier, I asked the head nurse for a cot or at least a recliner but was told neither was possible and that I could stay down the hall in the family lounge. "Please," I wanted to say. "I need to be right here, in the room just in case."

By 11:30 p.m., exhausted and with a whopper of a headache, I see things differently. I must go home for a shower and some sleep.

At midnight, I move cautiously through the darkness of our

house, having forgotten to leave on any lights. I turn on only the hall light and make my way upstairs, shedding my dress, letting it fall in a heap to the floor. I reward myself with a long, hot shower, the water streaming over my body, my mind in a glorious pause before I find my way to sleep. Wrapped in a towel, I step over my clothes, glancing down and not bothering to pick them up. Maybe it's then that I notice the stain, a shiny spot on the skirt of my dress as if I've wiped a finger smudged with butter or bumped against a weeping wound. No matter. All my thoughts are focused on tomorrow when I'll be back at the hospital in jeans and a T-shirt and tennis shoes, clothes that will allow me to sprint from one side of the bed to the other, out to the nurses' station to talk to the social worker, the physical therapist, clothes that say I belong to the legend of caretakers. The dress, after all, was only for today.

PART II

The Unknown World

2012

Chapter 7

THE NIGHT OF DAVID'S first shower, I watch as he walks slowly, laboriously, toward the bathroom, his swollen feet shuffling, his arms dangling at his side. When he sees the water gush from the tub's faucet, his brow furrows as if the water's dazzling force might hurt him. "Don't make it too hot," he says, voice pinched, his face a gray mask of worry.

"I won't." I kneel beside the tub, adjusting the cold water, then glancing up at him throned in a faded hospital gown: a frail, caged king, his borders narrowly drawn, his anxiety spearing the air. His feet are bare. His hair, still thick and shaggy, is smashed flat to his head.

"Relax," I say softly, rising. "Just stand still and don't worry." Behind him, I untie the ties and unpin the two drains clipped to the inside of his gown with extralarge safety pins, drains linked to the circular, almost calligraphic incision that makes a big smiley face across one side of his butt. I hold the drains—they look like plastic teardrops full of Kool-Aid—each connected by safety pins, admiring such a low-tech solution to such a high-tech surgery. When the hospital nurses showed me how they were attached to the gown, I said only, "Wow!" impressed with its simplicity l until I pricked myself with a pin's sharp point. Now as the gown drops to the floor, I turn the nozzle, letting water flow to the shower, a rush of moisture instantly thickening the air. David hesitates as if he's entering an unknown world, a slippery baptism that promises not redemption but only temporary relief, a mere swimming across the current of time.

"Watch the rim of the tub." I take his elbow and lean down to cup the rough pad of his heel in my other hand. I lift it so slowly my back begins to spasm.

"Don't go so *fast*," he says as if I'm rushing him. His voice, usually light and teasing, is now querulous and impatient, emphatic and demanding. It's the voice of cancer, the voice of pain. "The cry of the wound," I sometimes mutter, though I know I'm being melodramatic. During this first week at home, I feel estranged from my normal self, as if we've entered an eccentric groove of time or opened the door to a mysterious world that unwittingly swats at us, then clutches us, holding us close. There's no going back.

Just last month, David playfully grabbed me by the waist as I leaned into the fridge to get some juice, then teasingly massaged my butt, his fingers rubbing in capricious circles. "Fondling the Orbs," he calls it, as if I have the robust buttocks of a Renaissance woman, fleshy and soft and damp, instead of my hard, skinny little ass. The absurdity always makes me laugh.

"Higher," I say now, watching to make sure his foot clears the hard metal rim of the tub's shower frame. He grabs my arm, his grip surprisingly fierce as he lifts the other foot over the rim. Then he stands at the very back of the tub, water falling in a soft rain over his distended belly and the tops of his thighs, bouncing off his knees, then puddling around his feet. He glares at the water as if it's a threat, an enemy trying to trap him. "I'm just going to let the front of me get wet," he says as if I've demanded more. I nod, staring at the long caterpillar scars across the lymph nodes, thick, messy, mean-looking stitches clogged with blood, glue, and hair.

Once under the water, David closes his eyes, not moving, simply letting the water pelt him as if he's never been in a shower before, as if he doesn't know how to behave, what to expect, though he's always loved twenty-minute immersions. Tonight, I too close my eyes, opening them only to glance out the window, where I know the moon is shrouded by clouds, the air suddenly raw and chilled though the days are beginning to warm, the tulips bright and bossy and blooming each morning. It's early April, the last full month of the semester, and I have papers to grade and a thesis to read, but for now, I'm vigilant. I turn to watch the water splashing on his muscular chest where the once-dark hair has gone sparse and grey.

The shower doesn't last long. And yet every routine seems to take forever, as if we're children, untutored and awkward, reinventing the form. In a few weeks, we'll create a system, but tonight we're flying by the seat of our pants. After I turn off the water, I place a towel on his head, gently drying his hair and his face, then draping it there to hold the heat. I want to laugh. He looks like a naked man with a dishrag flung on his head. Instead, I say, "I'm going to put a towel around your shoulders," having learned in just two days that I must announce everything I do, or he'll be startled, the voice of pain rising hard and fast. "I brought Steph," I say lightly as I wrap the long blue cape of a towel around his shoulders, a towel one of us must have lifted from the gym years ago since neither of us would have bought a towel monogrammed "Steph." Occasionally, when we're having a bad night, one of us will archly insist, "All right, enough . . . let's get *Steph*!" as if only she might restore the fun, untangle the mess. We feel an odd fondness for Steph, as if we've appropriated another identity—blond and bubbly and absurd, one of those girls who paints her nails bright yellow and spends hours sweating on the StairMaster—a slightly foolish teenage identity that can only be adored and mocked.

Tonight, David doesn't smile. Instead, I dry his chest and abdomen, making the same soft noises I heard the nurses make, "There now" and "That's good" and "Almost done," while he's standing in the tub before we try the next trick: getting out.

"I'm freezing," David says once he's standing on the bathroom rug, his thermostat gone haywire. His body, usually trapped in an August heat wave, is now stuck on ice. I turn the fan to low and kneel in front, drying his thighs and calves and feet, the ankles mottled and swollen, the color of old lint. Next, I pat down his genitals. To keep myself calm, I tell him about a thesis I'm reading, how a young man's obsession with Bob Dylan and the New York Yankees provided a kind of safety net after his mother's suicide. David isn't listening, his eyes closed, but I need to hear the steady drift of my voice, the words humming and purring beneath the drone of the fan, my student's sadness tugging at the surface of my own. I need to do this because I'm going behind David to pat dry his back above where the tumor was removed, where the skin isn't quite skin, where a moody pink scar curves like the blade of a scythe. I don't dare touch that section. Instead, I pat dry the right buttocks and tell David he'll need to air dry while I get a clean gown.

It's only when I leave him—*escape* is the only word for it—that I breathe freely, blood pumping into my body as if I've been released into an oxygen-rich atmosphere. I want to rush up to our bed—the one we've slept in for thirty years—and throw myself onto the mattress, to yawn and sprawl and stretch without the slightest hint of worry. I imagine turning off the lights and sleeping, dangerously unconscious, pulling the covers over my head and selfishly ignoring my husband waiting downstairs on the bathroom rug. I imagine doing nothing, slouching on the couch and reading a magazine or watching *Downton Abbey*, a Diet Coke on the table, my feet stretched out in fuzzy socks. *Not a care in the world.* But no. David's new voice has pushed and pulled me, yanked me into a new world of fear and vigilance. Now I'm a watcher, a protector, a pilgrim. Now everything has consequences: sharp corners, loose shoes, twisted rugs, table edges, doorknobs, stairs, spills, even the trailing tie of his robe. Who would have known that this unknown world would be full of obstacles and booby traps, such sly, secret menaces? Trouble can be as simple as his foot coming out of his shoe, making him lose his balance. Or as unexpected as me turning too quickly and bumping into his back as he stands at the raised table, eating a piece of toast. Now I walk a wide radius around him. Twice a day I drain and measure the funky pink mixture from his drains; three times a night, I set the alarm to get up and check to make sure, despite the firm barrier of pillows, he hasn't turned over.

"Okay," I call as I come downstairs, nearing the bathroom. David holds out his arms and I pull on the clean, printed gown, tying it in back, then repinning the drains. He yawns, tired and ready to sleep.

I watch as he crawls—knees and elbows bent, back hunched—into the hospital bed, clean and exhausted, sinking down onto his right side as if, for the moment, it's his favorite position. He has his iPad on its stand, tuned to a movie, his earbuds in, the only way he can sleep. Soon, his eyes will close and for an hour he'll doze. For an hour, I'll work.

But first, a cup of tea.

When I come out of the kitchen, steam rising from my cup, I pause, watching David's eyelids flutter, his head tucked into the pillow, his hands drawn up, cupped together as if in prayer, just beneath his chin. A white sheet covers his feet and legs, three firm pillows fortress his upper back to prevent him from turning. The motor on the specially ordered air mattress hums its sedative drone, a low, purring sound. I stand watching, listening, staring at the dark hollows of his throat. I'm surprised by a shadow of desire: if only I could crawl in beside him and hold him, my hand tracing the muscle of his thigh. If only . . .

It's now that he opens his eyes and stares at me. It's a wordless moment, simple and serene, the steam from my cup drifting idly toward him. *Who are we?* I wonder, letting my eyes run the length of him, and then beyond where a branch from the crabapple tree hangs motionless outside the window. *Who are we now?* But that question quietly dissolves, for here we are, a man and a woman inextricably bound by the tugs and plunges of marriage, awkwardly shrugging off the old familiar life and waiting for something new to light the way.

Chapter 8

OUR OLD FAMILIAR LIFE was not always one of health. I've known for years that each of us has dual citizenship in the country of the sick and the country of the well, as Susan Sontag noted, an allegiance that swings back and forth, hitchhikers on this strange highway, taking whatever risks and precautions prove necessary for the trip. I know this because of my own history, a trip to the boundaries of exhaustion and a slow commute back to health.

For me, the descent happened so quickly I couldn't remember my other life, the life of the well, that ordinary *wake-up-in-the-morning-have-a-cup-of-coffee-and-get-on-with-it* self. One day I had a routine: I'd write for an hour each morning at the kitchen table at our small apartment in Santa Monica, go to work at 9:00 at Paramount or Warner Brothers, come home at 6:00, fix dinner with David, and then read or write until midnight. The next thing I knew I was too tired to get out of bed. Something had happened, but for weeks I was too woozy to know what it was. The flu, I assumed. A *bad* flu.

The truth is, my new life *did* begin with a flu, some virus weaving its way through the population of Los Angeles—where David and I had returned after a year in Seattle. For several days, David lay feverish and still in bed, sandwiched between the sheets, getting up only for full glasses of water and long pauses in the bathroom. I'd hear the toilet flush and see him stumble back to bed, too ill to talk. And then the fourth morning he emerged as if nothing had happened, fixed a pot of coffee, took a shower, and raced off to work. He'd been gone barely an hour when I felt the first flush of fever, an ache in my limbs, the sudden pull of exhaustion. I knew the drill. I called in sick and slid quietly between the sheets.

This new life began in 1982, the same year that Michael Jackson's *Thriller* hit the stores and teenagers drove in from the Valley, hanging out at Tower Records and Music Plus and Fat Beats. Adults fixated on another icon, real estate, which was booming. Everyone believed they could make a killing.

But I was too sick to make a killing. For weeks, and then months, I remained listless, my mind drifting, my head as light as scattered straw. My lymph nodes slightly swollen, my bones aching, I longed only to lie in the dark. Though I knew something had gone quietly haywire inside my body, the damage was so discreet that nothing definitive showed up on empirical tests. When I'd first become ill, I'd gone to the medical men: an internist, an endocrinologist, a neurologist, an allergist. On such visits I was told, "We can't find anything wrong except maybe some allergies." I was told, "Go home, young lady and drink some coffee." I was told, "It might be psychological. You seem an anxious sort. Try not to worry so much."

True, I didn't have cancer or MS or AIDS or any of the other horrible diseases I could list, and yet always there seemed to be a fever behind my eyes, a raw soreness in my throat, inflammation swimming through my blood, making me tired. Worse, my mind felt switched off, as if all the lights inside me had been turned down very low. Why *wouldn't* I worry?

I wonder now if it was because I'd become so curiously ill that so many of the things in my California world seemed absurd, or if it was merely a reflection of the times. Exhausted much of the day, I began observing rather than responding to the oddness around me, noting, for instance, that a homeless man slept under my car many nights, his head cradled near the left rear wheel, his legs sprawled, his flip-flops twisted; I noticed that our landlord, in his penthouse above our apartment, created a maze of newspapers stacked chest high, forming a passageway through his space to a wall-sized bird cage where eight cockatiels lived in ornate, stinking squalor; I was surprised that the couple next door, both engineers, dropped in to introduce themselves, the woman topless, her jeans short, neatly hemmed. I tried not to stare at the woman's breasts as I offered tea and cookies as if this was the most ordinary introduction to neighbors, *Let me just get the plates and napkins.*

I noticed these things but felt adrift, distracted, unable to react or comment. Or even to laugh.

LATE ONE AFTERNOON IN September after I'd been sick off and on for over ten months, I curled up on our blue-striped couch—we called it the "narcotic couch"—and gazed out the sliding glass doors at a smog-filled California sunset flush with colors of dusky rose and the faded yellow of a bruise. Behind me, the clock ticked loudly. The ceiling fan hummed, while just beyond the sliding glass doors a long rectangular roof provided me with a 180-degree view of the Pacific Ocean, a dazzling reprieve from our cramped, stuffy, apartment. On nights when I felt well, David and I sometimes danced out there under the stars, the day's dry air thickened at night by the humid swells of the ocean. The horizon was a thin, pale line illuminated by the tiny, diamond lights of a ship or darkened to an eerie flatness. Our next-door neighbors—the topless engineer and her boyfriend, who rented the other apartment opening onto the roof—worked late at their firm, and during the week, David and I claimed proprietorial rights.

Though I'd been lying on the couch for three hours, I hadn't had a restful sleep, only a heavy, dreamless collapse. I woke as tired and disordered as the moment I lay down. Now it was early evening, and I wondered where David was. He usually came home for dinner if he was working in his Venice studio, where he designed and made beveled and stained glass doors, windows, and skylights for clients, often bringing home takeout—soup or fajitas or a big salad. I wondered if he'd called or if I was supposed to know where he was.

As if I'd conjured him, the phone rang. It was 7 p.m.

"I'm finishing up a job with Roy and I'll be late," David said, sounding hurried and distracted. I heard the whine of power saws, the blur of talk, and some harsh scraping like industrial sandpaper against wood. "So, you'll be okay?

"I'm on the narcotic couch." Code to us already.

"Poor baby."

A pause. I wondered if Roy was listening in or grinning at David from across the room, holding out a tiny bag of cocaine. I wondered how much cocaine Roy had already snorted, how late they were going to work. David and I didn't do drugs, but Roy often stayed up forty-eight hours straight to finish a job, and even David, who averaged only five hours of sleep, couldn't keep up with him. Suddenly I sat up, nerves wired for trouble. "Where are you?"

"At Roy's studio," he said. "Remember, I'm working with him for a few weeks." And then quickly, "Gotta go. Gotta get something to eat. It will be a long night."

I settled back on the couch, relieved to know I could just lie here, idle, aching, letting the night absolve me.

AFTER LIVING FOR ALMOST a year in Seattle, David and I had returned to Los Angeles in the fall of 1982 with just enough income to tide us over for a few weeks. To our relief, our old landlord, the Money King, hired David immediately to manage some of his apartment complexes, and I worked temp jobs during the day, long, boring assignments that made the once-a-week, three-hour writing class at UCLA my dessert.

Within three months, David shared a studio in Venice with another glass artist, but he lacked contacts, and we needed money. The Los Angeles market for fine craftsmanship was extravagant and fickle, and we'd been gone for over a year, so it was fortuitous when he was introduced to a man named Roy, a man who'd become "all the rage" in the Hollywood world of designer-everything.

"Everybody says this guy's a wizard," David told me as we were fixing stir-fry in our small kitchen. It was one of my good nights and I was helping, cutting up broccoli and peppers and onions and measuring out the brown rice. "Some kind of maverick woodworker, you know, with a lyrical feel for the material." From what

David had heard, Roy built and refinished floors, making them look rustic, rough-hewn, and beautiful by distressing and sanding and then texturing them with five coats of gloss. He also constructed fireplaces and mantels and built massive beds that could have graced seventeenth-century French castles, beds held together with wooden pegs, the headboards thick and primitive and masculine. Later I'd understand that everything Roy built required punishing physical labor, weeks, often months of intense work, and, like everyone in Hollywood, he was always behind schedule, some finicky part of the work delayed.

A week later—invited to the desert to meet Roy and his wife—I was optimistic. It had been one of my good weeks. I'd worked four "temp" days at Paramount Studios and had finished a new short story, working through lunch hours and late into the evenings. If David could work with Roy—bidding jobs together or sharing clients—we'd be able to live in relative security and I wouldn't have to worry about my low productivity, my time on the narcotic couch.

That Saturday we drove southeast into the desert, the land as uniformly brown as a paper bag, only its tedious flatness dimming my enthusiasm. Nothing moved except a scattering of tumbleweeds in the occasional wind, the sky a relentless, searing blue. After two hours on the road, I wondered if we could be lost, as there were no landmarks to guide us, nothing but the gray ribbon of highway on an endless plain. Then a small market came into view, a lone gas pump out front.

"Land," David laughed. "We'll stop and get a Coke and check on these directions."

"Get me a popsicle. Raspberry if they have it."

"You'll be lucky to get cherry or grape." He smiled wryly as he got out.

Who was this man, this Roy, I wondered, looking out the window past the store at the barrenness, the cacti and stunted trees, the dull, dingy sand, this craftsman genius who lived in the desert? Would he change our lives? Would we like him? Would it matter? For the past four months, I'd worried so much about myself it was a pleasant relief to consider someone else. Surprising me, David leaned in the window, handing me a cherry popsicle, the wrapper already sticky. We both laughed, and the next thing I knew we were pulling into a graveled driveway where a white Corvette sparkled in the sun.

Rita, Roy's wife, took me in hand the minute we were out of the car. Maybe she saw me as the "wife," as someone easily amused, but perhaps I am being too cynical, too sensitive. She was a tall woman, lean and angular with dark blond hair and gray-green eyes that narrowed at the corners, not pretty in a conventional sense, but compelling, dramatic, a personality to be reckoned with. Roy was an outsized man with a large head, large hands, bulky shoulders, and long legs; he moved slowly, as if all his energy was held in check. Dressed in faded jeans and a beige shirt, he pushed at his unruly chestnut hair with thick fingers as he said in a soft, boyish voice, "Welcome to the desert, darlin'." A throwback from the 1950s. I smiled. By the time Rita had settled me at one of the tables on the spacious patio beside the swimming pool, David and Roy had wandered away toward Roy's studio.

Rita poured me a scotch on the rocks, never losing a beat in her commentary about some tycoon Roy worked for in L.A. She settled down beside me, informing me that she ran Roy's business, that it was she who took the crap, the bullying, the bluffs, the dismissals, the threats of litigation, "those nasty, aggressive phone calls from clients" when work ran over schedule. She looked poised, confident, and then her eyes narrowed. "This movie monster can't let a cunt tell him what to do, know what I mean?" She didn't name the movie monster, but it was clear it didn't matter. These guys were all the same, all worthy of her wrath. "Can't give *me* the money for the job, but he'd throw it away on some prick just like himself." I knew her curses were casual, simply part of the rhetoric, part of her tough-woman-seen-it-all pose. She closed her eyes, her head thrown back and I saw the faint lattice of lines radiating down her pale neck. "My god, women have it so hard," she whispered, then opened her eyes and sipped her drink. She stared at me. "But I'm not going to let them get me. It breaks my heart what I have to do but at least it's a hustle. I love a hustle." And then she smiled, her eyes flashing. "If I didn't have these pricks to deal with, I'd find some others. Yes sir, it breaks Roy into tiny pieces, but I *love* it." She took another sip of her drink. "I love my life!" she shouted. "I love my fucking life."

I smiled too because the scotch felt good down my throat and today I didn't feel sick.

"You have kids?" Rita asked, changing the subject so quickly it surprised me.

I shook my head. *I'm too sick to have kids,* I thought, though David and I had rarely talked about children. We hadn't talked about many things since I'd become ill.

"Too bad. I thought maybe you did. I always wanted kids, wanted a mess of them, but life is funny, isn't it . . . what you want at one time is what you can't get rid of fast enough at another."

I nodded, not knowing how to reply.

"I had one when I was fifteen. Nearly killed me having it, then when I got well, it was gone. Never really saw it. My mother put it up for adoption, but I didn't care. I wanted a new dress, some high heels. I wanted to see the world, get on the road and go, go go." She smiled as if remembering. "All I'd done was complain the whole time I was pregnant, and now I can't quit thinking about her. About her being lost." She sloshed whiskey in her glass, poured more, and took a long swallow. I wondered if the pronoun was important or if it had been a slip. "You won't believe it, but after that I went to nursing school. I used to be in charge of this program for drug addicts. Heroin. Smack. Devil-catchers." She stared beyond me, her face now saddened, older. I think she'd forgotten I was there. "And I lost again."

"Lost?"

"Yeah, they all died. Kaput with the needle. After all that talk I did

. . . Monsters!" She grinned suddenly, a foolish grin. "Well, I can't go back to that, so I stay here in the desert and try to get money out of these movie pricks for Roy."

I understood now that all Rita required was a captive audience, an occasional willing nod. I knew her stories would plot a familiar route: bad relationships, divorces, feuds, plastic surgeries (she confessed these in detail), debts, windfalls, collapses, perverse triumphs, untouchable greed, and resentment—a flood of suffering and redemption that could fill any daytime TV. Later, I'd wonder if money was her weapon of control. But money, I decided, was the result. For Rita, it would be face-to-face combat, a willingness to confront, to sink the ship, to play dirty . . . that was her sword. But I was getting tired. Listening had worn me out, brought back the old feeling of fatigue, and I was glad when David rescued me, insisting I see Roy's studio, a huge barnlike structure, as big as a warehouse built in a shelter of eucalyptus trees behind their house.

I clasped David's hand as we followed Roy. Dirty skylights opened the ceiling to the sun, yet in the dusty light its brightness was dim, esoteric. Other windows framed two walls, the desert stretching beyond in a smooth flatness. Roy stepped over a dusty piece of lumber, offered his hand to guide me, David right behind. Roy showed us the tools he used, mostly electric saws, cutting tools, a planer the size of my arm. Along the back wall, raw lumber, old and scrappy, pulled down from barns and condemned buildings, was stacked. It looked pockmarked, dirty. I thought it was funky, no good, but then I saw David's nod of approval.

"That's the stuff," Roy said. "The raunchier the better."

I walked through sawdust toward the wood piled against the wall. The wood's texture was battered, disfigured by wind and weather, the abuse of natural elements. Each piece was unique. Beautiful in its own way.

And then Rita appeared. She linked her arm through David's. "So," she said and smiled, tightening her arm, her fingers dancing lightly across his wrist, pulling him close so that their hips touched. "I think we'll be friends." She gazed not at David but at Roy.

WHEN WE LEFT THE desert, it was assumed that David would bid on some of the same jobs as Roy, perhaps sharing clients and thus working jobs together, though Roy's studio would be in the desert and David's in Venice, fifty miles apart.

On the drive home as David talked excitedly about the prospects, I tried to ignore the flicker of worry that nagged at such euphoria. Roy and Rita seemed theatrical and competitive, a calculated playfulness as if each was trying to claim us, not for ourselves but for some private agenda. To me, they seemed desperate, not for money but for something I didn't yet know. *Their lives are coming apart*, I thought and instantly knew it was true. I recognized this. My own life was coming apart, my days haunted, even when I was able to work, by a sense of fatigue and failure, a slow relinquishing of the self I'd known, the curious, ambitious self who wanted to be a writer. In Seattle, for the first time, I'd felt secure in the direction of my life. Though I'd been the rebellious, needy daughter for much of my life, the one who couldn't find a place to fit or an ambition to direct my intellect, in Seattle I discovered that writing stories galvanized me, settled me, as if I'd begun listening to a conversation I wanted to have. But once I became ill, there were many days when I couldn't sustain deep thought, couldn't puzzle out plot or the implications of character, my mind muffled by a fevered body, a broken immune system.

On the drive home, I closed my eyes, half-listening to David's thoughts and resenting his high-pitched energy. I knew that soon he'd be very busy, and the thought made me both grateful and worried. He'd get up at 5:00 a.m., walk out onto the roof in the early morning sun with a cup of coffee, gazing at the light haze over the ocean that blurred the horizon. He'd be thinking about a problem he needed to solve, and then for hours he'd be immersed in work, coming home near midnight. I'd be alone. I'd miss him. And like him, I too wanted the agitation of desire.

Maybe that's what kept me pushing against illness, made me experiment with different treatments and diets, cutting out all sugars and prepared foods, taking vitamin C and other supplements and getting allergy shots. There began to be days when I'd wake up to a veil of light streaming through the blinds and feel a sense of well-being, my body returned. "I'm okay," I'd think. "It's over." I'd wander out into the kitchen where David was making breakfast, pour myself a cup of coffee, and walk down the driveway to stand drunkenly in the sun.

Two weeks later I'd crawl, exhausted, into the stillness of my bed.

And yet for two weeks, I'd been a woman writing, working, reading, thinking.

AS I'D EXPECTED, WHEN the jobs with Roy materialized, David's life became hectic, charged with deadlines and meetings, designs and approvals as well as the work itself. To our relief, he was making money again, keeping us solvent while I managed to keep up with my night class at UCLA—my life support—and continued, in my erratic way, to be sick and then well, overwhelmed and optimistic, a lost cause and a writer.

It seemed that this way of living might go on forever. I don't know when it began to go terribly wrong or if we were simply caught in the downward spiral of the hustling ambition that made up so much of life in L.A. I try hard to remember. I remember that in early August, Roy moved his studio to L.A. to be closer to his clients, who'd become more insistent, even bitter, about deadlines, and David began to split his time between Roy's studio and his own. And then in late fall, quite suddenly—or so it seemed—Roy and Rita split up. I remember only that their fights were epic, full of threats and physical damage. Lawsuits were filed, cars driven up onto curbs and rammed into doors, wood splintering, glass shattering. Roy began doing coke all the time, working without sleep, his money gone, eaten up by lawyers and the chemical excess he needed to keep going. I remember David coming home late one night, exhausted by the sordidness, depressed by the weirdness of working with Roy. Roy, he said, was not just doing coke but that night had lit a crack pipe with an acetylene torch like someone *wanting* to commit suicide. "And all the creeps around him, the stupid fucks who work for him, were cheering him on as if it was some funny prank, ha, ha, just get yourself killed."

He slumped on the couch. "If I didn't need to get paid, I'd never go back. It's like being trapped in dark slime."

But he did need to get paid. All summer gas fumes from the cars parked in open stalls beneath our apartment complex wafted through our windows, making me sicker. Exhausted, I lay on the couch. Even when we kept the windows closed, there was always the lingering smell of gasoline and oil when we stepped outside, as if even the ocean breeze had betrayed us. We needed to find another apartment, but first we'd have to save a deposit and first and last month's rent.

AND THEN, SOMETHING CHANGED. One afternoon the ocean breeze was brisk and clean, and I felt a surge of energy, the waning of illness. I was working at home, rewriting a story at the kitchen table, when the phone buzzed. "I'm on the way to the doctor," David said, his voice high and faint as if he were dizzy. "The saw chewed off part of my finger. . . ." Then he slurred the doctor's address and hung up.

What part of the finger? Which finger? The whole finger? As I drove into Santa Monica, I thought of a severed middle finger, the fuck-you finger—bloody strips of skin and veins, callouses thickening the inside edge, the half-moon of a fingernail—dropped into a plastic baggy, an old shirt wrapped tight around the stump. But he'd said "part," so let it be just the tip.

When I reached the doctor's office, I saw David in the hallway, a nurse standing over him, her small, wizened face crisscrossed with wrinkles, her alert brown eyes sharp and focused. She barely glanced at me. She had the no-nonsense air of a marine sergeant as she tended him. "I'll need to see that," she said, pulling his hand toward her and removing the bloody cloth.

David looked woozy, started to sway, murmured, "Hail Mary, full of grace. . . ." Instantly, she whisked something under his nose. "Steady there," she said, and he shifted back into focus. Later we'd learn that she'd been a nurse on the Bataan Death March in the Philippines and seeing a bloody finger, the tip slicked off, didn't merit high drama. But as I watched her carefully clean the mess and saw David's confused, anguished face, a shiver gathered at the back of my neck. I felt the sudden pull of disaster, the unraveling of a panic I'd knotted and hidden somewhere deep inside. How would we survive now, two people trapped in the fringe of a life in L.A., our resources depleted, our energy sapped by the constant crush of getting by? Of course, we had no insurance. It had never occurred to us. We used every bit of our income to cover expenses. But I knew my anguish pushed beyond economics to the existential, as if for the first time I allowed myself to see that we were both fragile, physically and psychologically spent, our reserves depleted, our lives held together by the thinnest of threads. Though I'd felt untethered for most of my life, I'd also been driven, intent on overcoming and competing, finding my way and proving my worth. It had never occurred to me that I might falter until I got sick last year, my energy leaking out like air from a spent balloon. Now watching the nurse lead David into a treatment room so the doctor could patch his mangled flesh, I knew that behind all his intensity and concentration, he was as uncertain and terrified as I. It had always been there. I'd just never seen it.

I thought of Roy and Rita, the way they sabotaged each other, competitive and determined to make the other suffer. They too were fragile people, but fear had made them mean and angry and kept them fixated on punishment. David and I were different. I was sure of that. But our difference, I realized, also included a naiveté about financial stability, a reticence to assume the worst, to negotiate failure. When confronted by conflict or crisis, our instinct was to retreat, to turn away and wait before we acted. Perhaps this was the result of growing up with alcoholics or maybe it was simply a part of our temperament, a fear of losing control, of being pathetic, of making the wrong choice. As I stood outside the treatment room door, I knew, as if for the first time, that we had no safety net. I knew that we couldn't depend on good intentions or sudden fortune or virtue to rescue us. We had nothing but ourselves.

Listening to the doctor's voice talking soothingly to David, the shiver at my neck escalated to a chill. I watched David tuck in his bottom lip, then take a shallow breath. What would we do? What would happen to us now that David would be unable to work?

I HAD BEEN BROUGHT up to believe in the will, to assume that grit and determination and the driven self mattered. That night after we got home, while David lay medicated and asleep on the narcotic couch, I wondered if I could reclaim—as I'd heard that people often did in crisis—my old, driven self. I walked out alone onto the roof and stood staring into the darkness of the ocean. There were no twinkling lights in the distance tonight, no ships seeming to skim across the horizon, but the ocean breeze brought with it the smell of the sea, damp and musty and oddly pleasing. I leaned against the railing, uncertain if I had the energy for what lay ahead. For a moment I wished I were like Rita. I wished I could say, "I love my fucking life!" and mean the thrill of combat and controversy, the heat of the hunt. But I'd never be like that. For a moment I felt sorry for myself, for how frustrated and unprepared I was, how diminished by illness, how stupid and shamed by my situation. I wanted to whimper, to curl around myself, but then it occurred to me that this was what all the characters in the stories I loved recognized: the inadequacy of the self in the face of new circumstances, the terror of survival at every level of consciousness. I felt the brush of wind on my face, a burst of salt air. I imagined the swell of the sea, the heavy, white-flecked waves. Perhaps my fear was inevitable but endurable.

And then I saw a bracelet of lights far out on the ocean. Just a glimmer—or was I imagining it, wanting it? I narrowed my eyes, squinting. No, there were pinpoints of light skating in the dark, flickers of movement. Instinctively, I lifted my face to the night air. I knew this might be silly—Lights? So what? *You wanted those lights!*—but I told myself it didn't matter. As if the fact of them, the beauty and thrill of seeing them so many miles away, relaxed me, relieving me of some of my terror, I thought, *We can leave, we will leave, somehow, we'll get away.*

WHILE DAVID RECOVERED, I took on more jobs, pretending to be well even when I was sick, making myself do what six months before had seemed impossible. I remember sitting at a desk on the sixteenth floor of some insurance company, temping two weeks for an employee on vacation, feeling dull and irrelevant, a slug among the bottom-feeders, a placeholder at a desk. I'd been exhausted all week, going to sleep on the narcotic couch almost immediately when I got home and resenting the effort it took to dress appropriately each morning for such a boring job. One day after lunch, after I'd spoken to no one except to acknowledge the beginning or end of copy to be edited or typed, when I'd passed other workers in the halls as invisible as a ghost, I printed out a large sign and put it on my back: TYPING FOR THE MASSES, as if I'd entered the ranks of the socialist labor force. It brought a few punchy comments and some friendly laughs, and for the rest of the week I didn't feel quite so alone. Though I constantly admonished myself for not getting a better job—typing! changing commas! *I mean, really!*—I used all my "good" energy to write stories, to dream again.

After his finger healed, David refused to go back to Roy's studio except to pick up his tools. Instead, he worked on small projects and repairs. Though he didn't have many commissions, he'd become more cautious, and he had begun painting again. And now he came home for supper.

Maybe it was just that—a return to some kind of order, a life without the drama of Roy, a lessening of terror, that gave me the courage to apply to MFA programs in creative writing; that would be one way to leave. And on a sultry day in March a letter from the Writer's Workshop at the University of Iowa arrived, waiting for me after a day at another insurance company, my eyes still aching from staring at a computer screen for eight hours. I didn't want to open it and find out. "Oh, Christ!" And then I did, blindly, stupidly yanking out the single page of acceptance. Iowa, a place I'd never been and couldn't quite imagine! Thrilled, I ran out onto the roof and shouted to the ocean. "We're going! We're leaving! Fuck you! Goodbye!"

THAT JULY WE PACKED up our furniture and books and art supplies and drove across the country to Iowa City, Iowa, with its four-square farmhouses, its gentle rolling hills, its studious politeness, and perfect rows of corn. "Jesus, we'll be Midwesterners," David said as we passed through the flatness of Nebraska and western Iowa. To our surprise, Iowa City seemed a quaint place, almost a village, thrilling and new, a college town, a city of writers. As we drove the last twenty miles down I-80, I thought of Rita that day we'd visited in the desert. I saw her pouring more scotch, her eyes seared with sadness, and then as she took one swallow, her chin jutted out and she snapped, "The prick! I'll make him pay!" I wanted to laugh. That was how she survived, pushing, always pushing.

We'd left Los Angeles with such relief, there was only the sun's warmth on the roof to miss on cold, snowy nights in Iowa when the wind howled, and bare branches brushed furtively against our windows. I always hoped that eventually I'd see those difficult years in Los Angeles as useful, perhaps even necessary. I hoped I'd be able to extract meaning, to appreciate or at least mourn a painful, confusing time. After all, I still had days of inexplicable fatigue, what would come to be called chronic fatigue syndrome, a medical anomaly with almost no treatment and little medical sympathy. But this never happened. All I understood from those years was that I was humbled and had endured the mess and muddle of a marginal life.

After we finished unpacking our dishes and organizing our books, I gazed out the second-floor window of our small rental house in Iowa at the peonies and purple coneflowers blooming in a neighbor's yard, and felt grateful, even charmed by their beauty. Outside, birds chirped, the sky a blue-white haze while inside my small, still-empty study it was quiet and shadowed by trees. I glanced down at my notebook, words already written, a story in the making. Quickly, I sat down atop two stacked boxes and turned on the desk light to read what I'd come here to say.

Chapter 9

AFTER I FINISHED AN MFA at the Iowa Writers Workshop, I never imagined I'd return to Iowa City six years later as an assistant professor in the newly created MFA Program in Nonfiction at the University of Iowa. But in 1994, David and I packed up our lives in Tallahassee, Florida (where I'd gotten a PhD), and said an easy goodbye to the palmetto bugs, carpenter ants, and web worms, but felt nostalgic leaving the gorgeous live oaks and magnolias that shaded our street. "Goodbye," we yelled into the thick, humid air, a heat-glaze shimmering on the pavement.

In Tallahassee, David had moved from graphic and glass design to web design, and in Iowa, he quickly got a job with an architectural firm in the nearby city of Cedar Rapids while I began my trek up the academic ladder, teaching MFA workshops and seminars and undergraduate literature classes. Though the two of us were insanely busy in our demanding careers, we still secretly thought of ourselves as "an artist and a writer." *Doing our work* is what we called our mostly unpaid labor in art and writing, the creative life sustaining the imaginative rhythm and mood of the day. Luckily, in Iowa City, many people wrote novels, poems, essays, and plays or painted, drew, and sculpted in their garages while working at daytime jobs.

Once a friend's wife, exasperated, asked him, "Can't you quit being a *poet* for a little while?" He glanced away. Sure, he could get up from his desk and leave the pages behind, could go for a walk, meet for dinner, teach a class, have a conversation, an argument, could flirt and tease and sigh in boredom, but the "being" was in the thinking, the hearing, the listening, the beauty, and the longing.

And thus, it's not surprising that even in this new world of David's recovery—both of us trapped in the id of illness—I keep writing. I take notes, jot down images, and late at night I confess to my journal all my unvirtuous and unlovely thoughts as well as the sorrows and uncertainties and small triumphs that fuel the hours of my day.

AFTER ONE WEEK AT home, David can stand up long enough to eat, pee, and answer his email at a raised desk in his study. He can get himself in and out of the rented hospital bed in our living room, half sliding, half pulling himself into it like a large, damaged animal seeking shelter. He gets out of it with awkward knee and elbow bends and a scrambling push with his heels. Each time, as he grunts and grimaces, it's all I can do not to offer help. Instead, I act the sentinel, watching as if I'm part of an anthropological survey:

D looks like a man trapped in a Francis Bacon painting minus the religious iconography.

D struggles, rising onto his knees, panting, his stomach swollen, sagging, his eyes closed as if to say, "No more, no more."

D's scrotum is a bulging sack, enlarged by edema, like low hanging . . .

I STOP, ASHAMED, AND try to erase the image, to protect my husband's privacy, if only from my own thoughts.

I think instead of who we were eight months ago, yes, a night in September as we fixed a late evening snack in the kitchen. I was stuffing pita bread into the toaster and grumbling about some petty transgression—too much spam mail, one of the copiers broken in the English Department, a colleague who'd been snarky. "An *awful* day," I concluded, though this was a wild exaggeration, grousing for grousing's sake. I glanced at David. "I might have to run away."

David nodded. "I see."

"In the middle of the night."

He glanced at me. "Yeah, I know what you mean." He pulled out the butter dish, opening it, then gave me a sly smile, his eyes seeking mine. "Sometimes the best part of my week is when I go to Walgreen's at midnight to buy new inner soles for my shoes."

I burst out laughing. It was the silliest thing in the world. Man in the trenches! I could see him trolling the aisles of Walgreen's, his midnight mecca, then standing reverently before the shrine of inner soles on the rack. He'd pick one, feel its softness, its firmness, then try another until he found "*the one.*" Benevolence in a package. Cosmic joy.

David laughed too, and then grabbed my hand, pulling me closer, while with his other hand he batted me playfully on the ass. "Gotcha," he grinned, our old game of ass-punching spontaneously resumed. *Alright*, I thought, my mood shifting. And just as easily, I twisted away, swatting his butt before running from the kitchen and up the stairs, still laughing, even shrieking as he chased after me, barely two steps behind.

NOW, WE SAY HIS butt is "privileged," off-limits, inherently private, a dystopia in transition. But we also co-opt it, make jokes about it, giving it its due, especially the lovely scar from the perforator plus flap.

"Let's take the 'flap' out for a walk," David says on Sunday at the end of that first week. "You know, introduce it to the neighborhood."

"Okay!"

And that's how we begin strolling slowly, arm in arm, down our sidewalk, David in his faded hospital gown that sags unevenly beneath a black velour robe. "Quite fetching," I say as it lifts in the breeze, "though the dark socks and moccasins are a bit of a sartorial disaster." The air is soft and clean and smells of freshly cut grass.

"It's my Easter outfit," David says.

I laugh—I'd forgotten it was Easter—then glance at the houses on our block as if we might rouse the neighbors and say hello: first, Ann and Alex's white two-story, then Tom's one-story with its fresh coat of lavender paint with green accents and white trim and a front yard ablaze in daylilies. It's an eye-garden, intimate and happy.

Mostly though, I'm looking down, worrying about gaps in the sidewalk, ridges created by erosion from rain and snow, places that buckle and pucker the concrete. If David stumbles, we'll go down together. Though he doesn't look it, he's got the massive bones of a fullback, a man who should be six feet four instead of five feet nine. If he jerks forward, his weight will bring me to my knees.

When I see the white fluted petals of a honeysuckle twining up a neighbor's black lamppost and a white satiny ribbon, I automatically think, *It's Easter, a day of good news!*

Three hours earlier, Dr. M called to tell us the pathology report was negative. No lymph node involvement! I want to leap in the air; instead, I grin at the parked cars crowding both sides of the street as if they're a marvel. That is, until I see the dilapidated sofa—ugly brown tweed, cushions stained, the skirt torn—left on the curb across the street. Who could possibly want it? It's ruined. Hopeless. I turn away, needing to blot out the new thought buzzing in my mind: 20–30 percent of this type of tumor recurs. It's sneaky, persistent, uncivilized. It can come back.

I glance at David. His face looks pale, the skin sagging beneath his eyes. I look away to the house we call "the witness-relocation-house" because we've never seen anyone enter or leave though the outside is tidy, even pretty, the lawn always mown, the hostas in thick, lush clusters beside the fence.

As we turn the corner, then walk down the alley behind our house, a neighbor's security light blinks on. David and I laugh. Duh, it's midday in Iowa City. *Where are you, burglars?* We're still laughing when Michelle, who grew up in France, stands up from working in her garden, her hands flecked with dirt.

"Oh, my, have you been ill?"

"Surgery," David says. And then he surprises me. "I'm going to be a cancer survivor." It's the first time he's uttered the word *cancer* in public, the first time he's hinted at a future.

He looks at me. And I nod as if the two of us are standing before a benevolent god.

Chapter 10

ONE MORNING, DURING MY usual 3 a.m. check, I walk quietly down the stairs and stand beside David's hospital bed, relieved to see him stretched out on his side, his right hand cupping his face, the four firm pillows behind his shoulders and upper back. He looks so peaceful, almost serene—brows relaxed, face softened—that I turn away and push the curtains aside, staring out at the dark, silent street. It's eerily empty and oddly beautiful, the ash trees thickening with leaves, the nearby houses huddled in sleep.

At 5 a.m., I wake up startled and tired, my right leg aching, my mind muddled. *I'll just do a quick check*, I tell myself, hoping to get two more hours of sleep before critiquing manuscripts for my graduate class. Halfway down the stairs, I yawn, seeing David with the covers pulled snug to his chin as if he's facing the ceiling, but that can't be . . . unless. I race down the stairs and shove his shoulder, trying to turn him. "You've *rolled* over. You *can't* sleep on your back," I rasp.

"What?" His eyes flash open, but he's incoherent, caught in a dream.

"You can't sleep on your back," I say softer now, but still shoving at his shoulder. He's too heavy for me to move.

"I'm not," he says, but fear makes him suddenly obedient, and he shifts onto his side. "I'm not."

To my relief, I see he hasn't fully turned—the pillows have partially prevented him—but it's enough to scare us both. After wedging another pillow onto the stack, I bring my own blanket down to the couch and set up camp.

By 7 a.m. we're both hollow-eyed as I check the wound, lightly touching the large semicircle of newly connected skin with the handle of a pair of nail scissors as I saw the plastic surgeon do (if two white circles show, the blood supply is intact). "It looks okay," I say, sighing, but David doesn't meet my gaze.

"The fact that I can cause this to fail, that I can self-destruct—" He doesn't finish the sentence.

Instead, he tosses aside the pillows, wraps two Styrofoam rollers in blankets, duct-tapes them together, and secures them to the bed, making a formidable, less comfortable barrier.

WE'VE MASTERED THE FIRST complication, but getting David to the hospital for his follow-up appointment is the second challenge. He can't sit down to ride in the car. He can't walk the five miles to the Oncology Department. Dr. M suggested I rent a van and put an air mattress in the back, allowing him to lie on his side for the trip, but David can't get in and out of a van. Frustrated, David says, "Jesus, just tie me to the top of the car like Romney's dog!"

In the end, the solution is simple: we take the bus. David stands at the front of an Iowa City bus, one hand clutching the handrail, the other gripping the grab-strap, his hospital gown floating below a puffy blue winter jacket. To get to the university hospital, we must take two buses, walking three blocks from our house to catch the first one, transferring to the second one downtown at the corner of Clinton Street and Washington, across from the campus, then walking thirty-eight steps from the last bus stop to the hospital's main entrance.

Now we're on our way back from David's first pre-op appointment. It's mid-April in Iowa City. For two weeks the dogwoods and cherry trees have been in bloom, but last night the temperature dropped to twenty-seven degrees, and this morning the wind shakes the trees, loosening the buds. Pink and white blossoms scatter across lawns and onto the sidewalks as the bus maneuvers from the university hospital through neighborhoods of two-story clapboard houses that sit regally on sun-bright yards. David's black-checked pajamas are hiked up at the waist and safety-pinned to his hospital gown so that the loose elastic in the pants won't touch his wound or the two drains. Though he's worn nothing but faded hospital gowns, today he's made a stab at respectability.

When the bus stops at Clinton Street and Washington, we wait for all the students to get off, most of them ignoring us, talking or texting on their cellphones. The bus driver lowers the step, and, like a Secret Service bodyguard, I leap ahead to clear the way ("Ain't nobody gonna touch your bum," I've been teasing). "He's been in surgery," I announce to the two men waiting to get onto the bus. Their faces look blank, disinterested, white iPod cords dangling from their ears. But when they see my husband's hospital gown, they each reach out and grab an arm, easing him onto the sidewalk. Though I know he could have done this alone, I am so moved by their help I cry.

Now we stand in the sun's warmth in the middle of Iowa City as girls in pastel coats and leggings and gangly boys in ballcaps hurry past. I feel a sudden childish excitement: for the first time today, this seems like a success. And we don't have to hurry.

MARRIAGE IS WHAT I'M thinking about as I glance at David standing apart from the others at the bus stop. I notice his hospital gown is tucked up on one side beneath his coat, the back dangling and fluttering in the wind. I have an impulse to straighten it, to tend to him, but his face looks strained, cautious, and tired. Aware of how many times in the past week he's said, "Don't *help* me," I stay where I am. Since the surgery, we're like two people dropped onto a wilderness trail, wandering together on a route we didn't choose, uncertain of the dangers, wary of brief pleasures, forced to make up rules whose contingencies we don't quite understand. The one thing we know is that we're unprepared. Some days we cling to each other, surprised by our intimacy. Familiar tasks, such as preparing and eating a dinner of stir-fry and salad, pull us so close there's no need for words.

But there are also frazzled days when each of us feels lost and alone—more alone, I think, than we've ever been. Before we boarded the bus to the hospital this morning, I called to David from upstairs, "Did you get your coat?"

"Why are you always *hurrying* me?" he yelled back.

Surprised by his defensive tone, I stood at the top of the stairs, thinking, *I don't know you at all.*

On such days, I say one thing, he hears something else, and instead of solace or understanding, resentment and anger thicken between us. On such days, I never know what to do. My first instinct, I confess, is to flee, a voice in my head yelling, *Go, go, go*. My second instinct is to be bossy, hoping he'll comply with what I want. Resolution, I've learned, comes only after the hurt feelings, the anger and twisted rhetoric, have begun to exhaust us, and we break down, starting to communicate our deeper, more honest selves.

I step into the sun, shading my eyes. There it is: the Seventh Avenue bus, our final one.

Usually, I sit in a seat next to where David stands, but on this bus that seat is occupied so I must take a seat opposite him, several feet away. Still, I'm relaxed because the oncologist was pleased with David's rate of healing and secretly excited that we'll be home in time for me to fix a snack and review my notes for an afternoon thesis defense.

In the bus window's reflection, I'm smiling, and even imagine pumping my arm and shouting, *We did it!* like someone in a movie. Then I glance around, embarrassed, as if I've done this and meet the eyes of a young man in a North Face jacket seated two rows away. Blond and blue-eyed and probably in his thirties, he smiles a sweet, shy smile. I nod, then stare out the window. As the bus shifts gears and turns, I see David wince with each jerk and dip of this bumpy ride, his grip on the strap tight. When I glance around, the man in the North Face jacket is now grinning at me, and I smile back, thinking there's something needy about him. On another day I might pull out a book to signal distance, but today—maybe because of the good news at the hospital—I want no such defenses.

"It's finally getting warmer," the man says, as if we've been having a conversation. There are no riders between us. "It was cold this morning, but now it's okay."

"I had to put a sheet over my fern last night," I say because I come from a part of the country where such innocuous communication is part of the norm, an "exchange of pleasantries," we call it in Alabama, a way of being friendly and noncommittal in public.

"The flowers don't usually bloom this early," he continues, referring to the unusually warm spring we've had. "But they seem to be doing okay." Each time he says something, he smiles like a child asking for a lollypop.

"Let's hope the tulips didn't get killed by the frost last night." I never know how to disentangle from such conversations, and yet I'm enjoying getting to chat with someone without worrying about being misunderstood. To my surprise, the man gets up and moves to the seat across from me. Though he looks normal, I think he might be mentally challenged. His sentences are simple statements of the obvious. His face is open and guileless, and I can see that he's lonely and wants to be acknowledged, if only by an older woman on the bus.

"I like tulips," he says.

David turns, readjusting his hold on the strap and glares at the man with open disdain. "My husband and I have just come from the hospital." I nod toward David as if to defuse the situation. "This is our first time on the bus." By now I've adopted the man's short declarative sentences.

"It's a good bus," he says, ignoring David's gaze. "I take it every day." He leans a little closer, and for the first time I see something mischievous in his blue eyes, a flash of desire perhaps. I'm not sure what he wants, but I sense he's about to get up and sit beside me.

I reach up to pull the cord one stop early, then gather my purse and book and stand up. "Enjoy the ride," I say, giving the man a wave and a smile as the bus comes to a halt. David moves slowly, slowly down the steps. Each footfall jars his incisions and for a moment at the bottom he pauses with one foot in the air, half in, half out of the bus.

As I follow him onto the curb, I say, "Thank God, we'll get home in time for me to fix a toasted cheese."

No sooner does the bus pull away than David turns to me, his eyes burning with accusation.

"What? What's wrong?"

"What do you think you were *doing*?" he demands. "You let that man sit by you. You talked to him, but you don't talk to me."

I almost laugh, incredulous at the absurdity. *"What?"* If David hadn't come from the hospital where he was poked and prodded, I *would* have laughed. "Oh, honey, *please*. There was something not quite right about that man. Surely you could see I was just being kind."

David's gown blows in the wind and his blue coat makes his eyes look brighter. His hair, clean for the first time in a week, lifts in the wind, and then frames his face, making him seem boyish. I think of how anxious and drawn he looks each night when he's standing in a tub of hot water while I knead his calves, then wrap them in hot towels, tucking in the ends at the top so that he looks like a naked man in wet knee socks.

"I don't care." Still aggrieved, he refuses to look at me. "I didn't want you to talk to him." He fiddles with the coat's zipper. "It made me jealous."

I'm married to a jealous man. A sick, jealous man. Perhaps I should welcome his feistiness, be relieved he can feel this emotion, but I'm suddenly irritable. This feels like an old fight we have about loyalty: though we never doubt that we love each other, there's always the question of how much and how willingly that love is given. Who wants more attention? Who feels slighted?

"We talked about flowers," I say. "You heard it all." And yet even as I say this, I realize I was flattered. How absurd, but there it is: me a desirable woman, a girl on the bus.

The traffic light changes to green, and we cross the street; just two more blocks to go before David can crawl into the hospital bed and lie on his side and I can sit at my desk.

"But you *talked* to him," David says again, "and you walk three paces ahead of me."

As he says this, I realize I *am* walking three paces ahead of him. He has to walk so slowly it's hard to regulate my stride. I do for a little while, but then, impatient, I push past him. Now I stop and think how quickly we move to defend ourselves. *Haven't I taken good care of you?* I might say. *Haven't I been the most solicitous, the most dutiful of wives? And given this, don't I have a right to the insignificant pleasure of chatting with someone on the bus?*

I can imagine his response: *I'm the one who's been critically ill, the one who's had to suffer doing the most ordinary things, sleeping only on one side and waking with legs cramps and pain. I'm the one who has to shit standing up.*

He's right. That last part alone will win the contest of hardships and though he has the high ground, in marriage the high ground doesn't always matter. I long for us to be the couple joking in the kitchen: the half-asleep woman pouring her tea; the man teasing her as he brews his espresso. Instead, we are two people on the sidewalk, tired and petty. Anxious, I glance away from him, and that's when I see it: just beyond a wooden fence, near a set of narrow grey steps, a tulip blooms, red and languid in the sun. As suddenly my irritation dissipates.

David stops too. He looks so fraught, so fragile in his anger over the fact that I've gotten three steps ahead. "I always wait," I say, but his eyes remain distant, wary. His posture says he still wants to fight. I walk to him and take his arm in mine. He gives it grudgingly, his body stiff, unwavering. I hold him close, and we walk silently for the rest of the block until we turn the corner and see our house, a beacon of comfort and relief. Rest. Food. Sleep.

"We'll be okay," I say, patting his arm and hugging it tighter.

He says nothing. I keep my steps aligned with his, *slow, slow*, as we turn into our walk where, on each side, the hostas shoot up in thick green bursts. Carefully, we climb the four steps, stopping to rest at each one. As I move ahead to unlock the door, I hear the radio of a passing car and the drone of a distant lawn mower. I see our neighbors' dogs chasing each other in their backyard. Ordinary life.

"Thanks for getting the safety pins," David murmurs as I put the key into the lock.

In that moment, I remember how conscientiously he bunched together the fabric of his pajamas and gown, how carefully he fastened them with the safety pin, how he looked up at me and beamed at this small success.

"You're very welcome," I smile as we step inside our house.

Chapter 11

A WEEK LATER, I go out for the first time in months to have dinner with friends, a sense of normalcy I've lost. The night feels like a feast as we talk about writing and books and the ordinary frustrations of our lives, interrupting each other, ordering dessert, then coffee, then more coffee. Honor is her generous, reigning self, full of ideas and projects and funny stories of people in New York. Mary looks like a young girl with her new haircut and short bangs. Mary's telling us about a book she's working on, a book about how creative people use time, how the way each of us defines time presents a subjectivity of the self. I'm instantly curious, but it's the story of how she makes time for other people as a part of her writing life that intrigues me. For Mary, writing is personal but also intimate and social. Not only does she check in with a writing partner every day—a way of connecting psychologically as well as intellectually to discuss the work they're planning to do or can't do—but she also writes once a week with another writer, making a date for creative play.

Listening to her, I think of working at my desk late at night for an hour after David is asleep, of writing in my journal about the unholy parts of myself, of cribbing ideas on note cards to be elaborated later. I'm not good at writing with a partner, my sense of creative play coming alive when I'm deeply alone, but I wonder at the limitations I've intuitively imposed, as if my life has no time for anything but teaching, critiquing student work, and helping David with recovery. What I've learned is that in the middle of cancer nothing takes precedence over the story of recovery. And yet, while the metaphor of cancer is considered "a disease of overproduction, of fulminant growth," as Siddhartha Mukherjee writes in *The Emperor of All Maladies*, the metaphor of our lives has become one of constraint and narrowed focus, our obsessions diverted to pathology and practicality. For months, I've been both intensely alert and buried in fatigue, as if I exist only in contradiction.

We weren't always bound by constraint: I remember August evenings many years ago, weeks before I started the MFA program at Iowa, a summer of fireflies and late-night bike rides, of sitting on the front porch of our rental house in Iowa City, a pleasure that had been impossible in Los Angeles. One night we idled on our front porch after dinner, David playing with a neighbor's dog, then sitting beside me on the steps and eating ice cream as I stared into the darkening sky, surprised by how relaxed I felt, ignoring my writing, and simply dawdling.

I glanced over at David, lifting the last spoonful from his bowl. "Did you ever spend time like this, I mean, not putting creative work before *everything*?"

"Sure," he said, setting his empty bowl on the steps.

"Really?" I thought of how he often worked late into the night, ambitious, relentless, creating websites or making prints. I didn't know this part of him. "Do you miss it?"

"Well, I miss making granola."

"Granola!" We both laughed at how dated that was.

"I watched the sunset every night," he continued, his voice nostalgic. "For a year."

"An entire year?" I asked coyly, knowing how much he liked to exaggerate.

"Every night."

Now I was curious. "In Santa Cruz?"

"No, in Gualala and Manchester, up in northern California."

I knew that David had lived for several years in northern California with his girlfriend in the early 1970s before they moved to Santa Cruz and then to Los Angeles, where he and I met. I remembered that when we drove up Highway 1 the summer of 1981, my brain felt charged with happiness as we entered Jenner, a small coastal town in Sonoma County near the mouth of the Russian River, a town like Manchester: an outpost, a sanctuary with no economy to support it.

As I stared at the pink and white flowers twining up a neighbor's porch, I let myself imagine David as he might have been at age twenty-four in rural Manchester. In northern California, he told me, he'd meditated every day, baked bread and made vegetable soup, and been part of a close-knit community. He'd even played flute to the goats! I imagined him softer, calmer, perhaps reading Suzuki and designing logos during the day, then sleeping eight hours at night. And, of course, a proud granola chef!

It won't be until two years after his diagnosis with cancer that I'll wonder how this simple, committed life might have changed him, healed him, pulling him away from the feverish music scene in San Francisco and perhaps relieving some of the upheavals of his distressed childhood. Did those years of meditation help him regulate his hypothalamic-pituitary-adrenal (HPA) axis and balance his immune system? Did they make him more self-aware, leading him intuitively toward the man who would enter and change my life?

Calming down.

Relaxation.

Pleasure.

THAT NIGHT AFTER LOADING the dishwasher I open the door from my study to the deck, the smell of spring in the air, the stars receded into a blanket of blackness, the moon hung low, ripe and full. I remember those nights in Los Angeles when I climbed up on my trapeze and began my flight to nowhere, swinging wide, then wider, swinging from the back of the studio, up and up, and out into darkness, the velvet thrill of flying. *Letting go.* I close my eyes, imagining, my body soaring through the air, my mind loose. Suddenly, I feel more alive than I have in months. In a rush, I go upstairs to find David, who's checking his email at his stand-up desk. I take his hand. "Come," I say, and I lead him out onto the back deck, then down the steps and into the yard, where the yellow tulips are closed for the night, the ferns beginning to unfurl, a neighbor's clothesline swinging in the light breeze. We don't say anything. We simply stand in our yard, watching and listening, our story always moving and changing, full of surprises, diversions, and detours, but our breath tonight soft and warm and sure.

Chapter 12

THE STORY. ISN'T IT always a delicate balance between possibility and fatalism, self-knowledge and self-delusion, control and struggle? In our marriage, David has often been the optimist, the one who believes we can walk hand in hand into the forest and surprise ourselves while I imagine complications, uncertainties, the roaring of the unknown. To me, there's always a contingent reality cloaked in mist, a story beneath the story, a plot to be unraveled.

One night as we're sitting on the couch, I tell David that in literature the story beneath the story has a sequence: first, it's hidden, then glimpsed but not clearly seen, until finally it flickers like a light buzzing on and off, leaving a rhythm of clues.

"Well, sometimes it jumps out of the closet," David teases.

"Yeah, horror stories." I shake my head. "We don't want *those*."

THREE YEARS BEFORE DAVID'S diagnosis with cancer, there's a glimpse of what's been hidden, then a sudden bright flickering. It began in early October, the day after David bought me a red kettle, shiny and sleek with a full loop handle. "It's small and bright," he said, "just like you."

Pleased, I immediately put the kettle on the stove so it would be the first thing I saw when I came into the kitchen. And yet, the next morning when I glanced at it, I felt both immediate pleasure and shame because I'd already forgotten about it. Did I tell David how much I liked it? Did I hug him, kiss him, stand on his toes and make him sway with me, both of us too tired to do much more? I couldn't remember. I remembered David rushing out to his car, already late for work, his face pale and drawn from lack of sleep. He'd had too many late nights, and we were both exhausted from months of work, our moods as gloomy as the weather.

All morning, the wind blew leaves across our yard. Outside, there was an upheaval, branches and sticks roiling across the dead grass, newspapers caught in the shrubbery, a McDonald's wrapper and a Starbucks cup tangled in the dying hostas. Leaves piled up on the sidewalk, in the walkway, and caught in the cracked corners of the porch. I glanced at the sky, such a flat, dirty grey, like old underwear. I was supposed to be sitting at my desk, writing an essay about pleasure, something thoughtful and illuminating for an anthology on Carol Gilligan's latest book, *The Birth of Pleasure*. Instead, I stood frowning at the living room window, watching the world go by, idly wondering if David's energy was flagging, if he was compensating with extra coffee. When I'd gotten up to pee at 3 a.m., I glanced into his study: he sat at his computer, head in the turtle pose, the sides of his black bathrobe dragging on the floor.

I yawned, suddenly tired myself. And that's when I saw the two little girls from next door streak by my window in their pink puffy coats and dark leggings, their hair tangling in the wind. They stopped near the ash tree in my front yard, twirling in the leaves, exuberant, shouting, happy as if there was no such thing as boredom or exhaustion, their arms lifted, tossing leaves at each other, kicking and scattering them. Then they turned and waved at me before rushing back toward their house. I leaned against the clean laundry I'd dropped on the couch, the warmth of newly dried towels softening my knees. As I lifted a sage green washcloth to my face, smelling its cleanness, the pile felt like velvet against my skin.

Only then did I turn toward my study, ready to tackle pleasure.

THAT NIGHT, MY ESSAY begun, David home, our dinner eaten, we slouched on the couch, the towels folded and put away, the two of us released from our respective careers, the lights off, pillows plumped in our laps. It was so peaceful sitting in the dark, it felt easier to talk, to let go of the anxiety that kept my shoulder in spasm and David's lower back aching. "Couch time," we dubbed it, as if it were a new passive therapy, cheap and seductive, with no transactional requirement. *Just sit. Relax. Talk.* I closed my eyes. I wanted to tell David about the girls in their puffy coats because he liked the next-door girls who told us gleefully about dog poop and spiders and sometimes made us cookies, but I didn't want to break the spell. I felt dreamy, drowsy, almost rapturous. *This*, I thought, *is pleasure*, and so I was startled when David said quietly, "I found myself crying at work today, crying in the bathroom, but I don't know how I got there."

What? I opened my eyes, but he wasn't looking at me, only staring at his lap. He hadn't mentioned crying before, not in all the years of our marriage. A flickering.

"It was awful, uncontrollable . . . like I couldn't stop." He sighed, then turned to me, his eyes cautiously searching my face. He looked pale, sweaty, shadows deep beneath his eyes.

A flood of worry washed through me as I watched his face, wondering how I'd failed to notice those blurred rings of fatigue.

"I don't know why I was crying." His voice was softer now, barely audible. "For the first time, I was really scared."

I scooted closer to him and took hold of his hand even as a part of me longed to turn back to dreaming, to girls in puffy pink coats. *You're super tired*, I thought, remembering how late he'd worked last night, how little sleep he'd had in the last few months. "Do you remember anything before the crying?"

"No," he said glumly.

For a moment, I was silent, wondering if something had happened at work, if there was a quarrel or conflict that he wasn't telling me about. As creative director, his role was demanding, stressful; there was the usual competition and jealousy within the creative team, but in the last month he'd rarely mentioned them.

"I think I might be going crazy," he said. "I think this is what crazy is."

"*No.*" I was insistent. I sat forward, facing him, taking hold of his hands and pressing them inside my own. "You're *not* crazy, but you're *really* stressed, and you haven't been sleeping. You *have* to sleep. People without sleep can hallucinate, can come unglued. You become a walking zombie." What he needed was regular sleep, not the four-hour stretches he'd been getting, not catnaps and coffee, not twenty-hour workdays. I'd make him take melatonin tonight, make sure he went to sleep before me and slept eight hours. I'd fix us oatmeal and hot milk and lay down beside him, watching, waiting for his breathing to settle. I knew how to be vigilant even if this meant weeks of attention. As if I could mend what was clearly wrong—*he needs to sleep*—I stroked his hand, his skin soft despite the dry winter cold, and we both leaned back against the couch, quiet for a moment as a burst of wind rattled the windows.

In barely a whisper, he said into the darkness, "I've been suicidal."

Instinctively, I sat up, my brain capsizing, my body cold and still, everything changed. "Oh, honey."

I held my breath as he told me about days of driving back and forth to his job in Cedar Rapids, the infinite boredom of the morning drive, the trucks hemming him in, the cars cutting him off, the energy draining out of him, and all he could think about was how to slide his car into an embankment or a bridge abutment, anything with concrete that might *do the trick*. He closed his eyes.

"Don't," I said, squeezing his hand, pulling it to my body. And then I said it again, softer. *"Don't."* I stared at his face in the darkness.

"I won't." He tightened his grip on my hand. "I couldn't do that to you."

I touched his face, his shoulder, ran my hand slowly down his arm, caressing, easy, easy as my mind leapt into overdrive. I wanted to ask why, when, how, to claw my way beneath the story, to *understand*, but that wasn't possible right now. This wasn't sleep loss and anxiety. This was the Mississippi River with its churning currents and mighty floods. This was the story beneath the story, a terrifying plot that had just jumped out of the closet and awakened us with its screams.

THAT NIGHT AS I lay sleepless in bed, I thought of the Japanese lilac tree we'd tried to save last year. It had toppled in an early spring storm and leaned against our back deck, a dense clump of leafy branches covering the Weber grill as if it were merely resting before lifting itself back to an erect position. It hadn't been uprooted. This was a tree we'd planted when we moved into our house, a tree that gave privacy and intimacy to our deck so we could sit outside and talk while watching the moon. The tree was a dazzling sixteen feet tall.

When the man from Tidy Tree Service arrived, dressed in jeans and a slicker, his face was darkened by afternoon shadow though it was only late morning. He studied the tree for two minutes, then said bluntly, "Chop it down. It will never live. I've got the tools in my truck."

"No," I said, surprised at my own certainty. "Not yet."

"Your choice." He frowned as he rattled his keys. "It's now or later. Now would be cheaper."

The second man, a friend who worked in landscaping, was less emphatic. "Might live, but it's chancy," he said. "I think you'll end up chopping it down."

That night it rained again, and I imagined the tree's roots loosening, weakening, the earth too saturated, the roots wrenched and tired.

The third man, a tree saver who looked older and slightly tired himself, sighed, then said, "This will take some doing, but it's worth trying." And that day he trussed the tree with a brace and guy wires, then said in a careful voice, "Let's hope for the best."

To our surprise, that summer the tree leafed out as it always had, healthy and resurrected and reclaimed.

How I wanted this metaphor of resilience, though severe depression rarely bows to metaphor. Instead, I closed my eyes, wondering if I'd ever sleep.

WITHIN TWO DAYS, DAVID began telling his story to a wise therapist, revealing some of the difficulties of his childhood and the complications of an unstable family. I knew that David needed the supportive bracing and guy wires of a good therapist—a man we called Dr. K—a psychologist whose compassion and insight helped David hold fast to firm ground. Though David's first appointment was scheduled for the requisite fifty minutes, his visit extended to two hours, a generosity that would continue for months, allowing David the time he needed to reveal and grapple with his story. When David came home the first night after therapy, he was quiet and somber, his face contained. He looked as tired as I felt, and we wandered into the kitchen. I'd been starving after teaching a three-hour graduate class and had already eaten dinner.

Now David held out a bag of pills. "Sanity meds," he said, surprising me with a sheepish grin.

We looked at each other, then laughed. What else could we do?

"Somebody has to take them," I said. "What flavor?"

"Let's see. Wellbutrin, an antidepressant, and—" he rummaged in the bag, pulling out another bottle—"Zolpidem for sleep."

"Pretty good." I grabbed a cookie, wanting something crunchy and sweet, instant pleasure. "God, you must be hungry."

As David lined up the bottles of pills next to his bag of coffee beans, I fixed him a cheese and avocado sandwich and a salad, then sat down with him while he ate. After he'd finished eating, we did couch time, the lights out just like two nights before, our shoes kicked off, our bodies slumped, David's head against the pillows, his breathing regular as if already asleep. "I like this man," he said, surprising me, "the psychologist, I mean, but I can't talk about it, okay."

"I know." Though I was insanely curious, I tried hard not to ask about those sessions, respecting that telling the story of one's troubles, especially of one's childhood, also meant reliving it. A vulnerable place. A mess.

"You couldn't afford to make any mistakes in childhood," the therapist told him, and it was this one sentence that David repeated often, as if just saying it clarified and lifted a burden. Conflict in his family required a scapegoat, and he'd been first man up: *the bastard child plucked out of foster care, the mother's mistake, the stepfather's burden.* Though I still knew very few details about David's family, I began to understand that to survive his childhood, he had to squeeze through the cracks and constantly shift focus. But in doing this, he learned instinctively to keep his feelings tamped down, to hide, divert, digress, disguise. He had work to do: make no mistakes; avoid vulnerability; protect what is cherished from outside influence.

And, of course, if you can't make mistakes, your only choice is to become submissive or subversive. Or both.

THREE MONTHS AFTER DAVID began therapy, we drove to Barnes & Noble one evening to look for a computer book David couldn't find at home. It was one of those crisp, cold nights before Christmas when the air stung our faces, and just getting inside the store felt good, rushing from the car into the warmth and hum of lights. Therapy, sleep, and antidepressants had blunted the edge of David's sadness and contained his suicidal thoughts, and with the buzz of people in puffy coats and boots, teenagers flushed and rowdy, children noisy and gigging, I felt relief. While David looked for his book, I sat in the café, ordered tea, and began reading a novel, so engrossed I didn't notice him beside me until he laughed.

"Oh," I said, putting down my book.

He nodded, sat across from me, and started to read. I decided to run to Eddie Bauer's to buy a down vest, assuming David would get an espresso and settle in. "I'll be quick!" I joked because he knew I hated shopping, often simply pointing to an item, my debit card ready.

When I came back twenty minutes later, David was no longer sitting at the table, though I saw his book beside an empty espresso cup. I wandered the aisles, looking for him. When I finally found him, he was in the children's section pacing back and forth, anxiety carved into his face.

"Let's go," I said quickly. I zipped up my coat and we pushed out into the freezing night.

"I can't do this," he said.

"We won't do this," I said, and we drove toward home, both of us quiet, cars flashing past.

"My mother was always depressed," David said suddenly, surprising me because he rarely talked about his mother. "She basically went to bed and left me to bring up my half-brothers." He didn't look at me but out the passenger window, as if talking to the dark. "I hated it. Hated that she was depressed. Hated that she just lay there, not making dinner, not washing the dishes, not taking care of her kids." He glanced at me, then said in a tight, small voice, "I always had to stay *in*. Her depression kept me *in*."

He'd told me some of this before, but never so vehemently. What I remembered wasn't about his mother but how he'd once teased his brother, sing-songing, *"Johnny is a human. Johnny is a human,"* until his brother ran crying to his mother and begged her, "Tell David to stop calling me a human."

As I drove into the outskirts of town, down the slight hill toward the Iowa River, I thought about David's mother, a woman David hadn't seen in over forty years. I'd never met her—David didn't want me to meet her—and yet she called our house every few years, always surprising us because David had changed his last name, had never given her our number, and we'd moved many times in the last twenty years. Another surprise: on the phone she was gregarious, the kind of person who could talk for hours, filling in silence with anecdotes of her day, stories of the neighborhood. She never mentioned how she'd found our number or why she'd called, and she never asked why David didn't call her. Instead, her voice was inclusive, easygoing, almost coy, as if we talked to her every week. It was this ease that irritated and confused me, this implication of intimacy, this assumption of normalcy.

As we neared our house, David said quietly, "I don't want to be like my mother."

"You *aren't*," I said. "And you won't be. From what you've told me her depression was never treated."

He stared out the window. "I hope not. I was just a boy. I'll never forgive her for keeping me in."

KEPT IN. I THINK ABOUT this now, so many years later, because it's one of the hardships of cancer recovery. After surgery, David is primarily housebound, a man walking around the kitchen and living room and dining room in hospital gowns and pajamas and moccasins, his world defined by caution and avoidance, restriction and pain, wound care, and diagnostic appointments. In the past, if he wanted to do something, he wanted to do it immediately: let's go to the library, the movies, the grocery store, let's go eat Thai food, get French fries, right now, C*om'on, let's do it*! Impulsiveness! For years, this has been one of the thorns between us—this desire for immediacy, for getting out of the house—but now cancer dictates a different world. Recovery demands planning and restraint, self-consciousness and concession, watching and waiting.

Cancer is the new mean mother.

It keeps him in.

Chapter 13

OUTSIDE MY BEDROOM WINDOW the trees are wrapped in fog. Silvery threads of rain coat the glass. It's not yet dawn, and I don't know why I'm awake. I rub my eyes, pulling the sheet closer around my shoulders as I sink back into bed. And then I remember—*the 5 a.m. check.* I push aside the covers, grab my glasses, and glance at the clock: 4:55. I've awakened before the alarm. *Trained.*

I pause at the top of the stairs and gaze out the window into a pale grayness. It's Sunday morning. For the past two weeks I've been stressed and distracted, but as I watch the fog drift, the lilac bushes becoming visible, then veiled, I tell myself that today will be better: David won't be cranky from lack of sleep; I won't do laundry or dishes; we'll fix waffles, then watch something on Masterpiece Theater, me in the leather recliner, David standing with one hand on the back of the chair for support.

Though the living room is dim—shades and curtains drawn, lights off—I see right away that the hospital bed is empty. David's probably in the kitchen or the bathroom or maybe in his study, checking email at his stand-up desk. Sometimes he gets restless during the night, or his leg cramps, and he'll pace for a while to relax the muscles, roaming the house like a nocturnal tour guide: here's where we've made a thousand cups of espresso; here's where we caught that sneaky mouse; here's the pile of mail we shift from the table to the counter and back to the table. This morning, I prowl the house, calling his name. He's not in the kitchen, not in the bathroom. I climb the stairs and open the door to his study, expecting to see him standing at his computer, hospital gown hanging below his down vest. The room is empty.

There's one more place he could be: in the basement, putting clothes into the washing machine. But when I open the basement door, there's only darkness. I flick on the lights and call his name as I descend the steps. *Nothing*. Back upstairs, I'm surprised to find the front door unlocked. For years we never locked it, thinking the habit fussy and prim, but now there's a halfway house across the street with a group of thick-bellied men sitting on the porch at all hours. Several times this winter a police car and ambulance have arrived at that address, sirens blaring. We began locking the door.

When I step outside, the trees glisten with rain, and the wind blows their limbs against the roof. The light is soft and ghostly, with spooky fog that rises from the earth, erasing boundaries. Still in my pajamas, I walk toward the street. The hostas poke their noses through the dirt along our front walk. I don't see anyone, but even the outline of cars parked ten feet away is hazy because of the drifting fog. Softly I call David's name, feeling like the heroine in a thriller when something awful is about to happen. As if I've conjured the possibility, I imagine him wandering aimlessly in the fog in his hospital gown and slippers, happy to be lost, free of confinement, no longer kept in. He likes to wander, to ignore all directions, to throw away the map when we're driving across country, to miss turns and signs because he's distracted by the tug of a thought, the lyrics of a song. He's ruled by impulse and intuition; when his brain says, *Go*, all the neurons wave happy green flags.

But that's silly. Just yesterday in the bathroom, his face grew clouded with fear, and he insisted I get inside the shower with him to dry him off. "Go slow," he whispered, as if the nap of the towel might hurt his skin.

I watch the mist rise from the ground, shrouding the street, a pale, yellow light skimming the tops of the trees. That light. . . .

I race back inside and upstairs to his study. His camera, which usually sits at the far end of his desk, is gone. Anxiety floods my veins, followed by anger: he's gone on a 5 a.m. photo shoot not less than eight hours after he scolded me for not being careful with his incision. I glance out his study window and imagine I see him on College

Street, leaning forward, his eye to the camera as he frames a shot. He inches closer, closer, but the concrete is wet and slick, and before he can help it—

I jerk away from the window, but I can't stop imagining dire possibilities: He's stumbling over an uneven sidewalk. He's missing the step down from the curb because he's been distracted by the red tulip at the edge of a neighbor's yard. He's moving in to get a shot of an oak tree and then backing up too quickly on the damp grass. When he fits the camera to his eye, he becomes oblivious to everything outside the scope of the lens. Lost in time. Green flags fluttering.

Back downstairs, I turn on the porch light and step outside. I call his name softly, then a little louder and with insistence. My jaw is clenched. I try to relax it. *Why would he do this to me?* I imagine him standing just inside the perimeter of a neighbor's yard, staring at vines tangled through fence posts, the leaves jutting out, when a police car stops nearby. He doesn't see the two policemen approach, asking him to step toward them, to put down his camera, to provide identification. He tries to explain that he's just taking photos; unaware of how ridiculous he appears; unaware that in the past month two men have gone AWOL from the psych ward at the university hospital; unaware even that he's trespassing. Again, they ask for identification, and he gives them our address. They stare at his nightgown and say, "*We'll drive you there.*" His face tightens. Sometimes he still calls the police "pigs," as we did in the sixties, his distrust of authority firmly grounded in the experience of being detained in 1966 for having hair down to his collar. Now, I imagine, he tries to tell the police that he's had an operation and can't sit down for six weeks.

Will he hike up his gown and show them the big smiley-face incision on his butt cheek with its two teardrop-shaped drains? Will he say ironically, *You know, I just might have an expiration date, so I'd better get this photo*—a joke that will evoke no smiles? What can he say except that he's an artist, and this is what artists do: tramp out into the unknown when the light seems right and the spirit is willing?

Shit. I sit down on the front steps. I'm making myself crazy. I should go looking for him, protect him, but behind my worry and fear lies a silent fury. For the past two weeks we've joked that his condition is improving while mine is declining. As a caretaker, I've subordinated my own life—writing time, sleep, teaching prep—in order to make sure he's as safe and comfortable as possible: nighttime checks, medicine schedules, showers, clean gowns and drains and dressings. Now I cradle my head in my lap as the dark mess of my resentment tumbles out: *I don't want him to do what I can't do*. It's such a creepy thought, I know it's true. The idea of David being pulled by inspiration and impulse while I sit here, anxious and empty, makes me angry. It's the old story: How dare you venture out into the world and get lost while I wait and worry? How dare you indulge your creative life while mine is buried in errands and laundry, appointments, and bills?

As raindrops fall from the overhanging branches, splashing my ankle, I'm no longer worried about his safety. I'm worried about myself, a woman envious of her sick husband.

MORE THAN THIRTY YEARS ago, after David and I fled the chaotic bustle of Los Angeles, we boarded the Black Ball Ferry from Port Angeles to Vancouver Island while sheets of rain slapped against our ponchos and flooded our shoes. Only our books and snacks—held beneath our ponchos—remained dry. Once we'd settled in our seats, I took out Gore Vidal's novel *Burr*, which I was two-thirds of the way through, and Sartre's *Being and Nothingness*, a book on existentialism I thought I should read if I wanted to call myself educated.

"Can I see your Sartre book?" David asked.

"Sure." I watched as he opened the first page and began to read. I expected he'd soon get bored and put it down, since he had his own stack of books. I continued reading *Burr*. But when I glanced over twenty minutes later, he seemed absorbed.

"What are you doing?" I asked. "That's my book."

"Oh, are you reading it?"

I said no, but I was going to read it next.

David looked at *Burr* and saw that I still had a sizable chunk left to read. He said he'd read the Sartre while I finished the novel.

"You can't," I said, surprising us both. "*I* have to read it first." I put my hand over the book.

"Why?"

I stared into the distance, where rain blurred the horizon. "Because it's mine," I whispered.

"That's ridiculous!" David stood up abruptly, tossing the book into my lap, and walked away. But then, just as suddenly, he came back and stepped close to me. In a voice so low only I could hear, he said I was just too competitive to share. "You don't want to learn things you want to *possess* them. You're afraid that if I read the book first, I might know more than you, and you can't stand that."

I stared, stunned by how astutely he'd analyzed me. Humiliated by such transparency, I began to cry. I couldn't believe I was so warped and insecure that I didn't want him to know something I didn't. As he walked away into the interior of the ferry, I worried this would end us.

Miserable, I ate my beef jerky.

Twenty minutes later David returned carrying two cups of coffee. He gave one to me as if nothing had happened, his hand briefly touching mine. I stared at his thumb on the paper cup, remembering how, weeks earlier, he'd pushed aside a clump of hard dirt with that thumb as we'd lain laughing and kissing in an alfalfa field. "You don't need to be competitive with me," he said now, leaning closer. "I want you to learn as much as you can. As much as you want."

I'M MAKING TEA WHEN I hear the front door open, and my entire body tenses. David appears in the kitchen, camera in hand, looking self-absorbed and happy, oblivious to any complications caused by his early-morning jaunt.

Rather than feel relieved that he's back, I'm still angry. "Where have you *been*?"

"Taking pictures," he says, surprised at my tone of voice. "It's the light. I had to capture the light. I had to—" And then he sees my face. His body softens as he comes closer and tries to hug me. At first, I resist, my arms stiff by my side, but then I let him draw me in, my nose to the hollow of his neck, and I remember how last year, his body still whole, he walked out onto our front porch in a blue shirt—*only* a blue shirt—and I laughed from the porch swing.

I smell the rain on him, the musty dampness in his hair, his robe. It's oddly pleasing. When I pull back to gaze at him, he looks like a man who can survive anything. I feel torn between pushing him away and saying, "Let's have *breakfast*."

"I can probably sleep now," he says.

"Don't ever do that again."

He nods, yawning, then picks up his camera and starts up the stairs.

THOUGH THE POPULAR NOTION of marriage is that it's a partnership, a spiritual and sexual joining of two selves, that definition seems too benign, too constrained for all the feelings that fuel our union, all the mixed emotions and raucous decisions that define the way we have lived. David and I constantly connect and disconnect, fall in and out of each other's favor, alternatively crave the other's attention and long to be alone. It's true that we like the same jokes and make fun of the same people (whose traits often remind us of the worst parts of ourselves). We both require solitude and silliness, have fetishes about food—though never the same ones—and prefer a double bed to a queen or king, our bodies overlapping, entangled, thrown together. David once told me I needed to protect him from myself. I once insisted he was a self-righteous egotist and gave him a priest's collar and a mirror to seal the deal. "You don't listen!" I'll yell when I'm upset, and then he does listen—intently, even his breathing attuned to mine. And yet beneath all our habits and quirks and vanities, I secretly believe that what pulls us together is recognition: we understand each other's need to burrow deep into ourselves and become something more.

While David is upstairs, I wander into my study and peruse the bookshelves. There it is: *Being and Nothingness*, pushed between two paperbacks. I never read it. And yet I've packed and unpacked it with every move: from Los Angeles to Seattle to Los Angeles, to Iowa City to Tallahassee and back to Iowa City. I pull it out. The cover is worn, wrinkled, and water-stained. Staring at it, I realize I've misperceived my own story: I always told myself that the girl on the ferry would, in time, with the man's help, overcome her sense of intellectual inferiority, her need to know more, more, more.

Now I see that, instead of fading away, that feeling of insecurity is a live-in companion. I gain release only when I'm immersed in creative work, hunkered down, my daily life fading as the words ignite. Through the years, I've come to know that David is the same, released from his own captivity only when he sees the light loosen the mystery of two blue garden chairs in the weeds or the angle of a crooked, rusting fence. His morning trek was his way of defying cancer's demands, dismissing despair. For two hours he wasn't a man recovering from a rare malignancy, restricted and cautious and scarred, but an artist getting lost.

And of course, that is the problem. I want to get lost, too.

Chapter 14

WHO AM I BECOMING?

I write that sentence and stop. I can't seem to go forward.

Instead, I pause, wondering how I've learned to give and withhold tenderness, to feel so defensively competitive, to want so much more than seems available to me. Is marriage always a battle for power and balance, a struggle to claim your territory and also share it, or are we all Beckett-bound for ashcans, in locked combat until the end?

I think of my parents. Their marriage, a conventional marriage, lasted fifty-eight years until my father died in 2000. For years I was convinced I'd shaken myself loose from their legacy. Wasn't I a feminist, a writer, a professor teaching in Iowa, France, Italy, and Australia, living a wilder, more progressive life than was available or desired by them? I had divorced in my twenties, had several relationships, then lived openly with David before marrying him, shunning much of Southern middle-class life. But maybe I hadn't traveled that far. Maybe I'd stayed emotionally under their wing, repeating instinctively the lessons I learned as I watched them.

As I'm thinking about this, my ninety-one-year-old mother calls to tell me that a hard rain ruined the flowers on my father's grave. "They were all bunched together in places and just drooping in others," she says.

Oh, Mother, I have so much to do, I want to say. Instead, I listen.

"I threw them away and went right to Trees & Trim, where I found some red hibiscus with brown cone flowers for accents," she continues. "They were so pretty and in such a beautiful urn, I took them to the register even though they were over two hundred dollars, more than I could afford."

I remain silent. Last summer when I visited, she and I sat together with an account book at her kitchen table, going over her expenses to see what she might cut. Utilities. Groceries. Car insurance. House insurance. Dental care. Lawn care. Shoes. Underwear. Gas. Christmas presents. Not once did I think about flowers for my father's grave.

"I got to the register"—her voice brightens—"and guess what?"

A pause.

"They were half price!"

Until my father died, my mother never worried about bargains, never checked prices or used coupons, never denied herself flowers or cocktail dresses, patio umbrellas or sofas—never even balanced a check book. "Overdrawn," the local banker would announce drolly to my father every few months, and my father would simply shake his head and replenish her account. Now, she's elated with the bargain of her red flowers for his grave. "I drove several rows back to see them, and oh, honey, they just looked so nice."

As she talks, I remember that every time we've driven to the cemetery, she's fretted about the grave's upkeep, anguishing that his tombstone—a limestone Celtic cross—isn't more dramatic and imposing, that it doesn't represent him properly, doesn't validate his status in my hometown. He died of pancreatic cancer, a relatively quick, quiet death at home, his suffering minimized by medication, all his family gathered around him to say goodbye.

He was the love of her life and she the love of his, I thought last year as she and I circled the flat, unattractive cemetery, careful to turn into the grassy path toward my father's grave. Maybe I'm being ridiculous. And yet here I am, longing to believe in the romantic inevitability of my parents, the hard reckoning of their union despite all its scrapes and gashes, its metaphorical blood and gore.

"We spend most of our adulthoods trying to grasp the meaning of our parents' lives: and how we shape and answer these questions largely turns us into who we are," Phillip Lopate wrote in one of my favorite essays.

He was the love of her life and she the love of his. I'm no longer sure the truth of this sentence matters. What I know is that no two people could have been so aligned in their life's goals and so different in temperament, so bound by upward mobility and so fractured by social desire, so obsessed with success and so conflicted by pleasure.

After saying goodbye to my mother, I sit at my desk, the door open so I can see David sleeping in his hospital bed. I think about them. My parents.

Who were they?

MY MOTHER, A SERIOUS, introspective person, always insisted, "I don't like parties," apprehensive of any fuss *outside* of family events: Christmases, birthdays, graduations, and anniversaries, activities where the assembled could feast on her rich banquet of food and unwrap elaborate, expensive presents while eating red velvet cake on good china. For most of her life, she was captive to the decorum of the Southern class system, an entitlement based on family lineage to which she had no hope of easy admission, born as she was to miners in northern Alabama in the early 1920s. Her story had always been a bit of a legend to us: at age sixteen, she pushed her way into the larger world by going to the University of Alabama on scholarship, surprising herself with her intellect and her energy, delighted to learn her way around science labs and hospitals, dietary kitchens and shiny dance floors—this last, I imagine, with guilty pleasure—yet never losing the shadow of poverty that had burdened her childhood. It was her bad fortune to come to mature adulthood in the 1950s small-town South where women—shuttled back into the domestic sphere after the war—were judged by their husband's professions, their household luxuries, and their beauty and finesse at entertaining.

Ironically, my mother blamed her lack of social confidence on her looks. With raven hair, hazel eyes, high cheek bones, and an almost perfect figure, she could look startlingly glamourous or simply pretty, a reality she never quite grasped because of the flaw of her teeth. They protruded and were made fun of in childhood. Too poor for braces, she'd corrected her overbite in her early twenties with a dental bridge, and in her early thirties, perhaps to compensate, she bought closets full of clothes and scads of beautiful high-heeled shoes: brown lizard, black satin, blue suede, white leather, pink silk slingbacks, four-inch heels embossed or beribboned, the toes so sharply pointed they often looked menacing.

"I've always had pretty legs," she'd boast when my sister and I marveled at the shoes, giddy to try them on. "I need pretty things."

Pretty things brought her up to par.

My father, by contrast, was gregarious, witty, overweight, and naturally affectionate, loving nothing better than to work all day at his clinic and go to a party at night, flirting and dancing with all the women and drinking with all the men, certain that my mother would drive him home. His pleasure, of course, depended on my mother's dependability. For him, social life was a compulsion and a necessity. Also born into poverty (the Mississippi variety of bakers and factory workers) he wrestled himself from its grip through college and medical school, assimilating easily into small-town middle-class life as his medical practice flourished. "Oh, sweetheart, your father delivered every one of my babies," a woman said, squeezing my arm and smiling adoringly at my father as we stood in line to pay for an apple pie at the counter of the Friendship Café. My father, always a sucker for praise, grinned and teased, "Well, Mrs. S., you certainly kept me busy," while patting her shoulder.

And yet despite his success, my father felt the constraints of the Southern class system in a way quite different than my mother. He'd learned in his childhood to deflect from conflict and controversy, and in adulthood, he determined to avoid it by impeccable behavior. "Never be in the wrong," was as infallible to him as "pretty things" was to my mother.

The solution: an exemplary family. Why not be admired and successful, tenacious and charming, pushing ourselves to the top of the heap? Wasn't that the path to happiness?

Often on Sunday, dressed early for church—*always early!*—my father waited impatiently in the car with us kids, drumming his fingers nervously on the steering wheel, whistling a tuneless song, checking and straightening his tie in the rearview mirror. He'd been at the hospital with a patient until midnight. "Dammit, where is she?" His eyes flashed toward the door as if his stare might conjure my mother. *Late again*. He gnawed on his thumb, peeling a hangnail. When she finally emerged, locking the door, and then hurrying toward us in a silk dress and alligator high heels, she looked up only as she rounded the front of the car. Just as she passed the right headlight, my father beeped the horn. Always, my mother jumped, her shoulders jerking in cartoon fashion, her purse swinging. Always, my father laughed, released from his sulky mood. "Got her!" he'd wink triumphantly at us kids. Because he did this so often—almost every Sunday—the repetition is telling: a threshold crossed again and again with the exact same results—my father exasperated, then teasing; my mother surprised, then exasperated—as if they had enacted a conspiratorial pact. "Oh, Johnnie," she'd say in an aggrieved tone as she opened the car door, her lips pursed, his stretched into a grin. Their world righted.

IN MY LATE TWENTIES, I declared my parents' marriage *hell* (a "fucking joke"), the kind of "old style" marriage defined by inequality—dominant husband/subordinate wife—with all the trappings, I assumed, of inner loneliness, unspoken desires, and economic/sexual barter. Once I asked my mother if she ever talked to my father about their life together, about sadness or worries or private pleasures, or even why she liked the red caladiums in our front yard better than the white. She looked stricken, then merely embarrassed. "No," she said quickly, turning away, "we never talk about such things." And then after a trip to a medical convention in San Francisco, she confided wearily to me that she'd not only packed my father's suitcases but carried them on the trip. To my horror, I could imagine it: my father striding briskly ahead with his short, determined steps, my mother trailing behind like a valet, while he checked the tickets and talked to a colleague. Twice a week, she ironed his handkerchiefs (white cotton, light starch), and his underwear (white cotton, no starch), folding the boxers into perfect squares, all stacked neatly in a pile. As compensation—or perhaps he simply liked to indulge her—he gave her unlimited credit on her credit cards, always complaining with bluff irritation when the bills came in but never demanding a budget or cutting her off. She spent every penny.

My mother, I came to understand, needed not my father's energy—she was indefatigable—but his insistent direction, his demands, his gusts of need, her own private assertions foiled by a passivity I've never been able to unravel. It seemed as if something deep inside her had been restrained early in life, like a hand clamped tight over a mouth.

Only after we children had left for college did she declare her independence, returning to teaching science and biology in 1966 and remaining a beloved and demanding teacher for the next seventeen years. To shift the balance further—perhaps a final revenge for my father's masculine power plays—she began to serve dinner to him *last, after the grandchildren*. None of us questioned that she was still doing the serving, only that the order of business had changed.

In my forties, I saw for the first time the unspoken compatibility of my parents' routines. "Old bird," they called each other at breakfast, a joke between them, my mother still making the coffee, my father still paying the bills, the two of them getting up at 6 a.m. "Pass the sugar, Old Bird," my mother would say coyly, and my father would grunt, then flash a toothy grin and comply. They laughed at the same public fools, bitterly resented all criticism against the other from outside the family, and slept in the same bed for over fifty years.

In my fifties, I understood that they had endured and risen together and that this "survival and success"—securing a place for themselves as respectable and respected—had been a primary bond. "In unhappy marriages . . . I see two basic versions of reality rather than two people in conflict" and thus "a struggle for imaginative dominance," Phyllis Rose notes in her book about Victorian marriages, *Parallel Lives*. My parents' marriage had never wavered from their common belief in the transformative power of ambition, the necessity of sacrifice and loyalty and long hard hours of work.

Now, sitting at my desk, in my own threshold of uncertainty, I worry. Did I learn too well to see relationship as subordinate to work, work as defined by the will to succeed and the will to succeed as the most desirable thing—the *only* thing—in a person's life? In childhood, I remember that all our holidays were interrupted by my father's work, an emergency at the hospital, a house call, my mother weaving her way around the complications. As well, my father grumbled when my mother, sister, and I arrived after dark from ballet lessons in Mobile, indignant that he might have to make or even serve himself dinner. Vacations were work vacations, a medical conference in the mountains, in the city, at the seashore, something to expand my father's career. My parents rushed through their days, always pushing as if to prove they could work more than anyone else.

Is this what I too am trying to prove, why I feel such an urgent sense of deprivation? Is this why David's need to be creative, regardless of his physical condition, made me jealous, afraid suddenly that my own ambition is slipping?

I think again about David's comment to me years ago on the Black Ball Ferry: "I want you to learn as much as you *want*." But of course, there's always a story behind the wanting.

Ambition as first loyalty. The legacy of my family.

It's the old story of identification and subversion, complicity and revolution, the desire for self-expression shifting mainly in form. *I am like them. And I am not.*

I glance into the living room, where I can see David lying on his right side, now fiddling with the iPad, trying to find something to read. What about his parents? I wonder, curious if I'll ever know how he's like and unlike them (his mother and stepfather are both dead), what rituals and demands they followed. But it will be another two years before I'll know the deeper story of his past and the Dickensian hardship of that life, what was lost and what was found, what drove and frightened him, and what surprised him with pleasure.

Chapter 15

IT'S MIDAFTERNOON, FIVE WEEKS after David's surgery. I'm in the kitchen making a cup of tea and peeling an apple while David lies in his hospital bed no more than three feet from where I stand arranging sliced apples on a white dessert plate. A half hour ago—dressed in loose sweatpants and a shirt—he walked to the local co-op to buy coffee and animal cookies, almond butter and celery, his daily staples. Now, he's tired, slumped onto his right side. Every day he walks for thirty minutes—usually more—a straight trek to the co-op, then in a circle of our neighborhood with his camera, photographing whatever he sees: greenish-gray succulents wedging out of a stone fence, an overturned blue chair surrounded by yellow tulips, two skinny teenagers in faded T-shirts smoking on a back porch, their long legs slung out, a mangy cat asleep on one boy's lap.

"Come closer," he says now, lifting his head, his eyes finding mine. "I want to say something mushy." He's back in his hospital gown, the white sheet pulled up to his waist, his left foot kicked free of the covers. It looks alien, his ankle almost as wide as his calf with brown, tarry spots sprinkled like confetti across the bridge of his foot. *Nothing to worry about*, the doctors nonchalantly pronounce, as if he's following the wrong clues.

In one breath, David tells me he loves me. "But that's not really what I wanted to say. Closer," he insists, as if this is a secret. And so, I step right next to the bed. In the waning light, his eyes are almost grey with flickers of dark gold. "I just wanted to say," his voice goes low and husky, edged with emotion, "that this is the first time in my life I've ever felt safe."

His words are so unexpected, I simply stare at him.

"Going through this," he repeats, as if I've misunderstood, "it's . . . it's the *only* time in my life I've ever felt safe."

I glance at the cup, warm in my hand. I think of how much I've worried about safety, how every day's been fraught with danger, both the perverse possibility of more rogue cells and the necessary and precarious decisions we've made. *Safe?* I've never felt safe.

David takes my hand. "I knew you wouldn't let anything happen to me," he says in the same quiet voice. "I've never had that before."

I look beyond him out the window at a smoky blue sky. I know he doesn't mean that I "kept" him safe, that I prevented him from getting an infection or having lymphedema, from tripping or falling or bumping into furniture. He means, I believe, that I was *here*, that I "had his back," that I was the extra pair of eyes and ears and mouth, the one who called the ER, figured out the bus schedules, made the appointments, the one who researched the procedures and complications, the one who was watchful so that, for a few minutes, he could relax.

I nod, squeezing his hand, holding it lightly until his eyelids droop and he's fast asleep. Watching him, I wonder if he slept like this as a boy, collapsed in his bed with sleep-drugged limbs, one arm dragging the floor. Probably. Then again, I'm not sure. He's told me only bits and pieces of his childhood, odd memories, a sadness that emerges when it's late and something—a movie, a book, a child's feisty anger in the grocery store—prompts him to open up, more a rip in his psychic surface than a natural release. Nothing of whole cloth. Nothing I can quite see.

TWO HOURS LATER WHEN I leave my study to check on him, I pause, watching his eyelids flutter, listening to the low hum of the motor on the air mattress, a sedative drone. I stand watching, waiting, staring at the dark hollow of his throat. It's now that he opens his eyes and stares at me. A wordless moment, simple and serene.

Why was he never safe?

I gaze out the window where the whole world seems quiet, the ash tree's leaves greening in the sun, the bluebells migrating from my neighbor's front yard, cars moving slowly down our street. *Safe*, I think, saying the word like a mantra, *safe, safe, safe*. I need to know what dark undertows lie behind that word for him, what hidden stories, what unsayable things.

So much has happened this year that our world feels precarious, even fragile. And yet, strong currents seem to be pushing us toward an opening, a revelation, a shift toward the light, as if our hiding places are about to be exposed.

PART III

The New World

2013–2015

Chapter 16

EARLY ONE AUGUST MORNING, my sister calls. "Mama's being admitted to the hospital for a severe case of cellulitis," she says, her voice hurried. "She's weak and scared and I'm checking her in for IV antibiotics. Gotta go. Call me later."

I know that cellulitis is a common but potentially serious bacterial infection that can spread quickly to the lymph nodes and bloodstream, especially in a ninety-year-old woman. When I think of a needle plunging into my mother's veins, pushing through skin so bruised and crumpled it looks like old tissue paper, my pulse begins to race.

After my sister's call, I dial my mother's hospital room every fifteen minutes, only to hear an annoying ring tone. At 9 a.m., I decide to wake David so he can worry with me, and I can confide what I know: five days earlier my mother fell as she came down the stairs of her granddaughter's house, missing the last step and tumbling to her knees like a penitent, hitting her forehead and breaking her glasses neatly in two. A confirmed stoic, she knelt there a minute, then got up, placed a bag of ice on her knee, taped her glasses together, took a Tylenol, and thought, *no need to make a fuss*, until the pain—relentless and unequivocal—made her give in to the misery.

Because David wears a C-pap mask as well as earplugs—his "sensory deprivation rig"—I must wake him cautiously. Occasionally, he's had a scary startle response, as if he sees a primordial beast with fangs and claws, a red gnawing mouth. Neither of us has any idea why this happens.

Today I go through the usual steps: I turn off the white noise machine in our bedroom, carry a hot washcloth for his face and ease close to him sleeping on his back, the C-pap machine whirring, the covers drawn to his chin. Orange nubs of earplugs nestle in his ears connected by a tiny blue cord. Everything looks familiar and predictable: the darkened room; the white quilt; my pillow twisted sideways; his bedroom slippers on the floor, toes in opposite directions. I touch the quilt over his left arm, hoping this small gesture might wake him.

Nothing.

Next, I press a hand on top of the covers above his heart, expecting his eyes to flutter, then widen as he recognizes me. He'll nod sleepily and turn off the machine.

Nothing.

Once, last spring, I had to pull out his earplug, gently tugging the string until the nub popped out as I whispered his name. And just like that, he opened his eyes. No panic. No problem. Now I reach for the right earplug, but in leaning forward, I shift slightly and instead of touching the blue string near the orange nub, my hand grazes the top of his ear and brushes his cheek. Before I can remove my hand, his eyes flash open and his body begins to shake so violently I leap back, flinching, afraid he's having a seizure. Arms flailing, his body jerks in convulsive spasms as if some demon's flinging him forward, then impulsively yanking him back.

"*David*!" The room spins with light, though I've forgotten to open the blinds. Is this a heart attack? A stroke?

Before I can react, he jackknifes into a semisitting position, left leg thrashing beneath the covers while he pushes at the sheets, trying to free his hands.

"Turn off," he gasps, motioning to the C-pap machine.

After switching off the machine, I'm surprised by the silence, no relentless hiss of air. "What's happening? What can I do?"

Somehow, he manages to yank off the C-pap mask and one earplug. He squeezes his eyes shut and rubs his calf. "Cramp," he manages. Still, his upper body convulses, but now it is more of a shuddering, the spasms ebbing. I lean in to help. *"Don't."* He bristles. I step back.

After opening the blinds, sunlight flooding the room, I watch as he massages his leg, waiting for his breathing to slow, my own fast and shallow. "Are you okay?" He glances at me, a smudge of relief in his eyes, then nods, dismissing me. *Mine to deal with. Don't worry.* This, I think, is the code of marriage, the recognition of gesture, urgency relaxed by a look, a nod.

And yet I worry as I dry my hair in the bathroom because months earlier when he startled awake, he glared and snarled as if malice or stupidity were involved. "Jesus, what are you *doing*? Look what you're *doing*!" he snapped, his eyes hard and scolding, as if *I* was the demon. In retaliation, I shouted, "Fuck you! Don't *yell* at me!" and slammed the door.

Today when he stumbles into the bathroom, he looks pale and vulnerable.

"That was *bad*." I watch him in the mirror, turning off my hair dryer.

He leans into me. "Just hug me."

"You've woken startled before," I say, caressing his neck, "but *never* this bad." His body, warm from sleep, smells musty, even a little sweaty. I tug on the ear I grazed, then kiss it, biting it a little, like I often do to make him smile. "I thought I'd have to call 911." I burrow in closer.

"My stepfather used to hit me in the face when I was asleep," he whispers, his voice so low I can barely hear. "He'd come in drunk and smack me awake. I was eight or nine."

I pull back to look at him. Gray hair shags over his forehead, his eyes are still puffy at the edges. "Why didn't you tell me this before?"

"I just remembered." He looks surprised and then confused. "I just remembered," he repeats as if struggling to understand.

ONCE WE'RE DOWNSTAIRS, DAVID'S silence is like an indrawn breath. Though I want to say, *Please, just tell me what happened*, I tread lightly. Right now, David wants coffee and a shower and whatever normalcy he can claim for the day.

And so it's much later when I tell him about my mother. As if I've just remembered, I see her crashing again to her knees on a polished wooden floor, then kneeling there, astonished, not yet hurting. "She's in the hospital. And this is the *third* time she's fallen in two months!"

"Poor Bebe," he murmurs. "She'll be ashamed of getting sick and being dependent." To my mother illness represents weakness, a slackening of will, a blight on the campaign of good sense and optimism.

While David eats, I catch up with my sister, an internist who lives in the same town as my mother. "She's okay," my sister assures me. "But if she'd waited another day. . . . Anyway, she's stable now, only tired."

"Should I—"

"Don't come," my sister anticipates my question. "I'll stay tonight and tomorrow. Come later. I'll need you later."

Relieved, I look past David into the bright light of our backyard, noticing a few tomatoes hanging on the vines in my neighbor's garden, blood red amid the fading green. So much has happened today that I long to run outside where fresh-cut grass sweetens the air and pop one of those tomatoes in my mouth, letting the juice dribble down my chin. Instead, there's nothing to do but go about our day: David up the stairs to work on a print, I with a pot of tea into my study. And yet sitting at my desk, I can't concentrate, my mind too distracted as I wonder why David remembered his stepfather's fists *this* morning, more than fifty years after it happened. Though I know the response to trauma is often delayed, I can't stop worrying about the possibilities. Was it because of a dream fragment, something physically violent or psychologically treacherous? Was it a reaction to the melatonin he sometimes takes for sleep? Or was it. . . . Could it possibly be because I touched his face? He once warned me about touching his face while he was asleep, and I assumed it was because of the C-pap mask, the way it could be so easily dislodged, but perhaps it was a sense memory, a faint vibration of the past, an unbearable fragment, not quite repressed. I stare at the pages of an essay I'm supposed to read, but what I see in my mind is David's stepfather stumbling into his room, staring at his eight-year-old stepson curled in sleep, one hand tucked beneath the pillow, the other hanging limp toward the floor, and in a drunken blur, slapping or punching him, then yanking him up by his pajama top, leaving him terrified and disoriented. *That'll show you!* Was this memory tucked so deeply inside that it remained barely a flicker of pain, tinder burning so low he had no clue it could ignite?

A light touch.

And then an explosion, danger everywhere.

"OH, HONEY," MOTHER SAYS that night, her Southern drawl faint, her voice frail, "I just want to go *home*, to get back to my own bed." I hear the longing—"my own bed"—and the sharp edges of pain and unfamiliarity—"I hate this place." She's being given two different IV antibiotics, the needle taped securely in place, a dark new bruise mercilessly spreading beneath the white paper tape. "I didn't mean for this to happen," she whispers, her voice full of self-reproach.

"I know. But you'll go home soon. You won't be there for more than three days." Of course, I don't really know. I don't know how a ninety-year-old body repairs itself.

Nor do I know how a child's mind repairs itself. Once the wild animals are unleased, can they ever be caged?

Ironically, that night David and I decide to watch an episode of *The Killing*, a popular crime drama set in Seattle. In the past year we've become disaster junkies, following BBC series like *Cracker* and *Wire in the Blood*, and *Wallander*, and the much grittier French series *Spiral*. Some nights, like cynical teenagers, we need hacked-up bodies overseen by snide, overworked, chain-smoking professionals to psych us up for three more hours of work, our faces bent to our computers.

We love making exaggerated jokes about the shitty weather in *The Killing*: steel-gray clouds and rain (worse than Iowa!), the streets dirty and desolate with homeless kids, druggies, thieves, hookers. Good viewing for two people sitting on leather chairs and eating Skinny Cow ice cream sandwiches! *Bring on the damage. Not ours, not ours.* And yet tonight's episode includes an execution scene that's so visceral we rush downstairs to the comfort zone of our white couch to unwind instead of going back to work.

Slumped beside me, David surprises me, reacting to the intimacy of the violence in the crime show, a scene so haunting it resurrects his morning's memory. "My stepfather used to punch me awake, then make me get up to 'have a talk,' which meant he sat in a chair, and I had to stand in front of him." David's voice is low, weighted, the words pushed out. *That dead stepfather is here in this room.* I see the man called Soup, drunk and brash before the intimidated boy, wanting to hurt, but perhaps also longing to purge some vengeance of his own. "He resented me. . . . I wasn't his son, and I was always a hostage in the situation between him and my mother."

I nod. I've seen only a few photos from David's childhood in Worcester, one of David seated on Soup's lap in a bare, empty room, David grinning as if he's just been given a sack of candy, his hair shorn, his ears sticking out. I want the stepfather to be wall-eyed, with pale, pocked skin, instead of working-class handsome, a six-feet-two Stanley Kowalski, a swirl of black hair drifting across his forehead above a shy smile.

"Once, when I was about ten," David continues, "after Soup had been in rehab or maybe in Bridgewater State to dry out, my mother sat me down in her bedroom and asked if I thought we should let Soup come back. I knew by the way she asked, you know, by her fake-cheerful voice, that she wanted me to say yes." David looks at me. "I mean, she wasn't in the habit of consulting me, but now she said it *all* depended on me, that she wouldn't ask Soup to come back if I didn't approve."

"Nothing manipulative about that."

"Yeah, and then the minute I said okay, Soup leapt out of the bedroom closet where he'd been hiding, whooping and grinning and hugging her, and my mother pretended this was a wonderful and oh-so-surprising reunion."

"They knew you wouldn't say no."

"They knew I *couldn't*."

I nod. Complicity: it is what abusive parents do to ensure control and the pretense of connection. *See, you wanted him back. You said so*. But letting Soup return, David admits, did none of them any good. "He believed his discipline was the 'law,' that he and my mother should act as a team, and the one time she interfered he broke her nose. After that, he beat her up all the time."

I listen, nodding, appalled. My family might yell in anger and slam down the phone, but we've never been violent.

"I thought it was my fault," David continues. "That all his rage came from my not being his son."

"You were his scapegoat." I lean closer, lightly rubbing his leg. "You know that don't you?"

David sighs.

But of course, he knows it and doesn't. I think of that scene in the movie *Good Will Hunting* where Robin Williams, playing the psychologist, talks to the boy Will (Matt Damon) about his father's abuse. "It's not your fault," Williams says, and the boy says, "I know." Williams repeats, "It's not your fault," and the boy says, "I know." Williams says it again, "It's not your fault," moving closer with each utterance until finally the boy breaks down because the logic of the intellect can't "undo" the trauma of childhood. The child sees causality as intimately personal, every act an extension of the self.

Is this the story behind the story: his mother's complicity and his stepfather's brutality, the child sacrificed, betrayed by both? I sink back into the sofa, thinking. For the first time I have an inkling as to why David never claimed his family and why he had to leave at sixteen: the only way to belong was to collude with their manipulations and deny his own feelings.

I READ RECENTLY THAT if a threat isn't vanquished, the amygdala becomes hyperactive and continues producing stress hormones even when the threat has subsided. To avoid pain, a threatened person often dissociates, literally "takes leave of the body," the memory stifled, the body numbed, and yet once the threat recurs, the past quickly invades the present, creating new havoc out of old.

Each morning now I watch David sleeping, wondering if the memory of Soup's fists clarified his startle response or if it revived the old fear of deserving those fists. After all, when he jolts awake, he's an eight-year-old boy trying to protect himself, not just from the fists but from what the fists imply: *you're wrong, wrong, wrong*. Is it possible his anger on waking is also a form of resistance to a time when he was helpless, unable to defend himself, caught in the crevice of complicity? I hope so. I hope his adult fury is a decisive *no*.

But I don't know. David hasn't mentioned the incident again, and all I have is my memory and the notes I took that day, which, when I look back at them, seem sketchy and infuriatingly cryptic. For years I thought his anger, especially when startled, was personal—*about me!* His anger always hurt my feelings and caused many of our fights, though in reality, it had little to do with me. Instead, it was a violent collision with his past, a response to the monster, the intemperate brute. "The story of trauma . . . far from being an escape from reality," writes Cathy Caruth in *Unclaimed Experience*, "rather attests to its endless impact on life."

It's always been there. It's always there.

A haunting.

Sometimes just before I fall asleep, in that moment of quiet surrender, a thought floats up from my unconscious, something that's been unavailable to me during my waking life. I have one of those moments not long after David's awakening. I'm drowsing, sinking into a meditative ease, my body pleased to lie between clean sheets, my head on a soft pillow, when I think quite simply, *We're alike.* I wake more fully and lie in the dark, musing about what I mean. I've always known that David's and my stories—though vastly different in kind and degree—are psychologically intertwined. We were both depressed kids who grew up feeling restless and unworthy, never quite fitting in with our families, never sure that we belonged. I recognize in David what I know about myself: the need to be guarded, to be intimately wary of anyone getting too close. Too close might evoke humiliation and rejection, a damage that can't be repaired.

Freud believed that the" desire of consciousness" is "not to wake up," to remain asleep, ignorant, unfazed, and the great effort is to usurp that desire, to sneak past the censors. Though David's awaking was traumatic, there are other, more subtle moments of recognition for both of us. One evening, not long after David told me about Soup, he leaned over and impulsively kissed my shoulder, and in that fleeting moment with his lips pressed against my bare skin, I realized that for most of our marriage I'd thought of him as having the advantage, of being blessed with an ease I lacked for the simple reason that he was articulate and comfortable with strangers, capable of galvanizing his energy and intellect in public while I'm often plagued by shyness.

IT'S A TUESDAY MORNING, two months after that waking. I find David lounging on the couch, drowsing, the TV blaring, a blanket spilling onto the floor. His C-pap machine malfunctioned last night. Now I persuade him to go back to our bedroom, where I turn on the white noise machine and close the blinds. "Three hours," he says. "Wake me, please."

Once downstairs, I call to check on my mother. True to her nature, she's back to her routine—fixing meals, running errands, taking care of three great-grandsons two afternoons a week, though no longer climbing the stairs—and sleeping in her own bed. She's also returned to her stoic mode: "I'm fine. My leg still hurts, but the world must go on." Today, she tells me she's making a red velvet cake for my sister and then she's going out to buy flowers for my father's grave. "Hibiscus," she announces with satisfaction. I picture her kneeling at his gravesite, her hands busily arranging the flowers, fussing with the shape of them in the glazed white vase as she confides to him life's latest betrayal. "Johnnie, it's awful, they won't let me wear high heels anymore, not even the low kind you never liked, not even for my birthday."

At noon, I go into our bedroom to wake David. After that scary episode, we devised a plan: first, I open the blinds, switch off the white noise machine, turn on the lights, shut off the C-pap machine and wait.

Today he sleeps on his left side turned away from me, his C-pap mask already pulled off, his knees bent, his right hip jutting out. Once I've opened the blinds and clicked off the air filter, his eyelids flutter. He smiles. We talk a little bit while I'm standing nearby, his eyes opening and closing. He laughs at something I say, his chest rising. Then I sit beside him, my body pressed close to his back as I lean over him, my hands fiddling with his hair. We keep talking, about what I don't remember. Easy talk. Waking-up talk. I look at the way his gray hair is flattened, spiraling in all directions from sleep. I stare at the freckles on his eyelids. He's always had these, more visible in the morning, a light sprinkling near his brow. I see that he's still wearing his socks. Dark blue shot through with diamonds. One is twisted around his ankle. As we chat, my mind wanders to that awakening months before. I still shiver at the memory, but now it's a spoken rather than a hidden wound, something pulled from the shadows and a part of our lives. *It's always there*. Not a full story, but a beginning. "I should get up," David says, yawning, pushing at the covers.

"Not yet," I say, wanting to stay with the mundane. I lean down and straighten his sock, pulling it smooth around his ankle. "There," I say. "That's better.

Chapter 17

IF THERE'S ONE THING that literature teaches us, it's that we're doomed if we don't look back, if we close our eyes to the making of disaster, the foreshadowing of trouble, the consequences of easy solutions and avoided fears. We can't simply flee. It's true, of course, that Huck Finn flees; that Nick Adams flees; that Jewel Bundren flees. And yet Huck survives on a raft on the Mississippi by resisting repression, by going against his past and allowing himself to imagine a world beyond the iron grip of meanness. Nick flees to war, then returns to Michigan so traumatized he strikes out on a camping trip alone to find solace and renewal in nature, even as he stays within safe boundaries, careful and cautious. Jewel climbs out his bedroom window each morning at daybreak to till fields and tame a wild horse, claiming life and avoiding death.

ONE MORNING WHILE IN the middle of our breakfast David surprises me. "I hated Soup, but some part of me also wanted to please him." He sighs, shaking his head. "I thought there was something wrong because he didn't like me."

I nod, pouring hot water over my tea. Like the plot of a fairytale, this makes psychological sense: the desire to please the monster, to enchant what hates you as the *only* means of release. A child's logic. A captive's logic. A way of survival. But then, inevitably you grow up and see things differently, wondering how you might resist; and once you get a whiff of power . . . well, here's the dagger. But where exactly do you thrust?

IT'S BEEN MONTHS SINCE David's difficult awakening, and today I'm ready to gossip with a friend over tea at the Bluebird Diner, ignoring all worries about health and career and marriage. There's so much to catch up on—her novel and essays, my novel and essays—but just as I'm pulling into the parking lot, I hear a commentator on NPR discussing new research on depression and early childhood abuse with a group of scientists, one of those endless programs that crowd the early afternoon slot. *Enough*, I think. Yet I can't make myself turn off the radio when a commentator reveals that abused children in the study "had anxiety everywhere and that they couldn't put a contextual limit on when they needed to be afraid and when they didn't." I turn up the volume as one guest notes how the study "measures the extent to which childhood trauma translates into poor health in —" Then abruptly, the signal is lost.

What I'm listening to, I'll learn later, are the results from the University of Wisconsin study that used physiological evidence to show that "maltreatment during childhood can lead to long-term changes in the brain," weakening the connection between the hippocampus and the amygdala and leading to anxiety and depression. It's been several years since David's bout with depression, I mentally note, and though I catch only the tail end of the show, I scribble down the studies mentioned on the back of an envelope, something called the ACE Study and a more recent Wisconsin School of Medicine study where researchers used a special type of MRI to "measure connections between three areas of the brain involved in processing fear."

I hurry into the Bluebird Diner, where I see that my friend has ordered hot tea, her blond head bent toward the steam. She greets me with her bright, sardonic smile, but instead of our easy chat—the new Ferrante novel, an upcoming writing contest—I'm distracted, too caught by the implications of the NPR program to listen carefully. I nod occasionally, then admit that I've gotten sidetracked by some research on childhood adversity.

"The ACE Study," my friend says, forgiving me. She's had traumas of her own. "I've heard of that."

At home, I read about the ACE Study, begun in the late 1990s, an ongoing collaboration between researchers at Kaiser Permanente and the Centers for Disease Control and Prevention, that used seventeen thousand participants, the data gathered to measure "the extent to which childhood trauma translates into poor health and social well-being later in life." The ACE Study has an online questionnaire (used in the study) that I can download. From the study, I learn that the likelihood of childhood and adult suicide attempts increases as the ACE score increases, and that emotional abuse "exhibited the strongest relationship . . . to depressive symptoms among both men and women." Why didn't I know this? Is it possible that childhood abuse contributed to David's vulnerability to cancer as well as depression?

I read further, pushing my way through multiple articles on PubMed that confirm and deepen my fears: all types of child abuse are associated with an increased possibility of the abused child having an adult physical (health) condition. An article in *Health Reports* (Canada) states it very plainly: "Experiencing any type of child abuse (is) associated with increased odds of arthritis, back problems, high blood pressure, migraine headaches, COPD, cancer, stroke, bowel distress and chronic fatigue syndrome." It gets worse. Not only does childhood abuse relate to future health problems, but as the number of types of child abuse increase, so do the odds of most conditions.

After reading this, after marking passages with a yellow marker, I sit back in my chair, suddenly exhausted, deflated, until something inside me bristles. If David's just remembered the startle of Soup's fists, what other things has he repressed? Are there horrors he remembers but feels too ashamed to acknowledge?

I glance out my study windows, where light shimmers on the limbs of the katsura trees, where the heart-shaped leaves look ready to fall. I notice the weeds, vine-like and tall, growing out of my big, beautiful turquoise pots on the deck, aware that I haven't had time to create some beauty in our yard. More weeds are beginning to choke the hostas circling the deck. *I don't have time* is my new mantra, the one I cling to. Now I look back at the articles as if they too represent another mountain to climb. *I don't have time.*

And then a few days later, I do the simple thing: I ask David if he'll answer the questionnaire, and though I expect him to resist—"Hey, I'm doing okay, so let's leave everything alone"—he surprises me, saying yes quickly, then taking the sheet and sitting down to mark his answers. It's a simple, straightforward questionnaire that begins *While you were growing up, during your first eighteen years of life*: followed by a series of questions about physical, emotional, and sexual abuse, about alcoholism, divorce, drugs, and depression in the household, and ending with a question about whether a household member went to prison. There are ten categories for a yes (enter 1) or a no (enter 0) answer.

David isn't the least bit interested in the results, and after he hands me the sheet, he's off to his room to work on an art project. Alone, I stare at the sheet: it's a quick tally. He has a ridiculously high score. 8. A score of 3 is considered problematic. I stare at the questionnaire as if it's both revelatory and impenetrable. But now that I have it, I don't know what to do with it. It seems too stark, too intrusive, too private: 1. Did a parent or other adult in the house often . . . Swear at you, insult you, put you down, or humiliate you? or Act in a way that made you afraid that you might be physically hurt? 2. Did a parent or other adult in the household often . . . Push, grab, slap, or throw something at you? or Ever hit you so hard that you had marks or were ignored? 3. Did an adult or person at least five years older than you ever . . . Touch or fondle you or have you touch their body in a sexual way? or Try to or actually have oral, anal, or vaginal sex with you?

To make matters worse, I start reading the ACE Study at a time in the semester when I'm terribly busy reading graduate theses, when I stay at my desk working, usually past midnight, then collapse into our bed, certain my brain has atrophied and will never comprehend another thing. Perhaps I can't comprehend this either. Perhaps it's impossible to look closely at another person's life, to see beyond your own myopia. And so, I do this: I tuck David's ACE questionnaire into a file folder, where it will lie stacked with other file folders for many months. Nobody's business, I sometimes think, though I remind David to tell his therapist.

Still, I have the nagging feeling that I should *do* something, *say* something, that I should be responsible in some way. I just don't know what or how.

Occasionally I open the file and look at the questionnaire, but what I think about isn't the score but how David's blue-grey eyes looked alert and interested when I suggested he answer it, and how easily he complied, as if his past was no longer in hiding. Always my eye goes to a particular question, not the one about physical abuse, about being kicked or bitten or grabbed or hit with a fist, but the one that seems, in the end, more wounding.

While you were growing up, during your first eighteen years of life:

4. *Did you often or very often feel that . . .*
   No one in your family loved you or thought you were important or special?
   or
   Your family didn't look out for each other, feel close to each other, or support each other?

Abused and simultaneously neglected.

SOMETIMES WHEN DAVID'S BEEN especially tired or hasn't slept well, I'll bring a hot washcloth to his desk in the morning. "Close your eyes," I'll say and drape it over his face, letting the heat stream into his pores, seducing him back to life. Mentally, I can see him shoving his chair back and turning to me, deep shadows under his eyes, his expression one of flat emptiness as I layer the washcloth, molding it to his face. I tap it close to his hairline, shaping it over his brow and the bridge of his nose, tucking it under his chin. Always, he goes still, his body limp. Always, when I remove it, he says, "A human life has been saved!" And we laugh. Now he does this every morning, coming down the stairs, fixing his coffee, then turning on the hot water, heating a cloth, bending over the kitchen sink and raising the cloth to his face in a ritual of pleasure. If I've been up for hours and try to talk *before* he's poured his coffee, before he's administered the hot cloth, he'll mutter, "Not human yet."

Secretly, I smile.

What amazes me is that he didn't know the seductive power of a hot cloth in the morning, that simple, restorative act.

"It never occurred to me," he says. "I don't know. . . . Sometimes I just don't think about simple things like that."

But maybe no one ever suggested caretaking in his childhood, ever took the time to see what might comfort the body. Or the soul. Maybe a child can lose the idea of simple pleasures, remembering only what hurts.

And I think this too: maybe the repressed memory of David's stepfather's fists led me to the ACE Study questionnaire and maybe that questionnaire led us on a trek to David's hometown of Worcester, Massachusetts, and from there to a story neither of us could have foreseen.

Chapter 18

DAVID TOSSES HIS SUITCASE onto one of the double beds at the Courtyard Marriot in Worcester, Massachusetts, looking restless, ready to move. He takes out his camera, fiddling with the lens, zooming in, then zooming out. I've flopped onto the other bed, pushing all but one of the big fluffy pillows out of my way, so tired I want only to nap. We left Iowa at 6:00 this morning, raced through O'Hare saddled with carry-ons, then stood for nearly an hour in biting wind outside Boston International for the rental car shuttle. By the time we'd put our suitcases into the KIA Optima, a cold front had gripped the state: grey, swollen clouds, eddies of blowing snow, traffic lights bouncing in a strong headwind. It's late November 2013.

Now I'm pulling up the covers, tucking my palms close to my body, trying to get warm. My exhaustion feels medieval, tenacious.

"Let's get a double espresso and see if we can find my old neighborhoods," David says as if we haven't been trapped all day in cars and planes. He sounds absurdly happy.

"*What?* Are you kidding? We just got here." I don't lift my head from the pillow.

I watch as David goes to the motel window and puts his eye to the camera lens, aiming at the buildings next door though daylight is fading.

"Okay, okay. Just let me get a cup of tea." I drink my green tea slowly, lamenting that our moods are so out of sync. Then again, it's nothing short of a miracle that we're here in Worcester, where David grew up, in a place I've never seen, a place he remembers as a series of slum neighborhoods, of shabby three-deckers and cold-water flats, a city of shoe factories gone bust, their rusted wire fences surrounding empty warehouses after manufacturing crossed the oceans in the

1960s looking for a cheaper workforce. "A good place to *leave*," he's often said.

Now he stares at a city map and fingers the keys.

Twenty minutes later we're back in the rental car, ice furring the windshield, David's head swiveling as he tries to get his bearings in a city he left over forty years ago. "There!" he points triumphantly at a sign, barely visible. "I found Main Street." The streetlights are hazy in the snow, the signs almost unreadable, roofs of buildings like anointed drifts of white. I rub my hands together, trying to get warm.

"Main Street, isn't that the one—?"

He nods, then quickly shifts into a quiet, narrow street, cars parked bumper to bumper along the curb as we move slowly into his past.

THREE WEEKS EARLIER, I'D said casually, "I'm thinking about going to Worcester," as the pungent smell of coffee filled our kitchen on a late Sunday morning. I was on sabbatical, and it was the first chance I had for such a trip. "Do you want to come?" I buttered our toast, cutting it diagonally and sliced an apple, putting everything on a white plate.

Do I look crazy? his expression said as he sipped his coffee. We sat together in silence.

For months I imagined walking the streets of David's hometown, pushing through the heavy double doors of schools and cathedrals, hanging out in Shrewsbury Street, hoping to catch a glimpse of his features in the Italian shopkeepers, the butchers and delivery men, the shrewd maître-d's preparing the evening menu. Of course, what I really wanted were the twists and turns of story, the little sidesteps of memory, hints of a reckless affection or hidden vulnerability, a boy, perhaps in dirty sneakers with a ripped elbow seam in his new winter jacket. "You left Worcester for San Francisco when you were nineteen or twenty," I continued as if we were having a two-sided conversation, "and well, everyone in your family is dead except for your half-brother in Maine."

More silence. His mouth puckered.

"It's just that it made all the difference when you came home with me five hundred years ago because you liked my parents immediately, making it so much easier for me, and I've always wanted to see where you grew up and, you know, see it with you." I was making an appeal—no one can hurt you!—but did I really expect a simple yes? David hated Worcester, this place of "bad things," of betrayal and doubt, danger and loss. "*Wiss*-ter," he pronounced it, as if even the word had to be mangled. *He'll never go back*, I thought, glancing out the window, the Iowa sky blindingly blue, one of those crisp fall days in early November when I can't imagine the slap of a dry, biting wind. *We have to make new stories*, I wanted to say, but perhaps I was being naïve, overly optimistic, perhaps I was thinking of myself and what I'd learn. The truth is, I'd asked impulsively, maybe to surprise him, maybe as a forewarning that I was considering the trip.

Instead of answering, David began drawing the façade of a three-decker on the back of a Discover card brochure, erecting walls, a roof, and arched entrances that looked, to my eye, like the beginnings of a storybook castle. "875 Main Street." He slid the brochure toward me. "This is where I once lived in Worcester." I looked with surprise at the rough drawing because he'd never told me about this place. Then he pulled the drawing back, sketching twin brick turrets on either end of the building, accentuated by many-paned windows and double brickwork that complemented the arched doorway. "We had the second floor, the only *nice* place I lived there." He added decorative cornices, a cobblestone walkway, even a grassy lawn, all much better than my imagination, and then he paused, as if trying to remember. "I think—" he glanced up, sighing, "I think it was torn down to make a parking lot for a Thom McAn shoe store. Actually, I bet that everything I remember in Worcester has been torn down. It's like, you know, *Joseph Stalin is no longer here*."

I laughed. "Ha, then we'll go back to see monuments to the tyrant toppled."

"It makes me depressed to even think about it." Still, there was the hint of a smile.

I leaned across the table, touching his arm. "But what a win for me," I teased. "You know, rock bottom for you and a chapter in my book for me." Though he'd assured me I could write anything about his life, about our life together, some days I felt like a rookie archeologist digging and sifting through his past, trying to create a narrative with a few dusty artifacts, their meanings masked. Since I'd never been to his hometown and had seen only two pictures from his childhood, I told myself I was writing to try to understand David's story, but really, I was hoping to transform it into something I *could* understand.

He studied the drawing as if now that Worcester had been acknowledged, the shades on his memory were lifted. "My mother used to take a bus from Worcester to Sturbridge every three weeks to pick me up for an overnight visit when I was in foster care with Aunt Adeline and Uncle John because she couldn't drive. We'd stay here, in this three-decker." I knew that David had lived with Aunt Adeline and Uncle John for several years, had gone to first and maybe second grade in Sturbridge, had caught frogs and chased cats and hidden in the bushes like other little boys, but I knew very little about his childhood with his mother or Aunt Adeline. "It's where I came to live after she married Soup, after they took me out of foster care." He bent over the drawing again, adding double doors and windows. "My mother rented out rooms to boarders, but then Soup,"—he glanced up—"ah, such a noble man, so attuned to even the smallest social proprieties, rummaged through the boarders' rooms whenever they were out." David laughed derisively, shaking his head. "Come to think of it, that's how I first heard *South Pacific*, with Soup on a record player in one of the tenants' rooms."

And to my surprise, he began singing, his voice soft and tender. "Bali Ha'i may c-a-ll. . . ." But as suddenly he stopped, his eyes darkening as he picked up the drawing and stared at it. "No, I don't wanna think about that," he said quietly and got up for more coffee.

When David turns left on Pleasant Street, then right on another street, I see three-deckers packed close together with barely an edge of lawn. Some have front steps that butt right up to the sidewalk. Others have the width of a fire escape separating one building from the next. David pulls over, the engine idling, the heater blasting. He's suddenly quiet, staring at the buildings, ducking his head beneath the rearview mirror. I watch a flutter of snow. A softening. But what I see isn't the ugly, shabby place he's told me about with peeling paint and missing floorboards, but a pale-blue three-story building with dark decorative shutters, the porch given a facelift, a Christmas tree lighting the second-floor window with tiny white bulbs and candy cane swags. It looks warm and cozy. "Unbelievable," he says.

"The first toppling." I breathe easier, relieved.

David stares intently at the house as if he's gone underwater. "It's so changed," he says. "I mean, it's just sorta nice." We're both silent, the wind sweeping about in gusts, the street deserted, then a truck rumbling past. As we ease back into the street, I watch a man on the sidewalk in a dark leather jacket with cropped grey hair walking his dog, and then, an empty lot, evergreens rising like a high, dark wall.

When David lived here, Worcester was a working-class town, a manufacturing town, its population thickened by immigrants: first the Irish and the French Canadians, then the Italians, the Swedes, the Greeks, and the Albanians, all pushing into the city center, competing for jobs and edging out the newest arrivals. His ancestors, the Italians, came in waves at the turn of the century to work in the quarries and on the construction of the Wachusett Reservoir, willing to swing a pick and shovel for twelve hours a day, six days a week, to eat lunch in ditches with machines roaring and whistles blowing. They took over Shrewsbury Street from the Irish, opened bakeries and restaurants, rented the three-deckers and built Catholic Churches and schools.

From David's stories, Worcester was frumpy, exhausted, as dour as the Rust Belt, but before we left Iowa City, the internet told a different story: Worcester is now the second-largest city in New England, economically robust, revived by a sudden growth spurt. Later in our trip we'll see evidence of this: private roads winding into the hills where two- and three-story mansions nestle among firs and evergreens; high-rises and office buildings under construction, the wonderful Worcester Art Museum, Holy Cross College, and the sprawling University of Massachusetts Medical School.

"Why did your family leave that nicer place on Main?" I ask as we turn into another narrow street. "Was it because it was being torn down?" I can't read his expression, but when he speaks, I hear the old, scornful voice, the one he reserves for *Wiss-ter*. "Ah, that was the sweetness of Soup. He scared off all the boarders, poking around in their rooms, getting drunk and beating on my mother. Who wanted to live around that? Pretty soon, my mother couldn't pay the rent." He says this last matter-of-factly.

"So, every year we moved to a new place, a cheaper place, and Soup would promise to fix it up, you know, everything was going to be just great, *really* nice, I mean he worked construction, so he always had big plans, but the minute something good happened or he got praise—even if it was just someone trusting him to do a job—he'd get drunk. And once he started drinking, that was it, he never finished anything." We weave our way through a warren of streets where David used to live, all within a few blocks of each other. Snow is no longer falling, the air crisp and cold, the sky feathered with grey as I stare out the window.

Most of the houses we see are newly painted, the porch lights bright, the bushes trimmed, wreaths of holly on the doors. Already there's a snowman with dark coal eyes and a jaunty carrot cigar gracing a small patch of yard. "I don't remember this," David says, seeing a coffee shop, then a new building where a mom-and-pop shop used to be, the place he'd been sent to buy cigs for his mother. "I remember the streets, but"—he gives me a quizzical look—"Jesus, they've all been *gentrified*."

For a moment I wonder if he's disappointed—his story covered up, scraped clean and reconstructed without reparations—but to my surprise, he turns to look at me, a look so direct and naked it jostles loose what I hadn't expected: my secret relief that these houses aren't so sad, so humble with sagging porches and crumbling steps. Some insecure part of me was prepared to be embarrassed by that ugliness, to feel shame at David's shame, to fear seeing him as not quite the same man who lived with me in Iowa City, someone so smart and articulate that when we first arrived in Iowa City, many people thought he was the professor.

I turn away, gazing out the window, my breath an icy puff of air. Isn't that why we hold our shameful stories so close? Why my first instinct was to come alone?

NEAR DUSK, WE DRIVE through acres and acres of wooded parks, fir trees bundled in snow, brick buildings nestled into the hills, and then an old cemetery, somber and oddly arresting with its granite monuments and mausoleums embellished with fluted pillars and arches, the graves tucked into hillsides, a solemn stone angel resting over a child's grave. On impulse, we park. I wander down a small slope to look at an ornate Celtic cross, and when I turn, I see David with his camera framing the Madonna-like face of one of the angels, her eyes downcast, her lips pursed, her hair sculpted beneath the draped curve of her shawl. Snow gathers at her prayer-bent arms, scattering across her shoulders in lacy swirls. I stamp my feet to keep warm as David bends lower, moving in close to capture those clasped hands.

Watching him, I'm overwhelmed again by the thought that we wouldn't be here today if he hadn't had cancer, if we hadn't had to stop in midstride like two people pausing anxiously in the hallway to tell a painful secret. It's such a stark, intrusive fact that I stand very still, aware that I'm in a cemetery, alive among the dead with their unseeing eyes, their brittle bones, the crisp, cold air making me shiver.

WHILE DAVID WALKS TOWARD one of the mausoleums, I see the two of us sitting together last week on the green couch streaming Richard Linklater's *Boyhood*, a film we knew little about, having checked out only a few movie blurbs. "Let's give it a try," I said, but when we got to the scene of the stepfather, an alcoholic tyrant, enraged and screaming at his kids and stepkids, his fury lashing out while they cowered, heads bowed and eyes downcast, David hit pause. "I don't know if I can watch this." He stared at the still image on the screen, the stepfather's mouth caught in a distorted sneer. David's own lips were pressed tight, his eyes narrowed, not meeting mine. "It's not just that Soup smacked me around," he began, "but after living with him for a few years, I started confessing to things I didn't do." David's voice was low, tense. "If he accused me of eating all the peanut butter or losing a baseball or not coming home right after school or talking to Jimmy downstairs, who I wasn't supposed to talk to under any circumstances, I just said I did. He punished me so much I was like somebody battered by the police. . . . I could no longer stand up for myself. Sometimes I even convinced myself I'd done whatever it was he said I'd done because he was going to punish me anyway, smack me up against a wall or punch me." He sighed, closed his eyes, a heaviness to the air.

I stared at the stepfather's face on the screen. His eyes glare, a snarl twisted his thin lips above clenched teeth. He looked as if he could kill, as if he *wanted* to kill, as if he'd find pleasure or at least release by inflicting violence while the children stood meekly before him, looking shamed, dazed, as obedient as slaves. In that moment, I recognized visually what I'd only read about in books: how abused children learn to accommodate brutality, to accept powerlessness as a necessary fate in the face of danger.

I glanced away from the screen. "You were just a little boy. You had no choice."

David's eyes were fixed on the image. "I never let him see me cry. That was my only revenge." Abruptly he got up for more coffee.

Alone in the darkened room, I worried that the trip to Worcester might not be a good idea. David had walked away and closed the door on a place of bad memories.

As a light snow begins to fall in the cemetery, I watch as David turns away from the angel.

Now we've opened it.

Chapter 19

FOR YEARS, WHEN DAVID talked about his past, it was primarily about Catholic school: how much he loved daily mass with its liturgy in Latin, like an incantation from another world, and how much he hated the mean-spirited, knuckle-rapping nuns.

Catholic school. The 1950s.

As we set out from the Courtyard Marriot on our second day to find David's old schools, then to treat ourselves to the Worcester Art Museum, one of his favorite places, I try to remember what he's told me.

"Everything changed that year," he confided last spring about a school he attended in sixth grade, the year trouble gripped him, the year school made him anxious and wary. "I'd never been singled out before. The bad kid, you know. The problem." As he talked, I imagined David's Catholic school as an old Victorian building with brick-and-mortar chimneys and cramped attics, with high-ceilinged classrooms and a dim, silent chapel complete with kneeling benches and a pale, painted statue of the Virgin Mary.

"I mean, I got into trouble at every Catholic school," David continued, "but that was for truancy."

"Truancy?"

He smiled, his face relaxing as he reminisced, "Yeah, I spent long hours playing hooky and sneaking off to the Worcester Art Museum, where I could wander all over the place." It's here, he tells me, he fell in love with the bas-reliefs of Sumerian battle scenes, fixating on the garnet-painted chariots with their round wooden wheels and quivers of arrows, flanked by soldiers, their horses garlanded in fluttering red . . . and then the war gods in domed headdresses, their beards shaped like clusters of asparagus, their noses prominent, their wings high and elegant, spreading out in powerful curves. Sometimes the gods had animal heads, the arrogant, hooked beak of an eagle, a falcon, a condor, something so scary and fine, he stared in silence. He loved these stories carved in stone and woven into cloth, "so much better than learning about dangling participles or the propagation of plants or the death of Saint Justin and Saint Cecilia, even though the nuns insisted Saint Cecilia survived a beheading, which, in itself, was very cool." He came to the museum to stare at the bas-reliefs again and again, hanging out with the men going into battle, soldiers with defiant profiles, silent and stoic.

"I often spent part of the year in one school and then was transferred to another because my family moved around a lot, but even before sixth grade, I was branded as a kid who couldn't *behave*, couldn't sit still, couldn't, you know, act the good boy."

I imagine him that first day in sixth grade when Sister Florence yanked him to the front of the class before he'd had time to size up the bullies, the ones who'd push and trip him, who'd wait for him at the bottom of the steps, squint-eyed and ready, bodies bristling with meanness. He was confused. Sister Florence's stumpy fingers were clamped around his neck, just above his clean white collar, touching the bristly edge of his new haircut. Already, she was pronouncing him *A Problem* before the entire class of twenty-six kids he didn't yet know. "A Problem," she said, tightening her grip, her voice nasal and shrill, "but he's not going to be A Problem *here*." He watched her elderly face beneath the black wings of her habit harden into a wrinkled scowl, and then he glanced upward where a stain on the ceiling looked like a piece of peeled skin. "He's not going to be A Problem in *my class*, boys and girls," she continued, "because we don't allow troublemakers here. They shape up . . . or else." She might as well have held up a sign: STAY AWAY FROM THIS KID. He stopped squirming, a dark fury circling his brain as he shifted his gaze to the gaping kids, some with hands over their mouths to keep them from laughing, others zeroing in, sizing up a new target.

Automatically, he pressed his finger into an old bruise, one faded to yellow. It hurt only if he found its center, its secret heat. Touching it, a rough prickling sensation shivered through him and for a moment he wasn't in this classroom but standing in the apartment kitchen beneath the glare of a naked bulb, squirming under his stepfather's iron grip, a cigarette dangling from the man's lips, its red tip glowing, ashes drifting across his T-shirt as the man's big paddle hands clasped tight, then squeezed the soft skin of his neck.

At eleven, he was small for his age, but wiry and quick, with a good aim, a sharp tongue, a talent for remembering, and a sixth sense about the other kids. Within ten minutes of seeing a group of boys, he knew who would beat him up, who would jockey for attention, who would brag, gloating over victories, and who would try to fade into the woodwork—boys too small, too smart, too diverted to be anywhere but at the bottom of the pecking order. He'd never be one of those boys. He'd always need to push and shove. And yet as he'd walked to school this morning, gazing into the soft gray light, the leaves silvery with dew, dressed in his white shirt, all the buttons intact, his underwear new and tight, he'd imagined this school might be different. He might be different, just a boy with curious blue eyes and a crew cut, sitting somewhere in the middle row, reading about the 54th Regiment Massachusetts Volunteer Infantry in the Civil War and trying not to stare out the window at the squirrels chasing each other through the elm trees like bored, restless kids.

But no. Immediately, he was singled out. A *problem*.

Sister Florence's hand relaxed, patting him on the shoulder. He knew it wasn't friendly. It was merely telling him she'd finished with him, and he was to return to his seat, to merge with the rest of the students, as if that were possible. The boy in the second row held out a finger to jab him as he passed. Another boy with a straight line of eyebrow above his nose leered at him and held up a drawing of a hangman's noose. The girl with the freckled face who sat beside him pulled in her skirts as if even touching him might make her a problem too.

He sat very still, seething, though he pretended indifference, only doing what everyone else did, flipping to page twenty-nine and reading to page thirty-five, then opening his arithmetic workbook for exercises one through ten, though he was only waiting, waiting for school to be out, waiting to run clear of its boundaries, waiting to create his own surprise. He'd settled on that.

When the last bell rang, he darted out of class, racing across the street, and then slowed as he came to a nearby neighborhood, where he stopped in Sprags to browse the comics, count how many sodas he saw through the glass door of the fridge, watch the people buying newspapers and cigarettes, teenagers jostling each other, laughing, flirting. He'd been to stores like this all his life, sent out to buy cigs for his mother on Saturday morning. Later, inside Ciani's Market, he gazed longingly at the gaudy pink coconut cakes wrapped in plastic, but he had no money. Forfeited at recess.

Only near dusk did he dare walk back toward the school. He wasn't rushing. He idled, gazing in the windows of stores, at the display of fishing hooks, Monopoly and Sorry games, sets of Jacks and brightly colored hula hoops, and then wandered across the street and stooped close to the bushes that surrounded one side of the school. Squatting down, he thought of his favorite bas-relief, the one of the Sumerian soldiers: their faces fixed in profile, their eyes determined as they marched toward the enemy. He was one of them now, dressed in their armor, the hooded cap, the protective cape, a shiny brass plate pressing hard against his thick chest. Like them, he carried a weapon, though his were merely rocks stuffed in his pocket.

Hidden, he watched the doors. No one had gone in or out since he'd been crouched here. Craning his neck, he could see a group of tall second-story windows, but he wasn't sure if that was the classroom where Sister Florence had humiliated him. Those windows should have been marked with a large X or maybe the T of the cross, some sacred Catholic sign. Was it the *second* room from the end? The *fourth*? He'd only been at this school for one day. Suddenly his head felt heavy with sadness and disappointment, though he wouldn't have called it that. He'd have called it bad luck, shitty luck, rotten-first-day luck. To calm himself, he imagined Sister Florence standing at the edge of the woods, shaking with fear as the war gods turned their cold, unblinking gaze on her. He imagined her closing her eyes, her hands folded around a rosary, her lips praying. He liked this moment best, the tension in her face, her body shivering despite her clasped, prayerful hands.

Emboldened, he sensed the other soldiers fanned out behind him, each readying his ax, a few reaching for a spear, the one with the hooked beak giving him a nod. Quickly, he stood, glancing around. The streetlights were about to come on, the air lighter, cooler, the first hint of a breeze, tufts of grass pushing through cracks in the cement near his feet. He sucked in his breath, suddenly dizzy with the thrill of revenge, remembering how her hand, blunt-fingered and rough, the fingernails squarely cut, had grabbed him, surprising him. She'd smelled like dead leaves. Now, stepping forward, he drew his arm back and threw, hurtling an answer, an answer, an answer at each window until with the sharp shattering, splintering veins of glass, Sister Florence's grip loosened, releasing him, giving him back to himself.

It was when he picked up the last rock that he saw it, a bright flash, a blinking in the darkness; it was only a firefly darting, flickering just above the shrubbery. And yet for a moment he was the early-morning boy again, curious and interested and hopeful, his hand limp, the last rock loose in his palm. He wanted to capture and hold its fluttering light. It would be his to watch over, to take care of before the world narrowed, became riddled with restrictions. He moved quietly, stealthily toward it, his hand cupped tightly, close, then closer, until he heard the slam of a door. As if alerted, the firefly flitted away, toward a cracked window. "Hey," someone called, and then the suddenness of footsteps.

Instantly, he was back in the shadows, his body startled, still. He waited, surprised at how small he could make himself. His knee itched but he willed himself not to scratch. When he looked up, the firefly floated just above his head, suspended, as if keeping vigil. The air was so quiet he imagined he could hear it blink. But alongside that thought came a sharp squeal of brakes in the street and someone yelling, "Go on, you sonofabitch! Get *out* of the intersection!" As if given a secret command, he was up and running, his feet barely touching the ground as he raced around the corner, the last rock held tightly in his hand.

NOW WE'RE DRIVING DOWN a narrow street in Worcester, then left onto another narrow street. "It should be down *this* street," David says, leaning forward to see through the fogged windshield as we search for what might or might not be Oxford Street School. His face is flushed, his body wired with a restless energy.

"There!" I point to a small, rectangular street sign. Oxford Street, I notice, is a short, crowded one-way street with cars parked end to end on one side and small frame houses huddled close to the street.

"Wait, was this sixth grade?" I ask, thinking about the boy held tight in Sister Florence's grasp and those broken windows.

"Yep."

"But it doesn't *sound* like a Catholic school."

"It wasn't."

"What? I thought you always went to Catholic school, well, until Classical High." And I wonder, embarrassed, what else I've conjured.

He's driving slowly, his eyes squinting, scanning the houses and yards as if looking for clues. He ignores my question. And then at the very end of the block, where this street dead-ends into Pleasant Street, he notices the back of an old three-story red brick building. "That's it! I can't believe it. Oxford Street School," he says excitedly, his face revealing none of the misery I'd expected. "When we moved to Newberry Street," he says, his gaze fixed on the building, "my stepfather enrolled me in this school, the oldest elementary school in

Worcester, and insisted we go to a Protestant church. And I never went back to Catholic school."

I'm amazed at this flood of information. "But wasn't this the place . . . you know, where you broke all the windows? "

He nods, still staring at the school with an expression of pride. "This is it."

I stare at the building too, but I gaze at it if I've been mocked. It looks so benign, so ordinary, and there are not nearly as many windows as I'd imagined. And where is Sister Florence? I'm trying to shake free of my confusion and place him here, to see him plotting his revenge, an eleven-year-old boy, his mind charged with fury. "Did they ever find out that you broke the windows?"

"Nope. The windows were fixed the next day, and there were"—he pauses, smiling—"'no suspects.'"

"Whoa. You were lucky."

"The power in acts of vandalism!" he whispers conspiratorially, leaning close, then immediately he tells me that during this time he worried constantly, was tormented by fear. "I used to pull the fire alarms at the fireboxes, and no, I don't know why I did it so don't ask, I just did it, saw them and got excited or thought I could get away with it or did it on impulse or for fun, I don't know, maybe it just felt good to *do* something. But a man across the street saw me one time and tried to blackmail me, said he'd tell my parents and the police if I didn't stop."

After we park and step out into the freezing air, the sky already graying, I stare at the three-story, rusted-red brick building embellished only with a solitary brick turret, so different from my Victorian expectations. When David points to where his classroom was, the second floor in the L-shaped space near the back of the building, I laugh at how close to the street it is. *Really!* There are three rows of double windows, tall windows placed close together, the kind I remember from photographs of late nineteenth-century buildings. What bothers me most is that there are no bushes, no places to hide near this area, not even a dumpster, nothing but an empty parking lot of faded gray concrete. "There used to be a basketball net right there," David says, pointing, "for us to shoot baskets."

I nod.

"It looks so *small*," he says, with surprising tenderness, as he moves toward it. For a moment, I think he's going to touch the brickwork. Then his hand relaxes.

What startles us is that there's no sign for Oxford Street School. "I bet we missed it," I say, but then near the front, we see a professional white sign that reads, *RobRoy Academy: Schools of Cosmetology, Barbering, Manicuring, and Aesthetics.*

We look at each other and laugh. Unbelievable! A Cosmetology Learning Instruction Center. A joke on the past: a building no longer defined by punishment but devoted to the secrets and promises of beauty.

After David snaps a few pictures, including one of the sign, we rush back to the rental car, switching the heat on to high before turning right onto Pleasant Street. We ease into the flow of everyday traffic, the SUVs and sedans, sports cars and delivery trucks, checking the street signs like tourists.

"On to the art museum," David says, smiling as he moves quickly into the left lane. "Gotta check in with my Sumerians." I fumble in my purse for the directions, pawing through papers and keys and glasses cases, but what I'm listening to is his voice, the casual ease of it, the sound of ordinary happiness.

Chapter 20

I HAVE NO IDEA what to expect of the Worcester Art Museum, no preconceptions, no research, no gossip or jokes, only David's attachment to it, but when we enter the atrium, I'm stunned by its beauty, surprised by the flood of light from a skylighted ceiling that illuminates the huge Hunt Floor mosaic, a Byzantine work of art from the sixth century, spread across the center of the gallery floor. Instantly, I stop, staring at stags leaping, tigers rushing, their fangs sharp and white, alongside soldiers on horseback, their capes flying as they spear wolves and lions and beasts I can't even name. Posed at the center, a lone male figure in loose clothing and laced sandals cradles a long, impressive spear. Just what an excited, adventurous boy might want to see!

To my left, mosaics from the Assyrian and Meroitic periods don the walls, and when I turn to my right, the entirety of a small medieval chapel—transported from the Chapter House of the Benedictine Priory of Saint John in west central France and reassembled here at the museum—beckons. I stare at the stone vaulted ceiling—quadripartite vaults—then glance back at David, who nods happily at me, then wanders away. I see him stop before *Prince Arikankharer Slaying His Enemies*—the prince holding his enemies' topknots while a dog chews on a soldier's head beside his foot—and a wooden statue of St. George and the Dragon. A little savagery to get the blood going! I watch as David snaps pictures with his iPhone, capturing details and images and close-ups. A man in heaven: so many pieces of art to fall in love with again.

And this too, I think, is the surprise of the past.

AS I WANDER AROUND the small stone chapel, well-lit, but oddly intimate and private, I'm pulled by a disastrous memory from my own art-making past. In my midtwenties, when I was an MFA student at UCLA, a famous New York artist visited the Art Department for a lecture and workshop. I remember listening intently to him and becoming increasingly anxious: he was so articulate, his thoughts so nuanced, his abilities far beyond my own though he was barely older than thirty. I no longer remember his name or the focus of his talk, only that his confidence and expertise aroused in me such a deep sadness that at the end of the lecture I rushed out of the building, slumped on the low wall outside the Art Department, and wept. This was utterly melodramatic, a sense of despair that now makes me flinch, and yet that year had been tumultuous, not only because I'd left a small, traditional culture in Alabama—where the art needed to match the sofa—for an urban, liberal culture in Los Angeles, but also because I'd gambled that art would save me, would give me not only a profession but also a sense of confidence I'd lacked in the South.

To my surprise, when the famous artist emerged from the building, he came and sat down beside me. "Are you okay?" he asked, his voice quiet, thoughtful, almost intimate, as if we were friends. He was a small man, dark-haired and New York skinny. "Is there something wrong?"

While trying to dry my eyes, I told him that I didn't know how to be an artist, that all my art projects were failing this semester, and yet this admission only made me cry harder, embarrassment now wedded to sorrow. I was inside a hole and didn't know how to get out.

The man looked solemnly at me. To my surprise, he said, "Maybe you shouldn't worry so much about your projects. Look,"—he gestured toward the blue California sky—"it's a beautiful day. Why not go to the ocean, enjoy the waves and the sun, let the sand run through your bare toes. Art isn't all about work."

I gazed at him with dismay. *How could a failed art student enjoy the day?* I didn't understand. I was trapped in a labyrinth of "talent" and "judgment," so indentured to accomplishment and approval (the story of my upbringing) that enjoying a beautiful day seemed treasonous. Ambition had me by the throat.

Now I believe the famous artist was trying to tell me that you can't always *think* your way to clarity: yes, art comes through hard work and struggle—what David and I call "*doing time in the chair*"—but it also comes unbidden, a surprise, a revelation, a visit from the unconscious. Much of training is for readiness—a preparation in craft and self-awareness so that should an idea emerge, you might know what to do. And yes, a beautiful day at the beach, daydreaming and watching the rhythm of the waves, might be a catalyst for new work or it might simply be pleasurable.

WHEN I FIRST MET David in Los Angeles, he seemed entirely free of such conflicts, unfazed by the drama of success and failure in art. More than anything, art gave him a sense of self beyond the veil of criticism, allowing him to complicate his thinking and nourish his imagination. Maybe this sensibility emerged from his intuitive talent, a talent nurtured in high school by a conscientious teacher who insisted he be left alone to work on independent projects rather than follow a prescribed curriculum, and maybe this permission freed him from the weight of external judgment. This isn't to say David doesn't like feedback or love praise—*he did and does!*—but he never elevated other people's opinions above his own.

Instead of approval, David dedicated himself to obsession and risk. That is, he'd stay up all night to work on an art project, drinking coffee and eating apples, go to sleep for four hours, then take three hours off in the middle of the day to go to a movie, recharging himself with drama and popcorn before being pushed hard against a deadline. Once a deadline loomed, his focus was absolute: no phone calls, food, sleep, or talk; he survived on music and coffee. *Infuriating!* Sometimes, I'd stare at him sitting at his drafting table or before a canvas, his head bent to the work, his cowlicks rowdy and wild, his mind so immersed he looked like a monk in meditation. Only later would I understand that making art acted as a kind of tranquilizer, immersing him in the present, repressing all doubt and anguish about the past.

As I stand near one of the vaulted windows in the chapel, I think of the long hours David put in as an art director and web designer in Iowa, often getting up at 5 a.m. to revise a website, so busy he took photographs and made art only on Sundays or holidays. And yet once diagnosed with cancer, he carried his camera everywhere, photographing the oddities and surprises he found on his daily walks: broken fences, bridges splashed with graffiti, wildflowers spilling from a pile of rocks, birdfeeders, ladders, dogs, cats, geese, even cornstalks shimmering in shades of green, thick and lush against a relentless sky.

It's not until months after we've returned from Worcester that I notice a surprise, a particular fixation in his work. *Chairs!* In print after print, there are abandoned chairs, chairs compromised by weather or neglect, chairs for sale, for storage, for parties, for pleasure. In one print, two garden chairs lean against a fence overgrown with vines while a rust-colored bird pecks at a mound of dirt, its long, gawky beak next to a dented TV dish. In another, classic white beach chairs float idly in an ocean beneath a hazy blue sky as if *they* are on vacation. One image is so emotional, so stark and lonely, I can't stop looking at it: an iron kitchen chair overturned in a windswept field of weeds and goldenrod near a barbed wire fence, the sky a sweep of racing clouds, three telephone lines looming in the distance. Looking at it, I'm a voyeur gazing at an abandoned place, maybe the edge of a family farm, grass and weeds a hot summer green, a dark blue sky pressed beneath a fury of clouds. A private assignation of loss.

I look at these photos with excitement. *Of course!* For a man unable to sit for six weeks, what better way to ironize the situation than to fixate on what's been denied?

"I LOVE THIS MUSEUM," David says as we sit in the Worcester Art Museum coffee shop, relaxing with cappuccinos and sharing an almond croissant. It's late afternoon, the sky white and flat.

"I know," I say, pulling off a twist of croissant. "It's a *good* museum. I had no idea. It's like going to the Art Institute in Chicago."

"I think it saved me," he says. "Just coming here as a kid, even though I skipped school to do it, always changed my day. I could breathe."

"Here's to rescue," I say, lifting my cup for the final swallow.

"There's never enough." David sighs.

"Then exorcism."

I expect him to laugh or further the joke, but he only looks away from me, out the windows, where the wind is picking up, the tree branches lifting, the sky greying with cold. "Grace," he says softly, his eyes meeting mine.

Chapter 21

IT'S OUR THIRD DAY in Massachusetts.

To find Aunt Adeline, if only we can find Aunt Adeline . . . not the woman, of course, but the spirit of her, the house, the garden, the woods, the calm, claiming place of family where honesty and happiness ruled, a well-lighted path to a normal boyhood somewhere in Sturbridge, Massachusetts. Though only a foster mother to David for a few years, she was true family. My hope is that today we'll discover something concrete about her life, something that will nudge David's memory, unlocking whatever buried impressions or ordinary moments lie sealed inside.

Before noon we exit the Mass Pike out of Worcester onto a four-lane highway. Forty minutes later, we're cruising down a curving two-lane road, the highway dipping, then leveling off as we enter Sturbridge, a picturesque village with saltbox houses on one side of the street, small stores on the other, and fir trees dark against a gray-blue sky. Terraced houses snake up the distant hills, thick woodland groves beyond. Sturbridge is New England pretty with a gently sloping countryside and white clapboard churches, their spires rising pure and solid, looking utterly vulnerable against an empty sky. The population, I've read, is a little under ten thousand, a deeply white middle-class town with a famous living museum that recreates life in rural New England during the 1790s through the 1830s, the largest living museum in the region. But we're not here as tourists to see Old Sturbridge Village but seekers hoping to find the places David inhabited as a child with Aunt Adeline and Uncle John.

Especially their house. "It's in the Fiskdale area, near Long Pond, I think," David says as we drive down the main drag, the stores and shops brick-fronted and quaint. David's squinting, trying to get his bearings in this once-familiar place. What he remembers is a small blue-grey two-story house with a big picture window Aunt Adeline was so proud of.

Aunt Adeline.

"She was small and rather plain," he told me last year when I asked him to describe her. And then he began fixing coffee as if these words were sufficient. *Keep going, I encouraged, just tell me what she looked like.* "Well, she had brown hair just to her shoulders. She wasn't pretty, but pleasant looking. She wore house dresses, the kind a kid can't remember, just something patterned that went to her knees." Instantly, I saw my grandmother stepping out onto her narrow porch in Mobile, Alabama, in a printed dress, buttoned up the front and covering her knees, the buttons catching in my curly hair when I hugged her. "Aunt Adeline wore glasses. Reading glasses, I think." But he couldn't remember their shape or color. "My past is a blur."

And so, to me, Aunt Adeline remains in shadow. I see the bottom of her blue-printed dress and a trim ankle above a sensible black shoe as she's climbing the steps to her front door. I see her, a whirl of motion, as she shifts from the counter to the table to catch a lemon about to roll to the floor. I see her small, sturdy back bent and partially covered by a lace mantilla as she kneels at the altar of a French Catholic Church in Charlton, Massachusetts. Of course, I've conjured these images, and even in them, I never see her face, her gestures, her inclinations, never hear her voice or the cadence of her laugh. Still, I kept pushing my questions at David: *Did you ever see her cry? Did she put on lipstick for church? Did she show her teeth when she smiled? Did she ever get mad at Uncle John? Did she kiss you good night?*

David shook his head. "Sorry."

We wind our way along every street, driving up steep hills, around cul-de-sacs, and into no-exit one-lane roads where we back out *very slowly*. We find the red brick two-story school where David attended first and second grade with "1896" engraved across its stone entablature, but no streets nearby. We find Saint Anne's Catholic Church, which David remembers, though it wasn't the French Catholic

Church he attended with his foster family in Charlton. We drive up a curving, wooded street of elegant two-story frame houses with carefully stocked woodpiles out back and front doors tastefully decked with holly. It's a gentrified, upper middle-class street, unlikely to be peopled with families who took in foster children. David shakes his head. "Too fancy." Their house was near a small brook with a bridge he crossed every day on the way to school, but we can't find a bridge or a creek anywhere. All David remembers is that when the creek froze, he'd dawdle, the ice making everything trapped beneath look translucent, a semitransparent veneer.

"Dawdling. Not *you*," I laugh. My husband is known to go down every aisle in the grocery store just to see what might be new and surprising.

"Had to See Everything," he smiles. "My excuse."

As we drive, David surprises me with the story of his virgin trip to the dentist.

I raise an eyebrow, neither of us strangers to the dental chair. It turns out that when he was six years old, Aunt Adeline took him to the orthodontist, and the dentist put braces on his teeth because his front teeth didn't quite meet his bottom teeth. "What your mama would lovingly call 'malocclusion,'" he says, and we both laugh.

David says his jaw and chin needed strengthening, and besides the braces the dentist gave him a rubber strip to "work." "To sweeten the idea, he told me a story about poor little Eskimo children who used a piece of whale blubber, shaped just like my rubber thing, to learn to chew properly and stave off starvation. Evidently, they were model patients." He was supposed to use the rubber strip to make exaggerated chewing motions. He juts out his jaw and pulls it back, out and back, demonstrating.

"Nice," I say. "Did Aunt Adeline have to *make* you do it?"

"Of course." He gives me a look. "What six-year-old cares about his teeth? Aunt Adeline would say, 'David, did you do your "rubber strip" this afternoon?'"

I smile as a tiny bit of my husband's puzzle falls into place. When I first met him in Los Angeles, his front teeth angled slightly backward, as if he'd been to an overzealous orthodontist. Now, of course, I know it was more complicated than that: his front teeth protruded, his lower jaw was undeveloped, his back teeth were a wilderness of cavities caused by his craving for sweets. At the end of the twentieth century, children with an underdeveloped lower jaw will have reconstructive surgery, but not in our childhood.

"Anyway, the promo was fifty reps with that rubber thing placed perpendicular in my mouth twice a day, but I hated it because it kept getting caught in the brackets for the elastic bands on my braces, so I constantly lied." He glances at me. "My first performative denial of truly monotonous, boring things."

"But not your last," I say, reminding him of his refusal to vacuum.

He's about to reply when we turn into a circular road we've somehow missed, a short semicircle with no more than five houses tucked into the trees. David perks up, his voice almost boyish. "I think this may . . . this may *be* the road."

It's a narrow street curving into the side of a hill. We cruise slowly, scrutinizing each house, then David pulls over and parks so we can get out. The air smells like wood smoke and snow—*the breath of winter*, I think—but then the cold assaults me, and I scrunch both hands deeper into my pockets, pulling my scarf tighter.

While David studies the houses, I study him, fingering the button in my pocket, a dark brown button from his cargo pants, the kind he wears almost every day. "Da Uniform."

"This street looks like the one," David says, "but there's no house like Aunt Adeline's. Still, I don't know, it just '*feels* right.'"

I nod. The body remembers.

The cold's bristling chill stings my face. I stamp my feet, doing a little dance because my legs feel frozen, numb. I glance at David, who seems immune to the cold as he stares from the houses toward the roof of an elementary school, a school he attended for two years in the 1950s. Last night I lay in the motel bed exhausted after our trek around Worcester and watched David as he spread out the Massachusetts road map on the motel desk to check our route to Sturbridge, tracing his finger down the highway, the kind of planning he's never done. And in that moment, I knew that everything had changed. Though he'd originally resisted this trip, afraid it would be a disaster, once we arrived in Massachusetts, he became so energized, so directed, he wanted me to hurry, to go everywhere regardless of my exhaustion, my fear I was getting a cold.

I watched his button pop loose from his pants and fall to the carpet. Idly, I picked it up, meaning to put it in the suitcase. Now standing in the freezing cold on the street where David may have lived in a house no longer here yet once filled with the ordinary intimacy of family life, I think of the unraveling threads where the button used to be, a tuft of frayed ends around a bare space. On impulse, I take the button out of my pocket and let it slip from my hand, a talisman, into a crust of snow.

"I loved it here," he says, looking into ravines plunged in shadow, then up into the thick sprawling branches of an oak tree.

NEAR DUSK, WE'RE BACK in Worcester, driving down Lincoln Street, full of rush hour traffic and a blur of lurid lights, searching for the one place we haven't seen.

"It's a housing project," David frowns, staring moodily out the window of our rental car, his face in shadow, "the lowest of the low." A truck thunders past, throwing up slush. Housing projects: I think of skimpy curtains, roaches scurrying across the kitchen sink, dried ketchup on the floor. "All the kids knew when you got off the bus where you were headed. You were one of the untouchables." It's the first time he's looked strained since we arrived, his mood suddenly melancholic, as if a switch has been thrown. "There was no place to play, just institutional buildings with racks of clotheslines full of flapping laundry in the courtyard." He was eleven.

What I picture are gray brick apartments with small, high windows, but when we arrive, I'm surprised that the two- and three-story red brick apartments look as ordinary as student housing in our university town, neat and orderly and plain. Not pretty, but not shabby and depressed. David squints, craning his head toward the lighted entryways.

"They don't look so bad," I murmur, noticing a pink tricycle beneath a porch light and neatly shoveled walks.

"Yeah, they've added a few architectural flourishes"—he gestures to the arched, framed doorways and new concrete steps—"but nobody wants to live in government housing." He pulls the car over and we sit motionless in the dark. "This is where my mother got so depressed, she didn't get out of bed," he says in the tense, dismissive voice he uses when he talks about his mother. "She just lay around, not doing anything, not even washing her hair, and I had to stay in with my brothers. Every few days I walked two or three miles to get milk for them and cigarettes for her. I hated those goddamn walks in winter."

I nod, flexing my fingers. Even in the heated rental car, the air is chilled, the outside temps in the teens, the wind roaring.

"If she'd left that bastard, we'd never have ended up here." Soup, the stepfather, of course.

I glance again at the row of apartments, wanting suddenly to bid them farewell. *Joseph Stalin is no longer here*. Or is he? Memories, unlike monuments, rarely crumble; sometimes they twist and harden. Let's go, I think. Let's get out of here.

As we turn around and head back toward our motel, the sky a deep smoky blue, I try to imagine David as an eleven-year-old cooped up in an ugly room in that project or huddled in a cheap wool coat, walking down a highway scabbed with snow, cartons of milk in a paper bag. This is what I feared Worcester would mean: a trapped boy, his stepfather drunk, his mother like a warden, oppressive and silent under a cloud of unhappiness.

When we stop at a red light, I see tears in David's eyes. "I don't know why I'm doing this," he says, shaking his head. He looks away, opening a window, the cold air rushing in. "Just going back there—" I listen to the sharp sounds of the street trickling in, the screech of brakes, the hiss of tires, a bicyclist flashing past. "I used to think"—he whispers now—"that my mother was a prostitute or something because sometimes there would be a man in the house when I came home from school. I hated her for that." He looks away from me and I glance at his ungloved hands. They're red and raw with cold. "No kid wants to think that about his mother. I thought *that* was why I was in foster care, that she *did* something, but now, I don't know, I think, well, at least she showed up, at least she claimed me and didn't run away like my father. She refused to give me up for adoption." It's the first time he's revealed any compassion for his mother. Not forgiveness, but the beginnings of empathy.

When the light turns green, we move slowly forward, both of us quiet as we thread in and out of traffic, the windows cracked just slightly, cold air pressing against my throat. Secrets. In every family. So many secrets.

THAT NIGHT I'M RESTLESS. I can't sleep. Behind closed eyes, I see flashes of a mother sprawled on a double bed, the sheets damp and tangled, while a boy scrapes around the edge of a jar of peanut butter and glances at the flickering TV. Every time a gust of wind rattles the door, the boy tenses, waiting, but when the door doesn't open, he settles back, his attention focused on the TV.

Miraculously, David sleeps while I toss and turn, gazing at the glowing red numbers on the bedside clock. 2:32. 2:33. 2:36. I'm still anxious, the day sullied by that last stop, David brooding and sad, a shadow thrown over the trip. I hoped that together we could knock down those statues, that my being here would make things easier, the way years ago David had gone with me to visit my family in Alabama and simply by being there had provided a bridge for me to become a daughter again. How easily he talked with both of my parents, as if he weren't a transplanted Yankee but someone who could fit easily into their Southern rites: the big Sunday dinners, the family stories around the kitchen table, the spiked eggnog at Christmas, the sudden sharp words, the squabbling, the political arguments, the bad jokes. And there I was at thirty, not the woman who hadn't achieved the financial success her parents had wanted but a woman sitting at the round oak table with her father, eating a piece of lemon meringue pie and watching idly as he swirled ice in his drink. "Careful there, Pooch," he'd said when the meringue began to wobble on my fork. It was the first time he'd called me that nickname since childhood.

THE NEXT MORNING, I don't want to get up. While I lie snug in bed, David stands by the window in our room, staring out at a commercial building beyond the parking lot, a white bath towel draped around him. "Very senatorial," I remark, yawning, noting his wet hair scattered in every direction and the elegant towel bunched at his waist. He responds by shaking the water from his hair, fingering it into place, and telling me about last night's dream. "It was like a slideshow," he says, as if he's seeing it again, a flicker of images, "an improvisation of my former selves: me as a young child, me who loved but distrusted my mother, me who hated and feared Soup, me who was restless in school and shamed by our poverty, me who left home at sixteen." He sighs. "And alongside all these selves was a consciousness asking, 'Which one has the most to *gain* inside me?' as if this consciousness was trying to figure out which identity to claim, you know, which held the most clout." He pauses, his voice going lower. "Until, in the dream, I realized I didn't have to be any of them, that I'd simply been dragging them around with me."

When he turns to me, his face softens. "I'm not saying all these parts are gone, but now they're more like little dioramas in their niches and I can visit them, then move on. So, who knows—" He laughs a short, self-conscious laugh, "—maybe Joe Stalin *is* no longer here."

And then he adjusts his towel and stares out the window. "I always felt I had no origination, no place to be from . . . but coming back here, I . . . I feel different. That first night while we were eating dinner at the Sole Proprietor, I found myself saying, 'I grew up here,' to the waiter, and it, well, it was sorta okay."

Though I can't see his face, I remember the pride in his voice last night, the way he smiled, his words almost joyous, and I begin to relax, snuggling deeper into the covers, reveling in the warmth. "Come back to bed," I say. "Just for a minute."

Chapter 22

ONCE WE'RE BACK IN Iowa City, David's more energetic than he's been in months, while I'm like leftovers in the back of the fridge, nibbled and limp. One morning I wake so exhausted, I don't want to move, my throat tight, my body aching. I pull the covers up close to my neck and sink deeper into the bed, wondering if I have a fever or a cold, wondering what has caused this malaise. If only I could be like Virginia Woolf, for whom illness illuminated visions of poetry and mystical dreams instead of a person whose brain feels wrapped in cotton, her body listless, her dreams dull and scattered. I watch David take off his C-pap mask, then turn to me. "I can't do anything," I say. "My body's been kidnapped."

"Sleep," he says, having seen me like this before. A winter cold; a chronic fatigue crash; a sinus infection that wipes me out. For most of our marriage, I've been the "*sick one*"—sabotaged by illness—while David's been "*steady rolling*" until his rare cancer arrived.

All day I sleep, getting up only to take antihistamines and vitamin C, to eat soup and drink lemonade and glance at my vague face in the mirror, my skin pale, my eyes blurred, my breath ragged. All around me, time floats and thickens, the day absorbed by trying to wake up, until my doctor insists on prednisone, an anti-inflammatory drug that acts like a miracle cure, even as it leaches calcium from my bones.

My illnesses—chronic fatigue syndrome and environmental allergies—are laced not with pain but with journeys to the boundaries of exhaustion: fatigue pushes me to the lowest form of myself, not animal or vegetable but mineral: inert, unmoving. Most mornings I get up, take a shower, dress, have tea and breakfast, and sit at my desk. I tell myself to be hopeful because desperation often lurks nearby, the wings of illness shadowing my day. Many days, I *am* fine, or at least, good enough, and yet there are still "bad" days when I stay in bed, days that make me ashamed and furious about being sick, about what it snatches from me—my energy, my brain—and what it demands—sacrifice.

"LET'S GO TO A movie," David says on Saturday, a week later. He's standing in the doorway to my study, his hair rumpled, his eyes squinty from staring for hours at a computer screen, but his voice is excited. I can tell he needs a break. He loves movies, loves to sit in a dark theater and watch a drama unfold, his own life irrelevant, suspended, the fictional life made real. As do I. But right now, I have undergrad papers to grade and a book to critique for my Monday class. It's been a hard lesson: when I have a good day—alert and engaged—I can't afford a break.

"Sorry," I say. "I'm okay today so—" I smile. I don't have to finish. David knows the story, and though he looks disappointed, he nods.

"I'll catch the 3:30 show," he says. "Gotta get out of here."

"Go." I wave as he picks up the car keys.

In minutes, he's gone, the house silent except for the steady hum of the air filter and the ticking of the kitchen clock. I return to reading a student essay until a little part of my mind turns inward and I put down my pen, recognizing what people so often ask and I've so rarely acknowledged: Why did I, a writer, a snoop, a person wedded to the dynamics of family, know so little about David's past? In truth, after I got sick in Los Angeles, I was too shattered by the erratic nature of my illness—the exhaustion, the brain fog, the loss of self—to prod and poke at David's story, to think about any puzzle other than my own. Trying desperately to resolve my illness, I went to doctors in Los Angeles, then later in New York, Minnesota, and even Canada, hoping that someone somewhere could put me back together again. More than anything, I knew I'd have to make a living, knew that two people in the arts needed, at the very least, to have sellable skills, to be diligent and improvisational. Now I see that in trying to compensate for the “sick” self, I discovered my own stubbornness, an insistence that allowed me to be self-contained and hermetic, to focus on work over pleasure, which meant skipping parties and dinners and cultural events or going to the movies with David to sustain enough energy to “get on with it.”

Get on with it.

As I gaze out my study windows at the stark, leafless katsura trees and the pale blue light of winter brightening the old snow as it glitters near the garage, I wish, more than anything, that I could go to the movies, that I could go on a whim, a dare, a rebellion, could slouch in the seat next to David’s in the dark theater and let someone else’s story pour over me, seducing me away from my own. I let myself wallow for a bit in this speculative moment—I see my head resting comfortably against my seat, my knees braced against the one in front as I idly crunch on popcorn, my hand lifting rhythmically, almost unconsciously, David’s hand patting my knee, my eyes fixed on the wide screen as characters react to the circumstances of a plot, their lives stumbling toward trouble—and then I let it all blur into nothingness, a net of dreams fading to black. I take a deep breath, and then another and another, until I’m back in my study, neither a rebel nor a visionary but a woman who can savor a cup of hot tea, can read and enjoy a page of a student’s essay, making stars and comments in the margin, in essence, spreading out my arms to embrace the world I’ve made, small and limited as it is and yet irrevocably mine.

Chapter 23

WEEKS LATER, LIKE DUTIFUL pilgrims, we take elevator H to radiology for David's CT scans, then trek the length of the hospital to consult with the smart, feisty oncologist who insisted at our first meeting two years ago that we call him Mo. Grinning, he said, "I tell all my patients they can hit me once"—proffering his arm—"but only once." We laughed, though his joke seemed ominous, as if he'd just announced himself as the messenger of bad news.

Today, in radiology, we're directed to a different waiting room, a small, stuffy interior room with no door, no windows, and no sound except for the footsteps of passersby and the sharp, blustery blowing of noses. The room's crowded, a holding tank of motley people with puffy down jackets and bright knit caps. We take the only available seats, where directly across from us sit an older woman and man in jeans, boots, and faded sweatshirts, a couple who might be Iowa farmers. At a first glance, I wonder why the woman is wearing pink curlers, but as I'm taking off my coat and folding it in my lap, I realize they're small growths, like marbled pink gumballs clustered at the front of her head, strands of blonde-gray hair fanning out beneath. Quickly, I look away, though the writer in me wants to stare. Instead, I pull out a book.

Though I try to read, my concentration's shot, the words a black scramble. As David's name is called, the man to my left has such a violent coughing fit, the room is punctuated by his deep, ragged hacking. I glance up. He sits in a wheelchair, one side of his empty pants' leg folded almost to his hip, his face lined and leathery, yellowed with age and illness. I sink back, feeling guilty and unpardonably normal, as if I've been thrust into a Dickens novel with its wilderness of human misery. In this room, the integrity of the body seems to have been breached, the demands of disease insisting on capitulation, and yet we all sit here because we must, because we can.

Thirty minutes later I hear a low murmuring and glance up, gazing around the room. My eyes fall briefly on the woman across from me just as David waves at me from the door, his CT scan complete. I grab my coat.

"Prisoner number XX24, D. Wilder, has been released," he says, trying for a joke, but neither of us laughs. We're off to see Mo.

USUALLY MO RUNS LATE, and we supply ourselves with coffee and poppyseed muffins, sitting in this lovely waiting room with its muted colors and tasteful décor. It's almost a sanctuary—we could be waiting for something as incidental as a massage, a facial, could cancel the appointment on a whim, a wink, "Sorry, no time just now!" David puts in his earbuds, and I open my book, but to our surprise David's name is promptly called and we're in a treatment room thirty minutes early. I take it as a good sign. We've never seen Mo for more than ten minutes, just long enough for him to burst in, always doggedly upbeat, show us the scans, then give David the all-clear before he's off to another patient. "I live and breathe cancer," he said once in a voluble mood, his dark, intelligent eyes glittering in his buoyant face.

"Boy, you must be fun to come home to at night," I teased.

"My wife's a psychiatrist." He flashed a sardonic smile. "So, it evens out."

We laughed. I loved his funny frankness.

Now David chats with the nurse as she goes through the blood pressure, pulse, and temp routine, but I'm daydreaming, thinking about hot cocoa and buttered toast, and so I'm surprised when Mo comes in, his dark eyes wary, his face stuck on grim. Suddenly a needle of dread pierces my brain. He barely says hello. He's not going to offer a joke or a pun, not going to call us "young folks," not going to play nice. "The scans show two spots on your lungs," he says in a grave voice, his gaze locked on David.

I don't like this, I think, but I can't take my eyes away from his face.

He pulls up the test results on the screen, showing us what look like tiny white splotches near the middle of the left lobe of David's lungs—he points at them—and asks if David's had pneumonia or an infection in the last two months.

"No."

Now we're both sitting up, alert, uncertain how something can show up when we least expect it, when David's had no symptoms. How the hell are we supposed to know when to be worried?

"What does that mean, on my lungs?"

Mo turns, his jaw tightened, and I realize for the first time that I might want to hit him. "Once you've had cancer," he says gently, his eyes almost tender, "we can't rule out a metastasis. Cancer is ingenious. A maverick. But we don't know yet if these are small tumors; it might be nothing more than scar tissue. I can't be sure." His face loosens, as if he's shed weight simply by expressing doubt. "I'd like to think it *is* scar tissue because it doesn't look quite right, doesn't have the more precise definition of a tumor. A tumor tends to show up as a white dot all massed together whereas this looks looser, more splattered. But we can't rule it out. We'll have to wait for the radiologist to read it more closely."

Neither of us moves. We stare at Mo as if he's swallowed our voices. Irrationally, I feel as if David's been given this prognosis for no other reason than that it's never occurred to me that he could get lung cancer. Of course, this is insane—as if the incidence of cancer is tied to my consciousness—suggesting the sin of pride. But I can't let it go. *My fault!*

"I promise I'll call you tonight," Mo says solemnly. "We'll know more by then."

And just like that, we're walking out of the oncology unit, walking to ramp 4, walking to our parked car. Only when we're in a rush of cold air, the sky barely bruised with light does it occur to me what that low murmuring might have been: humming. I think the woman with a head full of tumors was humming.

ON THE DRIVE HOME the river looks icy, wind rippling across the frozen water. The bus ahead of us groans as it stops at the railroad crossing, then shudders noisily, shifting gears. Students stream out of the library, out of the gym and the communications studies buildings, young and healthy and oblivious. *Stupid students. What do they know? What can they possibly know?*

Today there is no sun, only gray. Winter has sealed us into ourselves, the earth frozen and bleak, a smothering dullness. The trees, black and silent, look lonely, naked; darkness hangs between the branches. We turn into our street and park. The front steps of our house are slippery with a crust of ice, the cold chafing at my toes, and suddenly, I miss the snow, miss the way it softens the day, the way it covers the land, hiding all the ragged, uneven edges. "Let it snow, please, oh, please let it snow."

In the kitchen David and I fix grilled cheese sandwiches, comfort food, neither of us saying much. After the last CT scan, we came home and fell into bed laughing. In the middle of the day. Fuck work! Fuck dinner! But today I slice cheese and think, *lungs*. I don't know a thing about lungs, those tree branches full of air. If the tumor came back, I assumed it would recur, like a homing device, at the original site, David's left upper buttocks. I imagined a second operation—though the idea of the surgeons cutting into those intricately reattached blood vessels made me cringe. I never once thought this rare cancer could metastasize to the lungs. And once there, why stop, I think now, why not a charged leap to the brain?

As I slice up squares of cheese and spread butter on bread, I realize how little I know about cancer, the disease itself, how protective and naïve my thoughts have been, how I've faithfully read articles on PubMed while secretly I've tried to slam the door on illness, as if by dimming the lights and closing the curtains, I can keep the bad things out.

WHEN THE PHONE RINGS at 7:10 p.m.—we've finished our cheese sandwiches and coffee—we stare at each other, paralyzed. Then, abruptly, David picks up the phone, turning toward the dining room windows. It's dark outside, a quiet world. No lights on in the neighbor's kitchen. No students walking down the sidewalk, their voices young and loud as they make their way home from the library. No birds rustling in the bushes. Everything is suspended. David mutters something, listens, and when he turns back, his face is pale.

"What?" I say, my voice unaccountably sharp.

"Scar tissue!" he murmurs. "It's only scar tissue."

I don't remember any more. I want to believe we play "Angel Eyes," the two of us dancing in the kitchen, swaying together as we move on the scratched grey and white tiles, a floor we always intend to replace with a wooden floor, something shiny and elegant and new once we have more money. But tonight, it doesn't matter. Who cares about the scratched floor?

David twirls me around, and then we break apart and I do my swivel hips for him—something I'm good at—a sexy bump and grind I've practiced since my teenage years.

My own kind of blessing.

Chapter 24

WE'RE IN THE KITCHEN preparing dinner. I'm washing broccoli and peppers while David seasons the salmon, the rice already steaming in the rice cooker. "A caseworker from Boston called today to say she'll be processing my request," David says, reaching for the roasted garlic.

I nod. After we returned from Worcester, David decided to get his foster care files, and it's been two weeks since he sent the form to the Massachusetts Department of Children and Families.

"But the surprise is," David continues, turning to me, "she said I'd lived with many foster families, and I couldn't get that phrase out of my head—*many foster families, many foster families, many foster families*—like I had repetition compulsion."

I shake water from the vegetables. "So, you didn't live *only* with Aunt Adeline and Uncle John like you remembered?"

"Nope."

I look at him slyly. "Well, now you've got a right to be really fucked up!"

When he glances at me relief flickers across his face, and he laughs such a big, happy laugh that I grin and do a little curtsey.

"Probably where I got my superpowers," he retorts, an old joke between us.

"Fucked up superpowers."

"But superpowers nonetheless."

I open the rice cooker to a billow of steam. *He'll be all right,* I think. *We'll be all right.*

WHEN THE FILES ARRIVE, David trundles them up to his study as if they're a secret, then retrieves them after dinner, placing them on the dining room table like a gift or a penance, I never know which, the manila envelope still sealed. "Let's read them together, okay?" he says, pulling out a chair. "I mean, I'm not pretending this will be easy. Probably like chemotherapy . . . gotta hurt to make you better."

I nod at his little joke, then we sit side by side in the heat of the evening, reading the beginning dates and summaries until on the second page we both stop, jolted by the words: *David received this date under Section 38: 12/20/48.*

"You were just a baby," I whisper, stunned by the news. "Not even three months old."

"It seems." He lets out a slow breath, staring at the page, and then he touches the words, running a finger over the sentence. "I never wanted to know about my past, didn't want to find out about my mother and why she let me go—" His face looks weighted, sad.

But instead of an easy abandonment, we discover how hard it was for his mother to live apart from him. *"Mother distressed that she will not be able to take him for day visits immediately,"* the caseworker writes only days after the mother has released him to foster care.

"She didn't want to let you go," I say, noting how again and again she asks if she can visit, if she can take David to her brother's place, if she can have him overnight, can get his picture made, buy him new toys, new clothes, feed him, dress him, sing to him, soothe him, every sentence a hum of desire.

David nods but says nothing. In the end, she was a woman alone, bound to minimum-wage jobs, to cheap rented rooms, and no help from anyone. She had to let him go.

That evening we get a late-night snack and then brush our teeth together, one of us inevitably talking even though the toothpaste is foaming and spilling and whatever is said must be repeated after the rinse. It could be any other night, but of course, it's not. The lights are too bright, the house too silent, the air too dry. Where is all the noise? Why am I still rubbing my mouth on a damp towel?

David puts up his toothbrush, then ducks into his study.

THE NEXT DAY, AFTER fixing coffee, David yawns and pushes the stack of files toward me. "You can read the rest of them now. . . . I mean, if you want." Last night we stopped reading after page fifteen (there are sixty-nine pages), and instead sat together on the couch, talking and not talking, leaning back and closing our eyes. "I finished them," he says now, "lying on the couch in my study." I imagine him sprawled there, trying to pretend he isn't stunned by this chorus of notes about himself, his mother, and his foster mothers.

I'm anxious to read the files, but for a few minutes I stare warily at them as if I'm about to yank off a Band-Aid and see red, wrinkled flesh. After all, this isn't a childhood but a case study, David's early years documented and interpreted by social workers and doctors, a clinical commentary with proscriptive expectations rather than an autobiography. *The 1950s.* Ugh, all that rigidity, that strict, gendered postwar morality, women financially restricted and sexually indicted, their identity and ambition constrained.

Though I'm ashamed to admit it, with the house shuttered and still, I slip the files from the envelope and feel a twitch of illicit fascination, a writer about to get the goods. I remember how earlier David's eyes clouded with tears (his mother's obvious pride and delight in him), how his interest sparked (the quickness with which he learned words, his *"diction and vocabulary are advanced,"* the caseworker wrote), how his mouth tightened (one doctor declared him *"mentally retarded"* when he was placed alongside a four-year-old with mental deficiencies). But it's different to read the files alone. The comments seem so personal—*Foster mother said that David understands that his foster father is not his real father, but he is not quite sure why he does not have a father like other boys*—and more bureaucratically distant—*eczema has cleared up; fractured right clavicle; buttocks badly scarred with sores.*

After rereading the first few pages, I'm still troubled by that fateful progression: child was "received" into foster care seven days shy of three months of age; child was moved to at least five different placements before he was three and a half years old; child was so distressed as the caseworker drove him to his sixth placement—Aunt Adeline's and Uncle John's—a journey of thirty-five miles from his former foster home in Worcester, that she feared he was ill.

"D. manifests great emotional disturbance because of being removed from one foster home to another. His hands are perspiring, and he seems to have a slight temperature. Visitor (case worker) disturbed to learn that mother and foster mother (the one he is leaving, the one he calls Aunt Alma) prepared David for his leave taking by telling him that foster mother (Aunt Alma) is to be hospitalized and that he may hope to return there at some far distant time when she may have recovered. Visitor attempted to point out to foster mother that this deception is unwise and could have far-reaching consequences for the child. However, the child is so confused that visitor does not attempt to give him any other explanation. On the journey to the new foster home David complains that he doesn't feel well and he is obviously extremely nervous."

TWO DAYS LATER WHEN the caseworker returned to check on him, he was finishing his lunch in his new foster home. *"He immediately tells visitor that he does not want to go in her car and wants to stay where he is,"* the caseworker writes. On the next visit, he was playing happily outdoors *"with his little cart and his tricycle." "Again upon greeting visitor,"* she writes, *"he shakes his head very solemnly and says he doesn't intend to go anywhere else."*

I'm sitting on the floor in my nightgown, the glow of the lamp a halo around me. "He doesn't intend to go anywhere else." Sadness. I put down the pages and another ragged piece of my husband's puzzle falls into place: he *hates* to move, *hates* to disrupt one household and start another, *hates* packing and unpacking, *hates* not just the physical act of moving but the preparation, the concept: leaving the familiar for the unknown. And not only that. He resists all fantasies about a new place, never indulging in "imagining what it will be like" or "who we'll be when we're there" or "how this will change us" or "what we'll miss or forget."

Because he refuses to conceptualize moving, his packing is always erratic and last minute, making the move a disaster, every departure delayed, the two of us shouting and insulting each other—"Come on, Jesus, *come on*!" I yell—because the movers are here and he's *still* not finished though he stayed up all night, sorting and discarding, half-empty coffee cups scattered around the room. "Leave me alone," he yells back.

I remember his face the day we packed for a temporary move from our house in Iowa City to Auburn, Alabama, where I'd be a Breeden Scholar at Auburn University for the fall semester. Though we took only clothes, books, laptops, and art supplies, the move meant renting out our house and driving fifteen hours from Iowa City to the southeast corner of Alabama. By the time David had crammed his photo equipment and suitcases in the car—two hours late—he was tense and distressed, complaining that he didn't feel well.

"It'll be okay," I kept saying, wondering why I always had to coddle and soothe. And then my irritation flared. "You're being ridiculous! Just stop!" All I wanted was for this to be an adventure, a pleasant little "getaway" from routine, but to him it was all rupture and trouble. *What's wrong with you?* I kept asking as we turned onto I-80 E, David slumped in the passenger seat, his shirt damp with sweat.

Our traumas, it seems, will never abandon us.

TO ME, CHILDHOOD MEANT a secure home and family in a small Alabama town with three meals a day, baths every night and stories read to us at bedtime or under the oak tree in our backyard. Insecurity didn't rear its head until adolescence. At age five, I could walk with my sister to the drugstore to get a coke float or sit sucking my thumb in my mother's flower garden, squatting by the caladiums while she finished making homemade ice cream, the clacking sound of the crank handle mingling with the shouts of the neighbor boys playing kickball. I knew that my mother would cook waffles or eggs and bacon every morning and that my father would return home from the clinic each night, fixing himself a drink and sometimes saying, "Com'ere, Pooch," patting the sofa beside him. To David, childhood was a series of temporary stops to unfamiliar places, a new mother always at its center.

"It was hard to realize I'd been placed in many homes, that I had no *home*," he said one night, not long after he'd read the files. Though his birth mother visited him at his first foster home four times a week, the files note, this was reduced to once a week after his third move and once every three weeks in the final move to Aunt Adeline's and Uncle John's. Each time the caseworker took him in her car, did he worry about who would give him food and warmth and a cuddle?

The first foster mother, the file suggests, is befuddled and sweet and young, the second one middle-aged and strict, the third one soft-voiced but mentally limited. From my reading I know that children in foster care, especially when they're preverbal, sometimes have difficulty forming secure attachments to new foster parents if they've lived in compromised environments with frequent changes. When this happens, children often become confused about how to behave, having lost two of the things a child most needs: the familiarity of habit and the security of being safe. Each move means "ruptured attachment," another break in trust, another experience of being unwanted or unloved, Cris Beam notes in a book about foster care, *To the End of June*. Did David learn to fear a change in mothering, to associate dislocation with episodes of sickness and stress and anxiety about the unknown? *Where were they taking him? Had he done something wrong?*

Days later, I'm shocked to read that "foster care children are twice as likely to develop PTSD as war veterans." I put the article down and stare out the window at the spill of impatiens hanging from my neighbor's back deck. *Breathe. Just breathe.* I begin rereading the ACE literature about how the HPA (hypothalamus-pituitary-adrenal) axis is "very reactive to adverse early experience" and that "foster children more frequently show 'atypical' patterns of cortisol production when compared with other children," which means the fight-or-flight response can go haywire, a twitch, a seam of fear, then panic swimming through the blood. I think of the body fragile and clenched, the brain marbled with dread, a subtle but ghostly disruption of the neuroendocrine system where nests of cells begin silently to rebel. I read these facts, but I can't take them in. Did David feel this powerless as a child or did he, by some miracle, fall outside of the norm?

In our life together he seems remarkably resilient: ambitious and friendly and comfortable with diverse groups of people, never shy or tongue-tied as I often am. His energy kicks up at English Department parties, writers' receptions, art openings, and community events where he's instinctively charming, his head tilted as he teases someone or makes a provocative comment, often moving physically near to people as if establishing intimacy though the talk is never personal or deeply revealing. "What did you talk about?" I often ask as we're driving home, jealous at how engaged in conversation he was with colleagues who seemed to laugh much easier with him than they did with me. "Oh, you know, we just played, batted the ball around," he'll say, never offering any concrete details. Such a response only makes me stew. *Batting the ball around, my ass,* I brood. It's taken me years to recognize that he wasn't being intentionally evasive or simply bullshitting and that the right term for what he was doing is flirting. It doesn't matter the gender because flirting is about winning favor, displaying charm; it's the ability to improvise, a natural instinct but perhaps a heightened one for a man who learned early in childhood that acceptance is conditional.

One Saturday afternoon we go to the Hy-Vee Grocery store in Iowa City to get broccoli and tomatoes and apples along with the usual household products. As we load our stuff onto the conveyer, the clerk says, "Well, hello there," to David as if they're old friends.

She's a pleasant-looking older woman with graying hair, glasses, and a flushed face. David smiles and chats about our purchases, about the discounts, and then they talk for a few minutes about the repairs recently done to her car. I listen, amazed. *He knows her*. He says something and makes her laugh. "You must be David's wife," she says, smiling, offering her hand, including me in their conviviality.

Why, *he's always creating potential family*, I realize as we gather up our bags and head for the car. It's instinctive to him, a kind of security, a way of being.

Years later, he'll give me another clue. In his seventies, he takes a nap in the early evening after we watch thirty or forty minutes of a TV drama. He lies back on the green sofa, shoes off, his head resting on a pile of pillows while I unfold the soft red and white blanket, unfurling it and covering him, then tucking it in at his feet and around his shoulders as if he were a seven-year-old boy. Every time I do this, his face relaxes into such contented pleasure, I can't help but smile as I sit on the edge of the sofa, chatting.

"I love for you to do this. I wait for it. It relieves *all* my anxieties," he tells me one night as I tuck him in. I nod, no longer surprised. This one gesture—a maternal act of care and safety—is what he missed for many years of childhood and still covets in adulthood. How could I have known?

What I do know is that anxiety isn't random. It too has a pattern. As does relief.

I'VE NOW DRUNK THREE cups of tea, one right after the other, and I'm overcaffeinated, suddenly wired and restless. Maybe that's why I'm incensed when I read the official petition for David's adoption by his stepfather, a report signed by the assistant supervisor of the Department of Public Welfare and distilled from summaries of the caseworkers' notes. On page two of this two-page document, the report says:

"During the period that he was under the care of the Department

he needed many foster home replacements because of his asthmatic condition, eczema, temper tantrums and slowness of being toilet trained. Handling him was more difficult because of the frequent visits of his mother, who overly indulged him. Throughout his care, there has been a question of his general normalcy."

I SLAM SHUT THE document. *What the hell?* It's near midnight, but I start pacing, restless and furious at what is so conveniently left out: that David was removed from his first foster mother's house after four months (he was seven months of age) because the caseworker stated that this woman was *"too young and immature to care for the child,"* that *"the child got little fresh air and sunshine and was always sloppily dressed,"* and that the doctor didn't feel *"that she carried out his instructions (for medical treatment), but let the child 'do for itself.'"* There is no mention that at this house, his carriage was placed on the back porch, where it toppled over and down the back stairs and the child broke his collarbone. There is no mention that the first foster home was closed down as *"unsuitable for all children."* There is no mention that he had severe eczema and such a bad upper respiratory infection, along with *"no training at all from the first home,"* that the second foster mother felt she was *"not capable of keeping him."* Within a month, he was shuttled off to a third foster home, in which the *"limited mental capacity of the foster mother"* and a four-year-old mentally retarded child gave the caseworker pause about David's adjustment, though he was kept there for several months—and labeled mentally retarded too—until another home could be found.

Though I can imagine David was a "handful" as a child, it might also be true that his stubbornness and tantrums allowed him to survive these places and become the thoughtful man he became. If he'd been a docile child, he might have been left with the first foster mother who let a six-month old "*do for itself.*"

But why am I in a tizzy about such vague diagnostic words as "general normalcy" when I know these terms were culturally imposed, defined by doctors who saw normalcy within the rather strict guidelines of postwar correctness: ease of toilet training, obedience to authority, participation with other children, cheerful affect, easily distracted from masturbation. I shouldn't care but I'm outraged on his behalf.

Idiots! I continue to march around the room, past the sofa and chairs, toward the front door, and back to the files on the dining room table, hoping only to tire myself out.

DURING THE WEEK THAT I'm reading the files, David and I go out to dinner with friends, people who will be sending their children, ages seven and ten, to a private school that costs thirty-two thousand per student a year, people who are educated and decent, whose wonderful kids will have every opportunity in life: to learn languages, to travel, to focus on their unique talents with the best teachers, the most modern equipment, with familial support. The man, a friend and former colleague, talks about his work, a novel he's writing and the research he's doing for another book, and when he asks what I'm working on, I find myself struggling, unable to talk about the memoir. "Fucked-up superpowers," I want to say, and for a moment I imagine blurting it to this man, so educated in entitlement and ambition. Instead, I ask him about his kids, about his wife's new job and his most recent travels.

Later, before I get ready for bed, I see David sitting at his desk, bent in a familiar posture toward the computer, studying a recent print he's made or perhaps just checking his email. He glances up as if surprised to see me, and smiles. Sometimes now I see the boy in the man, the freckles scattered across his eyelids, the quickness with which he adapts to new people, the entangled mess of his room as if each item tossed to the floor or the chair is a kind of claiming. *I live here. Home.* Though it might be a romantic notion, I like to think that the man I fell in love with—witty, demanding, surprising, tender, moody, irritating, and sometimes infuriating—couldn't have emerged from any other world than the one he survived. There's no way to know. I know only that for most of our life together there's been a space between us, his past shielded, a kind of protective veil I couldn't push through until he reached out to tear it open. Perhaps he couldn't look at his past until he'd been thrust into the gray-dark world of cancer. Perhaps I couldn't have shared it if I hadn't been there too, changing dressings, emptying drains, sitting those long hours in waiting rooms, watching the strained blue light fade to dusk.

I think now that cancer does this to some people, some marriages: once the illusion of normalcy is broken, what emerges is something sweeter, deeper, closer, as if the broken thing becomes, ironically, the healing thing.

Chapter 25

DAYS AFTER READING DAVID'S foster care files, I remember riding in the back seat of my mother's car one spring afternoon in 1958. I was ten. We were rushing to music lessons at Mama Dot's in Fairhope, a trip we made twice a week after school to our favorite teacher, a twenty-five-minute sprint from our small town, with treats already in the car so we'd be on time for our lessons. The day was warm, azaleas bursting into bloom along the side of the road, daffodils sprouting, goldenrod and bluebells crowding the ditches along Greeno Road. Today, when Mother turned off the two-lane highway into a dirt drive shaded by an oak tree, I was surprised. Just beyond the tree stood a small frame house with a tilted front porch, both badly in need of a coat of paint.

"I'll just be a minute," she said, gathering a package from the front seat. "There's a foster child here who needs medicine for impetigo." I watched as she knocked on the screen door, then talked for a moment to a white, middle-aged woman in a house dress and apron, who nodded as my mother spoke. I can't remember if my mother went inside, if she saw the child, though I imagine she'd want to see how the disease had spread and give specific instructions.

What I remember next is my mother on Greeno Road, heading toward Fairhope while I stared out the side window as the small house vanished from sight and the word *impetigo* scraped against my mind. *Impetigo. Impetigo. Impetigo.* I had no idea what it meant, what kind of disease it was, but I liked how the four syllables rolled off my tongue. I assumed that it was connected to poverty. It's what the small, dilapidated house suggested to me: people with barely enough money to survive—one bathroom for everyone, three kids to a bed, no washing machine or dishwasher, an old car, a rowdy dog, and children taken in for a small government payment.

And there it is: my ten-year-old mind had already acculturated the physical and psychological perceptions of caste.

Even now, over fifty years later, when I hear the word "impetigo"—knowing it's a bacterial infection caused by staphylococci organisms that usually affect young children aged two to five—I think of that house where a foster child lived, the word still aligned in my brain with a family who might not have been able to wash towels and clothes in hot water every day, to afford antibiotic cream or a visit to the doctor, who might have had no protection from the warm, humid weather of coastal Alabama or from discriminatory opinions. I think of a toddler secretly scratching at the small red bumps on his legs, confused by the pain. But I also think of my mother, the way she tried to make sure the poor and neglected in our county, people who might be exhausted and humiliated by their circumstances, by accident and illness, by trauma and despair, had medicine and treatment. Our lives were defined by my father's small-town medical practice, by patients showing up many nights at our back door, by nightly calls from the ER, as well as my mother's careful dietary plans for patients and her fervent community service.

Did my mother go into that home, remembering her own childhood in a company house in a mining town in northern Alabama, the bare walls needing paint, the faded curtains secondhand, the outhouse in the backyard, her brothers and sisters taking baths in an iron tub in the kitchen while her father slept before going back to the pits, or did she think about the new upholstered sofas being delivered to our four-bedroom ranch-style house in southern Alabama? But of course, I imagine it was both, the past always tucked into the present . . . just beneath the skin.

Chapter 26

I KEEP COMING BACK to our mothers. My mother. David's mother. In so many ways they shaped us, changed us, misperceived, and perhaps misunderstood us, just as we misunderstood them. To us, they seemed landlocked, stationary, while we hurled ourselves into the deep blue sea. How little we knew. Then again, we came of age in the 1960s, when the familiar seams of American life were unraveling, when families went to war over the length of a son's hair or a daughter's refusal to wear a bra. All around us, sons and daughters turned rebellious, leaving home and thrusting themselves into the unknown. I left home for college and then, at twenty, to get married. Though I wouldn't have said I was leaving my mother, I secretly believed there was nothing more urgent than to turn my back on the social safety and predictability of a Southern woman's life. True, I longed for a deep, burning love and appeared to live a conventional life, but I yearned for something more—call it the throw of a Frisbee, a surprise landing, a need to roam, to look in unexpected places.

David left home much earlier. "I had to get away from my mother," he said one night as we lay in bed, his voice low and tense. For thirty years I'd heard only his sharp, flinted words, the stories about his mother no more than a few terse sentences—"She sacrificed me to my stepfather. She let him beat me. She beat me too"—his anger flaring even as we sat together on the couch in Iowa City, the light fading, the wind up, branches tossed against the roof. Then, just as suddenly, the fuse fizzled. He shook his head. Old stuff. He didn't want to "go there," dragging himself back into his past.

And yet, each time he mentioned his mother, I resented her. I disliked her. I felt embarrassed by her, this woman who looked so working-class old and frumpy in the one picture I'd seen: shaggy hair, a beaky nose, dark circles shadowing brown melancholy eyes. A wicked witch! I thought, *You dumped him in foster care as a child and didn't protect him once he was yours again.*

Nobody deserved her.

BUT NOW, NOW THAT I've read the foster care files, the narrative has begun to shift, her story so much larger and more complicated than I could have imagined. True, I can't see her clearly, can barely scrape the surface of her life, but the difference is that I want—and *need*—to make her more than a monster. She died in 2000. She died and we didn't know it. Now I think the only way to resurrect her properly is to write what I've come to know, to say goodbye before I've even said hello. And though I don't have the historical documents or personal anecdotes to give her a proper eulogy, to chart even one hour of happiness, I like to imagine a night in spring as she sauntered down Millbury Street, the laundry done, the moon low and white over the trees, a new pack of cigarettes snug in her pocket.

I spread out all the information I have: a 1940 U.S. Census report (she was eleven); thirty-one pages of typed caseworker notes in a Health and Human Services file dating from October 19, 1948, to June 25, 1956, (the period that my husband—her son—was in foster care); a 1957 Worcester County Probate Court petition for adoption by her and her new husband, Orrin Campbell; a U.S. Social Security Death Index (she was seventy-two); an online obituary; and a few random pictures, one in which she looks so young and lovely I can't quit staring at it. In this photo, she's a slender woman, auburn hair swept back from her face, a bright cranberry sleeveless shirt bloused over tan shorts, one sandaled foot lifted as she leans into her new husband. Her skin looks pale and creamy, her thin lips pressed close, her almond eyes dreamy, almost sleepy, as if she's been coaxed up from a nap for this quick photo in an ordinary 1950s kitchen with its bright white cabinets and blue-gray tile. A paper towel rack is just visible behind her left shoulder.

Though she may indeed have been a monster, I know now that

she was also a motherless daughter, an abandoned girl, a jilted lover, a young woman caught in the crosshairs of poverty with a deep, hungry love for a baby she couldn't afford to keep.

HER NAME WAS ANN.

She is listed as Anna C. Trigiano in the 1940 U.S. census, though I don't know what the "C" stands for or when the final "a" was dropped from her first name. *Ann*. I say the name out loud. My own middle name.

She was the last of five children, born in May 1928 to an Italian Catholic family in Worcester, Massachusetts, immigrants from the province of Foggia, known as the "granary" of Italy and famous for their watermelons and tomatoes. The records show that her mother died when she was three years old and she was raised by an eleven-year-old aunt in a family whose social situation was listed as *"poor"* by social services, a 1950s code for economic and social dysfunction. When I read these words, I pause, alert to the genesis of trouble—*"mother died"; "raised by an eleven-year-old aunt"; "already in the system."* In one paragraph, the seeds of despair, the constraints of a future. I hold my breath: adversity often repeats itself in traumatized families, as if the child who becomes an adult remains locked in the peril of her childhood, tangled in its black shadow, unable to detach.

For years now researchers have acknowledged, even insisted, that problems in mothering were "the most dramatic for those who'd lost a same-sex parent at an early age." Here, a trope of inevitability, a helplessness that cuts like glass. Unmothered. Untethered. Unprepared. Where's the gleam in that? Maybe her mother's early death explains why she felt *"so unloved"* in childhood, why she described herself to the caseworker as developing *"a shy, inferiority complex with a defeatist attitude,"* why she seemed such an erratic mother, both detached and overly involved, trapped in her own twisted loyalties.

Maybe not being mothered left her empty. Maybe desire became demolition. Maybe it made her terribly hungry, reckless for any kind of love. . . .

But I don't finish that sentence. I look out my window, but there's only inky darkness, the air blue with cold.

Ann.

She left school and her father's house after the ninth grade—she must have been fifteen or sixteen years of age—"*because of my father,*" she confessed to the caseworker. After I read that sentence, I am indignant. I can't help but blame *him*: a shiftless worker, a gravedigger, a layabout, the files note—his stubby fingers reaching for a cigarette, a beer—and who knows, maybe a domestic brute and an abuser of girls? Regardless, her home was known to social services as a place of *"little security,"* where she felt *"unloved"* in an unsettled, shifting immigrant family dominated by men. At sixteen, she went to work in a factory, perhaps the Cudahy Packing Company, an Irish meat-packing plant on Franklin Street with its stench of offal and blood, sweat and chemicals. Though I can't know exactly what hardships or abuse she attributed to her father, I sense her urgent need to escape, the desire to slip from the old life into a new world. Just as her son will do many years later.

And this is the way I see her: a halo of smoke circling her as she stands in sturdy brown shoes just outside the factory gates at 6:58 a.m., a last puff of her cig before the grind begins. It's the summer of 1944, the whole world at war, puckered and burning, refugees crowding the roads of Europe, dreaming of cabbage, of black bread slathered with butter, the cloying stench of carcasses wafting in the breeze. And yet here in America with its energy and bustle, its humming factories, there are jobs for women—even for girls like her—with so many of the men overseas, the Allies preparing to enter Rome just as she, an Italian American girl, steps through the factory door into hot, dusty air.

A year later, I lose her. She's vanished from social service records. I have no idea what happened to her right after the war. Did she stay in touch with her sister, with the aunt who raised her? Was she laid off from the factory once the veterans returned, men needing and deserving good jobs, their welfare a national priority? Is that why she began waitressing, surviving on tips, on her feet all day, carrying trays, chatting up the customers—old men with yellow teeth and bored smiles; married men who demanded their coffee *hot*—prepping for the next day, the steady, methodical folding of napkins, the clinking of silverware, the stacking of cups, a little more knowing now at seventeen or eighteen or nineteen? She's petite but voluptuous, a wary girl but quick with words—this I sleuthed from my husband's comments—and an easy laugh. You can see I'm casting about; there's nothing concrete for me to know of her life—except that she was a waitress—until 1948 when she discovers her pregnancy, a fact she can't seem to tell the man she's fallen in love with and has been dating for two years.

The caseworker writes:

"Mother (A) talked freely about putative father and with a great deal of feeling. She said she had known him for over two years and he was a toolmaker, attending —— Institute during that time. A better job possibility had required him to leave the area shortly before she knew she was pregnant. She said she had heard from him in June (four months before the baby's birth), but at that time she lost the purse containing the letter and she was not able to write to him."

WHEN I READ THAT last sentence, I blush. It has the feel of a nineteenth-century novel, the tragic heroine defeated by the most mundane of complications: a lost purse. Oh, dear! And yet this is the middle of the twentieth century, and that lost purse, I suspect, is simply a detour, a face-saving excuse, an apt metaphor for so much more: the end of a relationship that once carried the potential for emotional and financial salvation. There's something so guileless about the comment, so vulnerable to easy critique that I imagine her glancing furtively away from the caseworker, embarrassed and uncertain if she's disguised the true state of things: she is alone and pregnant and abandoned by her boyfriend. The caseworker's notes continue:

"She fully expects," the caseworker's notes continue, *"that he will soon be back in Worcester and at that time she will inform him about the baby. It was apparent to Worker that she is hopeful that marriage to (the baby's) father will ensue."*

AND WHAT, I THINK cynically, could possibly go wrong with such a plan?

"I NEVER KNEW WHO my father was," David said casually one evening on a road trip to Alabama to visit my mother. Driving on Interstate 55, through the piney woods of Mississippi, I pretended no surprise, squinting at the highway while he tried to find the next exit on the map.

"Your mother didn't tell you *anything* about him, not even his name?"

"Nope. She refused."

"She didn't say what she liked about him or why they didn't marry?"

"Nothing. Not one word."

"That seems odd. I wonder why."

He didn't answer. "Exit 34," he said instead. "About four and a half miles."

NOW I BELIEVE SHE may have been one of those women who couldn't bear the loss, the betrayal, all hopes dashed, the man denying or simply rejecting the fact of a child. But perhaps she began to hate him too, to see that love can be duplicitous and slippery, can strangle the dignity of a woman while letting the man slip entirely free. I hope so. I hope anger singed her respect for him, but it's just as possible all the anguish turned inward, dulling and eroding the self, sneaking into her thoughts each morning to ambush her self-esteem. Perhaps she vowed never to mention his name, to keep him a private punishment and pleasure, a lifetime penance, the knowledge of his rejection like teeth sunk into her neck.

But she had the baby. Oh, yes! His baby. She had a part of him to love and delight in if not the man himself. He couldn't take that from her. Nobody could.

But of course, that too turned out to be a lie.

"I NEVER KNEW WHY I was in foster care so early," David said to me one night, several weeks after he'd read the foster care files. We were sitting across the table from each other, having just finished dinner, our napkins crumpled, our plates not yet scraped.

"Honey, your mother didn't have anyone to keep you while she worked, and she didn't make enough money as a waitress to hire someone to watch you." I tried to smooth out my napkin, my hands needing something to do. "Truth is," I said simply, "she couldn't keep you because she was poor." That's the real reason. Poor and alone. No family. No husband. No one to step in and help. Nobody to care. "After you were born, she stayed at the Girls' Welfare Society for six weeks, the file says, but I'm sure she could stay there only for a certain amount of time."

He looked surprised. "But wasn't there welfare—"

"No, they didn't have welfare for unmarried mothers in 1948, you know. Only for widows. They didn't have daycare either, at least not what we think of as daycare, though I think there was some childcare in New York and Philadelphia after the war. But not in Massachusetts." Back then, it was all sharp corners and straight edges, no room for ambivalence or surprise.

David stared at me, uncertain. "I thought I was *taken* from her. I thought, you know, there must have been something *wrong* with her."

"It was apparent to Worker how very proud the Mother was of her child and how much feeling she had for him. Mother evidenced sheer

delight in her intention of notifying all her friends and family about D (the baby)."

I THINK OF THE articles I've read, how middle-class unwed mothers in the 1940s and 1950s were so degraded by illegitimacy and so shamed by their families that they were strongly advised to give up their children for adoption while lower-class mothers more often kept their babies. And yet in postwar America, even for poor girls like Ann, marriage was still the prize, the only rescue. She might as well have been living in Jane Austen's England with Lady Catherine de Bourgh sniffing her body, pronouncing everything about her unworthy and inappropriate, while Mrs. Bennett fussed frantically to get her girls wed. And just as in Austen's time, the word *bastard* rang out a curse, "shame, shame, shame."

Bastard or no, when the worker suggested her baby might be a hindrance "*in terms of matrimonial possibilities,*" the "*Mother was quick to voice her feeling that she would like to tell the whole world about the baby and that she would under no circumstances keep him a secret.*" True, she must place her baby in foster care before he's three months of age, but during the first seven months of care, so the files note, she visited him four nights a week after work and took him to her brother's home for Christmas and his birthday. I imagine she thought she could manage, could make a go of it, sharing the baby with another woman.

But then suddenly the child's placement went to hell, the foster home was closed down for "unfavorable conditions," the baby moved and Ann's visits in the new foster home cut to once a week. I imagine her coming home from work and slumping down onto a chair, not bothering to take off her sweaty uniform or slip off her waitress shoes, her purse a heap on the floor. She sits and stares at nothing, unable to imagine how her baby will survive without her for six long days each week, and how she'll survive, her hands unable to hold him, her mouth unable to kiss him, her voice unable to surprise and soothe him. She slumps further, then suddenly, viciously, kicks her purse again and again.

BECAUSE I'M WRITING THIS and because I can, I decide to give Ann a happy moment, an hour of delight playing with her one-and-a-half-year-old son. He's pushing a shiny red fire truck across the floor, a toy she's just bought him though it will mean she'll have to scrimp on laundry soap and stockings. But as he bends down to a crawling position and runs the toy back and forth on her old wood floors, making "rrrrrhhhh-rrrrrhhh" sounds with his scrunched lips and saying, "Mommy, Mommy, look," she can't imagine why anyone would give a fig about new stockings. His hair sticks up in a ruff, his pants are a bit too long, but he's so gloriously occupied with the thick rubber wheels and the white plastic ladder that raises and lowers, she forgets that very soon she'll have to take him back. Back to his foster home, back to *"sleeping in the hallway in a house*, the files say, *where the older boy has taught him to sing out, "Bad boy! Bad boy!"* with such glee he too thinks it's funny.

EACH TIME MY HUSBAND comes downstairs to get more coffee I want to put this writing away. What the hell am I doing? I feel like I'm being subversive, appropriating what's not mine, rewriting the story of his mother, making it neater, giving it boundaries, tampering with it instead of merely attending to the facts: *she got pregnant, she gave birth, she put him in foster care, she reclaimed him seven and a half years later*. I listen as he turns on the water in the sink. I hear the refrigerator door open, then the swish of it closing. I hear the hiss and rumble of his coffee brewing, my hands paused, waiting. And then, just like that, he's gone back to his study, but I remain uncertain, wavering, not sure how to continue. Ann is elusive. A quicksilver presence. I can't see her. I can't know her. She was no saint. Of course, I'm making her up, embodying her, giving her purpose and consequence created out of the caseworkers' commentary and my own slender thoughts. But more than that, I'm allowing her to claim my sympathies. By giving her the benefit of the doubt, I've pushed past my husband's resentment, allowing the context of shadows and sociology, a feminist rebirth, a right to a voice. But why does this need to be done? No one's asked me to consider her as anything but an impoverished, conflicted mother who never got her act together. No one's demanding a eulogy or a vindication. And yet, after reading the foster care files, I lay in bed one night, dizzy with all the information, all the uncertainty. I closed my eyes, letting my thoughts drift, my mind untethered, and what I saw was Ann sitting in the caseworker's office year after year in her sensible waitressing shoes, a woman unable to let her baby go and unable to rescue him. I sat up and reached for my notebook: *the girl in the woman, the woman in the girl.* She was the center of it all. And didn't she deserve a story, not just the tired old story of the "fallen woman" but a story with a little charity, a small pocket of hope to even out the class barbarism, the misogyny of the late 1940s and 1950s?

I've no doubt that had she been born into the middle class instead of to the immigrant working class, she'd have had different opportunities—high school and maybe college, perhaps dancing and music, a room of her own and a closetful of clothes—and thus more choices, so many more ways to experience the world and perhaps so many more ways to fuck things up. "It's all about options," we say so casually today, the right to push against anonymity, to experience and value our difference, to thrust our thoughts into the air, saying *mine.*

And so, every morning I sit down to write about her. Every morning, I tell myself I should stick to the known, and yet the shadows beckon. What did she do with her private grief?

But perhaps I'm being romantic. Maybe she learned early to stifle the brooding, to get on with it, to avoid the mess of feelings, the push and heat of sorrow, enjoying instead her twenty-minute break from work with a piece of lemon meringue pie and a fresh cup of coffee. If I go this route, she's earnest and dutiful and repressed, a woman who accepts her lot, does her bit, and tries not to think too much beyond the present. After all, she grew up in an immigrant Catholic family in the 1930s and 1940s, crowded with brothers and sisters and uncles and aunts, with little space for adventure or difference. "And don't forget the misogyny of the older Italian men," David reminded me the other day. "A father's perspective was to keep everything in line and if that meant a little violence, some slapping about, well, who was to complain?" So, maybe after the birth of the baby, she doesn't need a stern patriarch to keep her in line, someone whose fury boils and explodes. She's already transgressed. She's used. She's done. So why not enjoy the lemon meringue pie, her feet propped on a chair, bare and plump in the warm afternoon sun?

WINTER. EVERYTHING HERE IN Iowa is either shrunken or dead—gone are the heart-shaped katsura leaves, the ivy, the geraniums, gone the red and pink impatiens, the lawn now khaki-brown or feathered white with frost, the trees mere sticks, branches rising upward and outward into skinnier and skinnier sticks. Only the fir trees blur silvery green in the late afternoon sun. When there is sun. But not today. Today the sky is empty, a gray swatch of color like lint or the inside of my purse, which is equally barren of money. "So much of possibility depends on economics," I told David last month in the midst of an argument about an IRA, and then more insistently, "Don't you know that to be *financially* independent is sometimes the defining moment in a woman's life? This isn't superstition or myth."

If I follow that lead, I see that David's mother *"agreed to pay $6/week to Family Services for his board in foster care out of a salary of $32/week."* Mmmh. My shoulders tighten at that exasperating figure: a $128 month salary from a factory in Massachusetts in 1948 (the average monthly wage for a male worker in 1948 was $216.56). Simultaneously I remember my mother's complaints about her monthly salary of $500 as a high school biology teacher in Alabama in 1951.

The comparison isn't merely the $327 difference in pay, but the fact that my mother's check was a secondary income added to my father's thriving medical practice. And yet, despite that reality, the whole of it stinks. Economic oppression *is* the dreary ballad of female history: for David's mother and my mother the world will not bend.

For three months, the files note that Ann dutifully pays $6 a week, but then *her salary is knocked back to $25 a week* and if she pays $6 for the baby's board, she has only $1 left to cover the cost of food and clothing and other essentials. And always something backfires: she hurts her back and must have osteopathic treatment for a chronic injury, losing four days of work; she leaves the meatpacking plant, goes to work at the Spanish Grille as a waitress, but quits this job to work at a girdle factory; when she's laid off, it takes two months before she finds a position at a hat company where she works as an inspector. The caseworker writes, *"She looks very tired and admits that she does not eat properly, smokes usually too much."* Inevitably, she's asked again to think about adoption—it's been two years since her child entered foster care, which is meant only to be a temporary solution. After all, she can't make the payments and she's without a plan. Be practical, I imagine the caseworker saying, observing her, noting the pallor of her skin, the dark circles shadowing her eyes. She's thinner, her dresses beginning to sag, her hair needing a trim. The worker prods her, leans closer. "My dear, you need to think about the security of your child," but still Ann shakes her head, telling the caseworker she just can't see her way to it, to letting him go. She promises she'll have a plan but several weeks later she's hospitalized for neuritis in both legs.

She is twenty-three.

LET'S SAY SHE FINDS a way to accept this life, to survive her frequent disruptions in employment and the child's transfer from home to home. Let's say she understands that if she can't live with her boy, she can at least visit him, hold and cuddle him, feed and change him and make peek-a-boo eyes at him. I imagine she knows how to make friends with foster mothers, women not so different from her except that they're married and with husbands whose labor doesn't quite make ends meet. She understands this. She understands crowded bedrooms, three children to a room, one bathroom, thin towels, diapers drying on the line, chipped bowls, dusty curtains, a pretty blue vase nudged high up on a shelf, out of reach.

But after several years, she gets careless, forgetting that she's at the mercy of another woman, forgetting that her presence in the foster mother's house requires being attentive, pleasing, never lingering, always asking permission and showing gratitude for the favor of seeing her baby, now a toddler of two, and then three. It's not that she does something outrageous or stupid. It begins with her being late for the appointment to see him, not getting the ride she expected and having to take the bus, now two hours late and earning a frown of disapproval from the foster mother who stands in the doorway.

Ann smiles, hoping to soften this bedraggled woman, understanding that she must humble herself, be penitent. "Oh, I've been such a burden and you've always been so generous to me," Ann begins, noticing the woman's slouched posture. She knows she must tell this foster mother that she'll only stay for an hour. After all, it is late afternoon, the sky a pastel blue, the air soft. Ann is about to commit to this scenario when her son toddles to the door, his cheek a sweep of eczema, his right arm in a sling because he fell out of bed and broke his collarbone, his mouth crusted with old milk, and she forgets all about this plan. It's as if the foster mother vanishes as she sweeps him up, "How's my boy?" Ann whispers, kissing his hair, dancing her fingers up his left arm, and then hours later, when it's past dark, she walks out the front door, secretly triumphant to have stayed with her boy.

"Worker feels that foster mother is somewhat jealous of Mother's love for D and that Mother, in turn, is jealous of foster mother for having daily care of the baby."

I WONDER IF THIS is the moment Ann realizes she's been naïve, walking through each day with her eyes half-closed, seeing only what she's wanted to see: obliging women offering her son to her for a few hours every week. Then again, her life isn't the ordinary world of getting up and taking the bus to work, having a smoke break and chatting with girlfriends, flirting with the cook or a customer, paying rent and utilities, buying groceries and cigarettes, but a darker, restless world, an uncivilized place of men deserting and fathers berating and caseworkers always asking *when, when, when will you be able to make a plan for your son?* as if she could simply sit outside in the evening and wish upon a star.

A plan is what you do if you've finished high school or maybe a year or two of college, had training in bookkeeping and dictation or plied some special talent: illustrating or drawing or hat design or sewing. To her, a plan means working extra hours at the Spanish Grille and trying to save a bit before the next layoff, the next bout of neuritis or bronchitis.

How is she supposed to make the unlikely probable?

And yet somehow, she does make a plan. It takes several years, but by scrimping and flirting—everything seems to require a bit of badness—she's able to *"rent seven rooms in a run-down three-decker,"* fix them up with repairs, a coat of paint, and some cheap leased furniture, *"and rent out rooms to boarders."* It's the first thing she's ever managed, and to her surprise, it works. She talks easily to carpenters and laborers, fixes them coffee, takes out icy lemonade on a sweltering day, handing a glass up to a man on a ladder who's resetting the window, aware that, for a moment, he's turned his attention to her, barefoot in blue shorts and a knit top, her eyes moist from cutting onions for the potato salad, her thick auburn hair pulled up, exposing her pale, smooth neck. Sometimes they stay later, do a bit of extra work, unclogging a drain, repairing a soffit, replacing a rotting step, chatting with her, catching her eye, and not charging her a penny.

At night she feels the warmth of a man, the rustle of bedding, and in the dark, she smiles. She'll get her boy back. She will.

But even with this entrepreneurial success, she can't get her son back. Most of her boarders are old men on pensions, their payment enough to cover the rent and utilities and furniture lease, but she still must work. As she's walking to the bus stop from the Spanish Grill, already tired, her feet aching, she thinks about the payment she must make for the plumber she had to call last week. Today's tips fill her pockets, but will it be enough? Will it ever be enough? And who will take care of her boy if she must slave away in the mornings and evenings?

As she approaches the bus stop, a man turns to glance at her. Instinctively, she straightens, accepting his approving gaze. He nods. But once on the bus, she closes her eyes, letting the motion of movement relax her, her feet still, her breathing quiet as she allows herself to know the truth: Getting her son back also requires a husband. She isn't opposed to the idea. And yet, for a little while, during that spring when the elm trees are dressed out in green, when lilacs and daffodils bloom, there is a softness that surprises her, like a little cushion of air surrounding her, protecting her. Her son is safe and growing, a sweet but high-strung, mischievous boy who lives a thirty-five-minute bus ride away in a small town, almost a village, where he tramps down the hill to first grade, kicking rocks and jumping puddles and printing his name in big round letters. *"(He) identifies Mother to the foster mother as his 'best girl,'"* which makes her grin. Sometimes he playfully calls her *"Ma"* when she picks him up for the one overnight visit a month and refers to his foster mother as Aunt Adeline, and yet now he seems quite happy to return to his foster family after spending a night with her, throwing her a kiss even as he runs to eat Aunt Adeline's chicken and dumplings. Though at first the ease of his leaving stuns her, this new cloud of possibility steadies her.

A house and a husband. It isn't exactly that she makes a plan, only that someone is already there, one of the carpenters, a big, strapping

Scotsman who's lingered more than the others, taking a little longer than necessary to sand a door. This, she was to understand, had been an odd job for him, something to tide him over while he waited for a construction job opening up in the summer. And yet, when she came home from her waitressing job, hot and sweaty, her hair pulled up, a few auburn strands loosed and tangled, tucked inside her collar, he didn't seem to mind being there, would often stay for a beer. Then more.

Now the construction job has come through and he's drinking, blowing money on Friday and Saturday nights, but always back to work on Monday. It's a way of life. Familiar. Familial. Preferable perhaps to having no one. When her son comes to visit, *"the man plays with the boy,"* laughs, and lets him sit on his big, wide lap. And hasn't she seen this man, Soup, catch a green fly in his bare hands and drop it casually out the window, then glance up at her and sheepishly smile?

How can she know—can any woman know?—that the very thing that is her salvation will also be her undoing? How can she know that though the husband will adopt the boy, he'll come to resent him and resent her for having him, will punish the boy for being such a pain in the ass without even a drop of his blood? How can she know he'll beat him, step on his hands with his construction boots, mock him, berate him, make him stand naked in a chalked circle for punishment? "I gave the kid a name, for shit's sake," he'll yell at her years later, as if he's the one who's been played for a sucker.

This man, who once seemed so easygoing, so playful, eating a huge forkful of birthday cake, thick with frosting, while holding her boy in his lap, will, in three years, become an alcoholic, crashing again and again into Bridgewater State Hospital's detox unit, while she'll be passive and hopeful, then devious and resentful, and finally depressed.

And yet in the summer of 1956, she's in the three-decker with its ruffled curtains, its rented sofa, its secondhand TV. She's attained the impossible: a husband, a reclaimed son, another on the way, even as the air of possibility now gusts past her, skittering down the block while she hovers in the doorway, exhausted, blinking, uncertain just how it is that she failed. For years, when her son looks at her, he seems hopeful and loving, but by age twelve, he's wary, then angry, and finally, at sixteen, he refuses to look at her at all.

"My best girl," she murmurs one night, staring into his empty room.

He's gone, his closet stripped of clothes and books and dirty socks. She stares at the bare mattress, the stripped sheets, aware of how time folds in on itself, and yet she doesn't cry as she pulls closed the door.

Full circle.

Chapter 27

YES, DAVID LEAVES, LEAVES home at sixteen and never goes back. How can that be? How did he survive, manage to get through every twenty-four-hour day, week after endless week? I couldn't have done such a thing at sixteen, my life so firmly tied to the emotional and financial support of my family, to comfortable beds and dinner every night, to travel and dresses and all the extras in education paid for by my parents.

But here he is, a boy alone and in high school in 1964 with only his head and his heart to carry him through a restless flight. Alongside his own drama, this is a pivotal time in America, so many doors swinging open and closed—the Beatles have just made their premier appearance on the Ed Sullivan Show, the first Civil Rights Act has passed, Ford's Mustang is galvanizing buyers, especially young men, the first draft card is burned, and later in the year the Gulf of Tonkin Incident and Resolution will change the direction and deliberations of our country, wrenching us apart in so many ways.

But what happened at 29 Congress Street in Worcester, Massachusetts, in a five-room upstairs flat?

The truth is, I don't know very much about the circumstances of David's leaving his mother's place on Congress Street because, like many people traumatized in childhood, his memories of crisis events lurch and fizzle, often frozen, inaccessible, his emotions in lockdown, his words the familiar, "I don't know. I can't really remember. Thinking about this makes me depressed." What he remembers are fragments, a riff of images, a tiny edge of feeling. What I've come to understand is that he left after "an explosive" argument with his mother, an argument in which he accused her of being a bad mother, ragging her about her behavior and her money, with naughty implications about where she got it, until she said, "Get out!" the very response he consciously or unconsciously wanted, since he'd already rented a room for eight dollars a week in a two-story red brick building several blocks away.

Oh dear!

Though David can't say much beyond the tone of the argument, what he visibly remembers is walking out the door of the flat and into the hallway, how dark it was, the dingy beige walls shadowed by dusk and the coming of night, the worn stairs winding down, down, down to the street, to a first glimpse of evening . . . and the rest of his life. He'd lived with his mother and two half-brothers on the third floor of this three-story flat for several years (some of them with Soup, now mostly gone, separated from his mother), and as he took the stairs he heard the dull shuffle of his feet, smelled remnants of cooking oil and old smoke trapped in the air, glimpsed newspapers and flyers outside certain doors, lights coming on, the rambling noises of TV. Perhaps this enclosed stairway leading to the unknown *was* the metaphor for his leaving. *Familiarity. Descent. Flight.*

Later, he'll tell me that some part of him wanted to force the leaving. He knew he had to get out, but he couldn't just *go* and needed to make it partly his mother's fault. When he tells me this, he looks away from me, out the window, where a March wind grabs at the bare limbs of a maple tree, the branches flailing against each other, fighting, and tangling and then untangling.

"But how did you *live*?" I ask, amazed that he survived, that he managed to go to Classical High School—studying French and biology, American literature and history—and then to his afternoon employment without ending up homeless or worse. Of course, what I really wonder is how he managed his fears, his longings, his deepest needs to be supported and loved and yes, to belong, to be part of something bigger than himself. Once, when I was in my midthirties and having a spat with my family, feeling hurt by some remark or incident, some dismissal that cut too close to the bone, a therapist asked, "Why do you go home? Have you ever thought about simply staying away?" Shocked, I stared at her with confusion. True, I was *furious* at them and had lived outside the boundaries of their lives, but I also belonged to them in the most primitive and fundamental way, a deep roar of feeling just beneath my skin. Then again, I hadn't been an abused child, hadn't lived in poverty, been beaten, threatened, or ignored.

Even though I'm a person who desperately wants to know the story beneath the story, the secrets, yes, the dirty little secrets of our pasts, I've learned to respect David's reticence, and we don't talk about those fears. For a long time, I didn't understand how much David needed to protect himself, how he often lived in "survival mode," every day a battle of wills, any memory of the past an ambush. But now that I've read the foster care files and he's allowed the bones of his history to emerge, I recognize the limits, the shadow of anxiety darkening his gaze, his need to look away, to distract. Instead of feelings, David tells me about his job at Aubochon's Hardware Store, where he worked for three hours each day after school and all day on Saturday for $1.25 an hour, minimum wage at the time, enough for rent, bus fare to school, and the hamburgers, fish sandwiches, fries, apples, and occasional ice cream cones he consumed at nearby shops. He's always liked gear, building supplies, nuts and bolts, and what I call "the guy stuff" of hardware stores, a place I avoid like the plague. He liked the job, but later that year found work at a dental lab for more money, making molds for dentures, a design job where he excelled, making the gum line look natural and the teeth in alignment, a job he took pride in, the dentist a gentle soul who diligently fixed the teeth of children with cleft palates. "But also eccentric," David says. "I mean, sometimes he'd talk about aliens, always in the most optimistic way, you know, like they would be our saviors."

We laugh at this, but even as we talk casually, making jokes about the past, I'm stuck on the gravity, the hard-knuckled terms of living alone in a rented room. What did it look like? Feel like? Smell like? What were his first thoughts when he woke in the morning, his last image before sleep? What stirred inside his body—his pulse rate, his breathing, the tingling beneath his skin—when he thought about his mother?

But I'll never know these things.

"It looked like all the rooms for old men you've seen on TV," he says, "a single bed, a dresser, a lamp, a window, a chair. A place to sleep." We leave it at that as he tells me, "I had some friends and places to go. Not close friends. . . . I mean, Classical High was mainly a middle- and upper-class school attended by smart, Jewish kids, but still, there were people to play chess with, to hang out with, listening to music and watching girls." Later that year he befriended a group of older boys, almost eighteen, boys not so different from him, working-class kids who knew the streets, knew how to avoid bullies, the thugs and drunks, how to get beer and jobs, to play music, and, later, get weed.

I nod. I always nod.

ONE NIGHT AS WE'RE settling into our bed, David turns to me and says softly, his voice so low I lean nearer, "I can't do this. I can't talk about that time anymore." He stares at me, his face drawn by sadness, his eyes shadowed with fatigue.

"We won't," I say, pulling him close. For years I didn't know his secret belief that he could bury his past or at least ignore it, but in truth, when we lived in the studio in Los Angeles, I too assumed I could toss my past into a psychic basement, letting it lie hidden in the dark while I obsessed over artwork, music streaming through my ears, the Santa Ana winds blowing sand through the air. Alas, "the past is never past," as William Faulkner famously said. It's always here.

After David falls asleep, I lie awake, my mind wandering, humming, replaying the stories he's told me. I imagine him at sixteen, getting off the bus, a slight, dark-haired boy bundled up in a two-year-old coat and gloves, walking the streets, his mind focused, even obsessed (he's often obsessed) with an idea, an image, a design problem, a political issue, and as I see him searching in his pocket for money to buy a hamburger, I'm startled by a revelatory thought, one that swims up through my consciousness. *What if* . . . what if it wasn't *only* the hard, hard fact of leaving his mother's flat and living alone that changed the direction of David's life but something more foundational. . . . The discovery of a new path, an unexpected jump-start to ambition and pleasure and obsession. *Music. He loves music—words and rhythm and feeling—the way it runs down the nerve and ignites the brain, revving, soothing, pleasing.* In 1964–65, the folk scene is everywhere, rock music bragging and building, and those older boys. . . . Yes, that group of older boys he knows, are starting a band, eighteen-year-olds going on and on about songwriting and lyrics, about pitch and rhythm, about Dylan and Baez and Lennon, about folk and rock and blues, playing records and listening, always listening, then talking, practicing, singing. It's with them that David gets on the scent.

First, he goes to various stores, trying out different instruments, then settling on the bass—"because it's the easiest," he'll tell me later—pretending he wants to buy so the salesman will teach him a few chords and let him practice, as he's never had lessons. He does this again and again until the salesmen become annoyed—he's wasting their time—but by now he's moved out of that rental room and into the house with the four boys forming a band. And then, to his surprise, one of them offers him his bass, teaching him everything he knows so that, just like that, he's being mentored, groomed, learning not only by practicing but also by watching, listening, and talking, learning by need, obsession, and then hope. To his surprise, he has almost perfect pitch and intuitively understands rhythm and tone. For him, playing music is like diving deep into dark water, a lake, a river, a stream, the bottomless bottom still to be touched. He's swimming with his eyes closed, his hands familiar in their motions as he glides away from the world above, discovering his talents, his affinity for pleasure, acquiring insight and confidence before he breaks the surface to breathe again the common air.

He learns quickly, and within six months he plays well enough to jam with the others in the house, improvising, creating something out of nothing, letting the moment, the instrument, and the mood in the room tell him where to go. "It's magical," he tells me. "I don't know anything like it. Playing music with people when you're young begins to supplant everything you do."

This, I think, *is how a boy saves himself.*

It's not where the hurt stops—that remains tightly coiled inside his brain—but it's where the heart swells, where the present takes hold with a feeling that says *I'm alive, alive, alive.*

I glance at his sleeping form, his head snuggled into the pillow, hair smashed flat, earplugs in, C-pap on, the covers pulled up close to his chin, his arms folded over his chest as if he's protecting himself. *Still.* I know that he played music in Worcester for three and a half years—clubs, cover bands, festivals—and then at age nineteen, he moved to San Francisco to start a new band, once again playing clubs and parties and even a huge arena after his band was named one of the "Best New Bands" in San Francisco. Until recently, he's kept a guitar in his study upstairs, practicing late at night, the sounds drifting and melodious from behind his door though he quit "the music scene" before we met, moving north to Mendocino, where he "played flute to the goats."

Playing music was, I know now, the key to David's survival, the act of creation releasing a kind of purity, a newness that surprises. It's the same with writing and art and theater, anything that transforms the old and broken into the promise of song. One morning as I gaze outside an upstairs window at a bottle tree—thin blue bottles thrust onto the empty branches—I'm surprised to see one catching the brightness of the sun, shining a deep glassy blue the color of a blueberry as if lit from the inside. *Yes, like that!*

Chapter 28

TODAY THE SUN'S COME out after days of rain. I leave the computer and step out onto my deck, the air fresh and clean, the sun warming my face. Okay, okay, I breathe with relief, glad to feel nothing but this. Pleasure. The leaves just budding on the trees, the daffodils and tulips in bloom. When I go back to writing about David's mother, I wonder if I've shifted the balance, made the intolerable tolerable, brushed a bit of color onto the cheeks of a sordid story. The truth is, I think I've only made myself feel better.

"I believe I should be able to forgive my mother," David said one evening last week while we were making a snack of rice cakes and almond butter in the kitchen, "because now I know from the foster care files that she loved me, and she. . . . Well, really tried." He looked both sad and relieved at the thought.

"She did," I nodded, understanding. And though I've been trying to resee her, to imagine her life, I haven't really forgiven her either. After working so hard to reclaim him, she seemed unable to protect him, to make him feel wanted and worthy and necessary in the world. Once she'd pulled it all together, everything just went to hell.

"Anyway, it's good that I got the foster care files," David said. "After reading them I don't feel so much like a victim." He washed the French press to make his evening coffee and began measuring out the dark roast and the exact amount of water. "And I don't hate her anymore because they let me see a different part of her." He glanced at me. "So, I'm glad you helped, I'm glad—" but he didn't finish. Maybe he couldn't.

"Me too." I handed him a plate.

After he poured the hot water into the press, he waited, staring at the brewing coffee as if meditating. Then he glanced up, giving me a rueful smile. "Family." He shook his head. "It's all Bosch and Breughel."

Delighted, I laughed. Yes, family—so full of dark paradoxes and grim depictions.

But I also think of his mother on the Greyhound bus riding out of Worcester on a Saturday or Sunday to see her seven-year-old son at his foster home in Sturbridge, watching the city's shoe factories with their rising plumes of smoke give way to the countryside, goldenrod and bluebells blooming on the side of the road, grazing cows in the distance, fat trees crowding the far end of a pasture. What must she be thinking, sitting alone on that bus for thirty-five minutes, going to see a child she hasn't put to bed or fed or talked to in three weeks? She's never seen him catch grasshoppers, do his arithmetic homework, or read his first series of books at a desk, never taken him to the dentist or to buy shoes. And yet when she's there with him, for two hours or four hours or sometimes an overnight visit, I like to imagine the uncertainty of her choices lifts. I like to think that she holds on to this thought, slippery as it is, her face softened, her shoulders eased, the possibility of connection there only because she's kept it alive.

"I'm glad," I imagine her whispering to him, summing up her plight. "I'm glad and I'm sorry." Five honest words.

Chapter 29

LATE SUMMER. FRIDAY NIGHT. We're trapped at a stoplight on the strip of a busy interstate exit outside St. Louis, Missouri. Exhausted, we've come to this featureless place for gas and food, hoping for the rescue of a motel room, only to discover no vacancies are to be found. It's almost 9 p.m. We've been driving for thirteen hours, having left my family in southern Alabama early this morning. Now David leans forward, gazing intently into the darkness. "Pull over," he says. "I've got to photograph *that*."

I notice a bright harvest moon animated by a slip of cirrus clouds in a smooth inky sky. I glance at him, then at the moon. "For god's sake, it's 9:00!" I'm crazy tired, my mind so dull I can't think of a better retort.

"Ah, com'on . . . *please*," he urges.

"I don't know why you have to do this," I grumble. "I want to find a motel. I've been driving—"

"Just give me five minutes."

Begrudgingly, I pull into the parking lot of a small, almost empty mall so that David can leave the car with his camera and walk toward a grassy field twenty feet away. I lean my head against the steering wheel, irritated, exhausted, my arms heavy and weighted, my shoulders aching. I must have dropped off because I don't remember David getting back into the car until he says, "I've got to get it from another angle." He's not looking at me but gazing across the highway, his voice rising in a dangerous hum of excitement as if he's just had a double espresso. "Up there." His energy grates on me. I want to smash it.

"Jesus," I repeat. "We don't have a motel room yet."

I watch his lips twitch, his face in shadow. "I haven't asked for anything on this trip," he says, "not a *thing*."

It's true. Though I've driven the entire way—my choice—David's been a good sport, navigating the trip, demanding nothing, taking occasional naps, but mostly keeping me company and walking endless circles around the car when we stop for gas. After the cancer surgery two and a half years ago, his legs ache on long rides—the muscles tight and swollen, his ankles spreading as if he has residual lymphedema, precarious and insistent. Reluctantly, I steer across the street to another empty lot. This time I don't fall asleep but watch resentfully as he shifts from place to place, setting up the shot, then moving again, setting up another and another, never once glancing back. "Come *on*," I yell out the window as a rush of traffic ruptures the warm night. Still, he doesn't turn. I wait two minutes, then yell again.

AN HOUR LATER AT a motel entrance, we're raw with fury, each thundering our wounds. "You're such a prima donna," I hiss. My neck, a knotted boulder, stiffens.

"I'll just sleep in the car," David sulks, squinting at the windshield.

"Don't be ridiculous," I say, irritated that he's being melodramatic.

"Don't tell me what to do!"

And yet we both get out of the car.

What is there to say about a motel room except for its blinking brightness, the light harsh after the highway's irregular darkness. It's a generic room: two queen-sized beds, a bedside table, a desk with plastic ads, a wide-screen TV, a fake-walnut chest of drawers. And now us.

Silence. We don't speak as we haul our suitcases into the room, turn down the AC, and close the drapes. In the bathroom, I brush my teeth and wash my face, splashing eye drops into red eyes, my mind swirling, while David undresses in the main room. "Sorry about that," he says when I emerge. He says this casually as if "sorry" will do, and I gaze at him stupidly because five minutes earlier I wanted to strangle him. He steps closer. "Sometimes there just isn't enough of me, especially when we're down south with your family," he says quietly, "but when I take photographs, it's like I'm getting myself back."

I nod. I understand. To be with my family is demanding, their emphasis often on wealth and success, less on creativity and play. And though I agree with David's perception, something remains charged between us, a messy, pent-up struggle that transcends apologies and explanations and makes me edgy. Perhaps it's my own vulnerability after a visit to Alabama, a belief that I must do more, that I've been plunged for too long in illness and caretaking.

Still silent, I toss my pants onto a chair, drop my shirt on the floor.

TEN MINUTES LATER, I'M lying on cool, clean sheets, my shoulders and hips soothed by darkness, a hint of relief even if my mind's still reeling. I close my eyes, *just let me sleep, please let me sleep*, and then David slips in naked beside me, wordlessly, insistently pulling me close, his lips on my cheeks, in my hair, on my breasts, and as suddenly we're making hard, pleasurable love, the kind of ravenous sex we haven't had since his cancer surgery. Maybe it's our anger redirected, pleasure consuming trouble, the fever of release after a week with my family. Maybe it's a return, however brief, to the people we used to be, young and resilient and arrogant about consequences. Or maybe it's an opening to David and Patricia after cancer, two people learning to grapple with the present, to fight and forgive, breached and weightless, even the air alive.

Beyond us, the air conditioner purrs, the clock drones its precise tick-tick-tick while SUVs and U-Hauls stream past on the interstate, the drivers sullen or high or numb, the world dissolving, but we don't care. Wrapped in clean sheets, our bodies finally loose, we sleep curled together, no longer restless or rebuked, the trip almost over, only four hours of driving tomorrow through northern Missouri and southeastern Iowa, to books and art and writing, to cooking together in our own familiar rhythm, the cupboards open, the oven heating, the green onions chopped. *Home.*

Chapter 30

"I HAVE A LAST name." David stands at the top of the stairs, grinning at me as I climb the steps, clean towels and an extra quilt in my hands. It's a cold day in late October, the snow piled high against the curbs, a crusty white mound blanketing our back deck. Outside, the wind howls.

"What?" For a moment I think he's joking, certain he'll make a wry comment about a crank email or robocall to some ridiculous surname. *Pavio. Partykooper. Liderwand.* Something world-class and cheesy. This has happened before. I'm waiting for him to laugh, to explain, but he's only half-smiling as he zips up his fleece.

"I JUST TALKED TO the social worker," he says as I arrive at the top of the stairs. The social worker, I know, is attached to the Massachusetts Family and Child Services in Boston, the woman who sent the foster care and adoption files he requested months earlier. Though we'd read about where and with whom he'd lived from the time his mother relinquished him at three months of age until the year she retrieved him when he was eight, there were places in the documents where names were whited out, paragraphs whited out. Whole paragraphs of his history.

"The social worker told me who my alleged father was," he says in a surprisingly relaxed tone of voice.

"Really?" I'm up the stairs now and have put down the towels. Though we've both wondered about the whited-out spaces in the documents (putative father) and the whited-out technical institute the man had attended, I'm surprised David called the social worker to ask about it. "Wait," I say, turning to him. "Can the social worker *do* that? I thought the privacy clause would restrict—"

"Yeah, actually . . . she *didn't* tell me. I guessed the name. I thought this one man might be who it was," he continues, "because I always had to call him 'Uncle' when my mother and I visited his house. I thought it was some not-so-secret secret . . . though my mother would never tell me."

Oh, how weird those visits must have been: his mother taking David at age eight and nine to visit this man who had a wife and two children. What pretense did she make? Did she seem nervous or awkward or was she stoic and reserved, capable of hiding all her feelings? Did she present herself as an old friend, sitting in the den with the man's wife and children, chatting about their kids' schools or neighborhood gossip or current events?

"Let's sit on the couch a minute," I say, shoving aside a stack of his clean clothes from the two-seater in his study. Settling, we hold hands, not saying much as we lean against the back of the couch, our eyes closed. "Do you feel relieved?" I finally ask. "I mean, that it's him."

"I guess," he says. "It seems okay."

He'd always hated his mother's refusal to reveal his father's name. "What, am I Oliver Twist?" he'd say as if he were a Dickensian protagonist without lineage or identity. But now it's settled. I want to believe that this man known as "Uncle" makes sense to David if only because he is (or was) an architect and David's always loved architecture. In every city we've visited, David studies the structure and style of buildings—old Victorian libraries and town halls with their twin spires and clock towers and the curved glass and postmodernist mosaics of new hotels and skyscrapers—taking numerous photographs and commenting ecstatically, while I stare at people, at faces and bodies, expressions and gestures, trying to assemble a story. Our first days of visiting a new place are a scramble of interruptions and non sequiturs, two people talking over each other. Though David's made his living in graphic and website design, architecture is the career he might have chosen if he hadn't run off to San Francisco at nineteen to be a rock musician, to erase as much of his past as he dared.

When I glance at him now, he looks oddly peaceful, as if he might be sleeping.

A FEW DAYS LATER, with David's approval, I type in the putative father's name on Google, hoping to find an address, a news bulletin, a social engagement, a retirement announcement, an obituary—but to my surprise, I come up with nothing, not a damn thing, though I have the geographical location from the file. When I tell David this, he merely nods. "Maybe I'm spelling it wrong." All we know is that the father's name is Greek or Albania or Italian, and though my husband heard it pronounced as a child, he's never seen it written. "I'll call the social worker next week and find out how to spell it."

THE NEXT WEEK I'M so busy with a conference in Seattle, then a friend's visit from Germany and two sets of student papers to grade that I forget about David's quest. And yet at the conference, a national writing conference, I'm reminded of the power of names. I see many people from different eras of my life: friends from graduate school, students from the first university where I taught, former students from my current institution, colleagues from other universities I've visited or collaborated with or goofed off with at lunch. "Patricia," I hear someone call out from the crowd. I turn when I hear the name—*I always turn*—even though there are five hundred people in every room and surely more than one Patricia. But a name so identifies, so marks you, that you close ranks and lose yourself within it.

And yet I haven't always been called Patricia. "Pat, try on this white tutu and make sure it fits for the recital." "Pat, quit worrying about your hair. Just let it go, stop it, we've got to hurry." Pat, the name my family used for eighteen years, sounds as foreign to me as a second cousin's name, though everyone in my family and hometown calls me Pat. A short puff of air! Sometimes I startle at the name, that persona of my childhood I left behind like slipping out of an old skin. In 1977, standing in the Sculpture Garden at the University of California, Los Angeles, I intentionally gave my name to the other graduate students as Patricia, my given name. There's something rebellious and restorative about changing your name, even modifying the shortened version to the longer one—*don't we all, at some point, want a new identity?* I'm not who I was. Or . . . I'm not *only* who I was. I'm leaving "her" behind. And yet in reality, I'll always inhabit parallel universes, will always be both Patricia and Pat, will always find in each a secret, shadow self.

"DID YOU EVER CALL that social worker?" I ask David a week after I've returned from the conference in Seattle. I'm sorting through papers on my desk, getting ready to write critiques. I'm not really expecting an answer because I know he's been finishing artwork for a client.

"Yeah, I did," he says, surprising me. "I called last week."

"Great!" I'm still distracted, trying to arrange the papers in order. "Did she tell you how to spell it? I bet it's an odd spelling."

"I had it wrong," he says, coming to the door of my study and watching me. "It turns out one of the names I'd given her wasn't his *first* name but his *last*. I completely misunderstood her and thought she was confirming both names."

Now I'm the one who is surprised. "Really?" I turn and watch his face for a reaction. He's said this with such quiet candor, I'm stunned by his calm. Wrong name. Wrong man. Wrong story.

David explains that when he called the social worker, he'd wanted to clarify the man's last name, establish the place where he'd worked in Worcester, the technical institute where he'd studied, and his ethnicity. "She wouldn't confirm very much, not even his name," he tells me, but she implied he'd been some kind of inventor, and it was possible he'd worked on the movable focus lens, you know, the zoom lens." Now we look at each other, eyebrows raised, as if there's a cartoon bubble floating above our heads: *"You must be kidding."* It's just too ironic. Too crazy. First, we thought the unnamed father was an architect, and now an inventor of photographic equipment. Who would make this stuff up? David's been obsessed with photography for much of his life, building a darkroom in the first two places we lived, creating fold-up dollies for his tripod, and learning digital programs to enhance and modify his work. He's the only one in his family who loves art.

And yet now he looks unsettled, as if by telling me, literally saying this revelation out loud, he doesn't know how to absorb the news. In many ways, it's much more disturbing, more unfathomable, than believing the man he knew as "Uncle" was his father. This new man he's never seen, never spoken to. This new man is a stranger, a mystery, and yet a man whose interests so relate to him as to be uncanny.

"Don't worry about it right now." I put my arms around him, pulling him close. But perhaps I'm telling this to myself as well. I'm shocked. I don't know what to think, how to act. I can't imagine what David feels. It's a new story. Perhaps an unknowable story. He'll need time to absorb it, to decide on its worth.

AND YET THIS IS not the end of the story. Two weeks after I look up details on the new name David gave me of his putative father, I'm stunned to find another man with the exact same name, born a few years earlier, in the exact same area where his mother lived. Suddenly, there is *another* possibility, though I can find no information about this man except for census data from his early adulthood in Worcester. All I know is that both men are dead.

When I tell David this new quandary, he nods as if he's no longer surprised about the paradoxes of his past. "Do you want me to keep looking, to find other databases? I mean, I can go to the university library and ask for help."

David sighs and shakes his head. "Not now. I need to move on."

His voice says he's weary of it all: the new information, the new emotions, the struggle to reclaim a heritage. *What the fuck?* And then he nudges me. "Come see what I'm working on."

Upstairs in his room, I stare at the new image he's tacked up on the whiteboard across from the couch. In the print, there are three faces . . . well, not faces but masks: the first is clearly a human mask, the other two are bird masks, their eyes ancient and penetrating and curious above stark, horny beaks the color of sand. Their surface is etched and shaded while the larger human mask is central, its gaze startlingly sensitive above wide sensuous lips and protruding ears, a face the color of bark, its decorative forehead a smoky white, a jeweled egg in an egg cup balanced on the top of the head. Off to the side sits a birdhouse, stark branches, a small wooden box, and beyond these, a milky sky.

David and I talk about this print, its style and composition, its subtle tensions. I admire the subdued, moody colors, the asymmetrical positioning, the staring eyes. I'm oddly moved by the image, pulled into those staring eyes as I go back downstairs to work on student papers. Concealment can be protective and necessary but also beautiful and revealing. Then again, with a mask, you're both known *and* unknown, a self *and* a self-in-hiding.

Chapter 31

DAVID AND I WATCH as two huge cranes move debris from a construction site outside the oncology waiting room window. We're here for the results of his CT scan, six months after the scan that showed scar tissue on the lungs, three years after his initial diagnosis. Around us, the waiting room is quiet, almost empty except for a gray-faced man hunched in his chair near the receptionist's desk, his hands folded limply in his lap, his eyes closed as if he's drowsing, and a woman in a pale green sweater and turban with bold, blue eyes, staring fixedly at her magazine. The furniture is soft and comfortable, the lights muted as if this is a place for rest and napping until the double doors swing open and a nurse calls out "Lawrence *F*," or "Sarah *K*" with such curt finality we all startle to attention, destined to follow her into the inner sanctum to be initiated into the secrets of the body.

Usually, David and I sit silently reading or listening to our iPods, pretending to be somewhere else, but today he's nervous and fidgety, running his hands through his thick salt-and-pepper hair, shaking his head, then sighing. He looks again out the window—the sky gray and dour, the trees just budding with leaves—then picks up a magazine. Immediately, he puts it back down and stares at the double doors as if wishing he could hide from the call of his name.

If only. I think of the story about his secret hiding place between the tub and the shelves in Aunt Adeline's house. In my mind I see him, a five-year-old boy crouched in the unfinished space of the bathroom closet, his mind flickering in the dim light as he listens to the hum of the pipes or the soft mumble of voices or the tingling of his own breath. Regardless, he's hidden away, shielded from discovery, good luck to anyone trying to find him.

"Elaine *D*," the nurse announces, the double doors flung open. For a moment the air tightens. When the small, turbaned woman rises, edging toward the door, David and I watch covertly, waiting, then drift back into our distractions. *Not yet. Not yet.*

Because I need to let my mind wander, I think not about my husband's hiding spot but about the other side of the story: Aunt Adeline prowling the house, searching for him. Does she call to him from the kitchen, "*Da-vid . . . Da-vid,* where are you, child?" her voice curious and hopeful? After a few minutes of silence with only the kitchen clock ticking, does she mutter, *"Where does that boy go?"* then wander through the house, down the hall, and into his small bedroom—the first room he's had to himself—his pajamas scattered on the floor, as if the outside world claims him when he opens his eyes? Does she knock on Betty's and Helen's door, the two foster girls who've lived with her and John in this house for so long she's begun to think of them as her daughters? She knows they're both gone—Betty to high school, Helen to work—but she knocks by instinct, then slowly opens the door to their made-up beds, the cloudy oval mirror and a flannel robe on the hook inside the open closet door. "David," she calls softly, her eyes sweeping side to side, searching, but only dust motes collide in the air with a faint smell of face powder.

There's no reason to go upstairs to the apartment where her seventy-five-year-old mother lives because the boy knows not to intrude—her mother insists on privacy—though he's drawn to the smell of rhubarb and apple pies and sometimes claims the stairs to play with his trucks or an assortment of rocks he arranges in endless combinations. Her mother bakes every day and brings down her treats for the evening meal, especially her famous pies.

The boy is most likely out in the yard or in the woods scrambling about, entertaining himself. He's good at that, at making up stories and play-acting different roles. She can imagine him talking to himself or charging into what must surely be a fierce battle with a stick, whacking at the bushes and pine needles, his arms scratched, his face scowling with determination. Whatever it is, he wants to win. She goes out the back steps and looks in the yard, past the small garden where the wild rhubarb grows, past the perimeter of the yard where the woods begin. Not dense woods, but scrub oaks, maples and pines and lots of bramble. "*Da-vid*," she calls again, louder this time. She isn't angry—it's not in her nature—merely perplexed.

Because he's been with her and John for over two years, she knows the flicker of his smile each morning, then his utter concentration when he tries to corner a frog in the pond or catch a grasshopper near the back door. At night he goes to sleep so suddenly it's as if a trap door opens and he falls through, his body deadweight. He came to them after a "failure to adjust" in his previous foster homes, where he seemed troubled, "unsettled" (his case file said) by both his birth mother's erratic and overly demonstrative visits and his foster mothers' slackness—overwork or incompetence, she doesn't know which. She knows only that he's been in foster care since he was a baby, a child placed again and again, here and there, shifted and shunted from one temporary place to another.

As I sit in the waiting room, I think of my husband as a boy who longed to claim a space for himself, a place of his own rather than one chosen by the authorities—state supervisors, caseworkers, caretakers, doctors—who managed his life. Perhaps in his hiding place he had his first glimpse of autonomy, the pleasure of solitude and protected privacy, good preparation for an imaginative life. He also had the assurance that Aunt Adeline would always search for him, leaving nothing to chance or carelessness.

"Aunt Adeline," I say, surprising David, but also myself; I didn't mean to say her name out loud, but now that I have, I keep going. "Just thinking about her, curious, you know. . . . I always want to know more." *Was she ever afraid of becoming too close to David, a boy on loan who could be taken away in a heartbeat?*

I expect David to make a face, but another surprise: he nods. "Well, she always talked to me," he says as if this is the heart of the matter. He shifts his knee closer to mine. "She taught me my alphabet and my numbers when I was five so I could write my name and read the words on the cereal boxes in the kitchen, especially Cheerios and Corn Flakes, and she"—his voice softens—"she listened while I recited them." He looks at me, then glances away. "She never yelled at me, and made sure I ate breakfast, had clean clothes, and baths every week."

I nod. This seems in some ways elemental: a caretaker who doesn't yell and provides the essentials, but also one who goes a step further, teaching a boy to read and write his name, to complicate himself. I know that when David was a kid, maybe nine or ten, he had a photographic memory, that is, he could watch a thirty-minute TV program, then recite all the lines of dialogue to his three-year-old half-brother, acting out each part—doing the grimaces and hand motions and accents—keeping his attention. He could listen to a recording of songs and remember all the words, the inflection, the pacing, the style, the shifts in syntax. Listening to words jolted his brain; with reading he was slower, slightly dyslexic before schools had resources or therapies for treating this disorder. Still, by the time he was in sixth grade, the school system in Worcester wanted to place him in a school for accelerated students, but when the principal asked for permission from his biological mother and stepfather to move him to that school, his parents refused. "Too much trouble," they said as if education was an inconvenience rather than an opportunity.

I think of Aunt Adeline as the opposite, a woman who recognized a child's stories as his way of making sense of the world, who probably saw learning as necessary, requiring both structure and attention. According to attachment theory, much of the success of a child's attachment depends on the caregiver. "Most children placed with 'autonomous' caregivers formed secure attachments," one of the articles I read noted, defining an autonomous caregiver as someone who saw relationships as meaningful and important, whose acts were responsive and contingent. "From the beginning," his caseworker noted,

"David has responded remarkably well to the foster mother." And it was Aunt Adeline who told the caseworker after David's first month that "he is amenable in every way to her supervision, and she believes he is making an excellent adjustment." The caseworker further wrote, "David has a great deal of affection" in this home, making him feel safe and loved.

Though I know it's romantic—my desire to impose goodness—I imagine Aunt Adeline in her kitchen, dropping soft dough by the spoonful into a simmering broth while David prattles on about his play with Buzzy in the woods. I see her hanging clothes on the line, putting methylate on cuts, tugging off David's cap in church, laughing at a repeated joke. Simple, ordinary acts for a boy who had been moved too many times and needed steadiness and comfort. In the beginning, foster care was referred to as a "waiting room" for the very reason it was meant to be a temporary solution, with temporary parents. But that seldom happens. David stayed over seven years.

"The only time I remember Aunt Adeline getting upset," David says, turning toward me, "was when I trimmed her bedroom curtains even with the sill."

"Uh-oh!" I laugh. "That couldn't be good."

"Yeah, my five-year-old aesthetic."

We both smirk, hiding our smiles. "I think she was surprised as much as anything. You know, just coming into the room and seeing those—" He's about to tell me more when the double doors swing open and the nurse calls out, "David *W*."

And just like that, we stop talking, the past receding, the present demanding our attention as we follow the nurse through the double doors, leaving Aunt Adeline's sheared curtains behind.

For twenty minutes, David and I sit side by side in a small examination room, silent, waiting for Mo, the oncologist, the nurse flitting in, taking David's blood pressure, his temperature, then flitting out. There's no pretense now, the air charged. The test results are about to be revealed, signifying whether cancerous cells are again hiding in his body, perhaps metastasizing to the lungs or the lymph nodes or the liver. We sit quietly, the overhead lights bright and annoying, the examining table formidable. No hiding places here. I feel David's body clench, his knee tight against mine.

"Hello, young people!" Mo's voice booms as he strides into the room. The air softens. Heat rushes to my face. "Everything's looking good," he says, smiling at us as if we've just won a prize while he nods for us to look at the scan on the computer. "You're good to go."

We've seen him for less than five minutes, but we can't leave the hospital fast enough.

HOURS LATER, I'M STILL absorbing Mo's good news while David, exhausted, sprawls on the couch, taking a nap. I too close my eyes, but instead of the doctor's voice, I'm pulled back to the finale of David's story. On the ride home, he picked up his memory of Aunt Adeline, detailing again the shock on her face when she came into the room and saw her curtains, gingham curtains shorn right to the sill, the scissors still in David's hands.

"I made them *even*." That's what he told her. And despite her irritation, I want to imagine she had to suppress a smile because he'd noticed her curtains, limp from monthly washings and hanging in this room for over three years. No one had ever said a word about them. Still, he knew better than to play with scissors. She held out her hand and, reluctantly, he relinquished them. She tried to look stern, but this too was not in her nature. Instead, she sat down on the bed. "Come here, dear."

Once he was seated beside her, they both gazed at the curtains. Strings dangled in places and there was a ragged gap at the end, but otherwise, he'd cut with remarkable consistency. Of course, she'll have to make new ones, but she understood that for him it was probably a way to create order when his own life had so little symmetry. "I know you wanted to do this," she began, "but you must remember to always *ask* permission first. You see, I made these curtains, and they matter to me. I like to open them in the morning, see the sunlight and the sky and then close them tight at night. I was proud of that." She paused, watching his serious face. "And remember our rule about scissors?"

He nodded.

"Now I'm going to put them away, and tonight you will tell Uncle John."

They both knew what that meant. When there was to be punishment, Uncle John was consistent. He simply said, "Start running," and David raced down the hall to the old Singer sewing machine, bent over, and waited for Uncle John to give him one swat on the behind.

"Come along now," she said. "You can help me set the table." He stared fondly at his work, but when she got up, he followed.

WHILE DAVID SLEEPS, I sip a cup of tea, steam rising to my face, softening my breath. On impulse I begin to search online for any information about Aunt Adeline. I can't believe I haven't done this before. I doubt I'll find much, but when a link pops up, I feel a certain pride. Opening it, I discover it's a death notice, a fact that elicits an unexpected ripple of dismay. *Adeline E. Partlow died in Southbridge, Massachusetts, on November 26, 1997, at the age of 88.* There is no obituary. There are no photos. There are no descendants, no survivors. There is no mention of a burial or a grave or a memorial. There is just a single line: a name, a place, a date of death, an age. I print out the page and imagine David adding a necessary word: *Mother.*

Epilogue

IN AN OLD ALBUM I find a black-and-white photo of David. He looks about fifteen. He's standing on the sidewalk in Worcester, wearing a dark suit with a white shirt and a tie, as if dressed for church. Behind him, a white picket fence. His stance suggests reluctance: his hands jammed in his pockets, his feet thrust a little too far apart. His face is sullen, his mouth pressed tight, his eyes resentful. It's an older man's face imposed on a boy's skinny frame; a hopelessness in his gaze makes me turn instantly away.

There's a corresponding picture of me at about the same age, an enlarged portrait that hung for forty years on the far wall of my parents' bedroom in Alabama. Every time I saw it, I'd stop, both pleased and shamed at the mask of social ease on the girl's face. She sits posed in a demure, gold-printed, sleeveless dress, her blue eyes shyly meeting the gaze of the viewer, her blond bouffant hair—a shade lighter than the dress—curled coyly behind one ear. She is smiling, a gracious Southern smile that suggests there might be nothing more important than being right here, looking at you. *Such a poser.*

Of course, it's impossible to imagine being fifteen again, trapped in all that teenage angst and suffering, always wondering if the world will have meaning, and yet what I remember is being depressed, feeling as unreal as if I were encrusted in ice.

"I always thought I was a bad kid," David tells me, when I show him the photo from Worcester. It's a summer evening, the ash trees shading our front yard, the fading light soft in the hot June air.

I nod. "At that age, I thought I was doomed," I say.

We both laugh at the hyperbole.

We're sitting at the table, finishing dinner. All day I've been thinking about my childhood and how rarely I told anyone what I was thinking or feeling, as if I knew intuitively to keep my interior life private. On impulse I ask David if he had anyone to talk to growing up when something happened at school or with friends.

"I never told anyone anything," he says quickly. He looks surprised at the idea. "I thought I was the person they said I was at home."

Trapped.

I look out the window, watching the night darken. If I opened the window, I'd hear the frantic buzz of cicadas, a startling sound that would pull me back to the past, the swampland of Alabama. I too remember feeling trapped, perhaps in temperament more than circumstances, as if something in my makeup didn't fit the story around me. My music teacher, Mama Dot, said I once confessed that I felt like myself *only* when I first woke up in the morning. I was ten. So many hours of the day to get through. By the time I was fifteen, I thought I lived under a social microscope, appearing inadequate and insufficient, a not-rightness I didn't know how to correct. To be a Southern girl in my family meant not only to make A's but also to be popular and optimistic and charismatic, and yet the social part seemed elusive, perplexing to me. I never told my family I was lonely. Instead, I put on a mask.

"I didn't tell my mother or Soup *anything*," David repeats, bringing me back to the conversation. I remember that the foster care files noted how easily he chatted in Aunt Adeline's kitchen.

By age ten, everything had changed.

No one listening.

Silence as protection.

The hiding place.

PERHAPS THE HIDING PLACE was necessary for both of us. The trapped boy. The masked girl. It was a place to keep ourselves secret. A place where we weren't defined by others' demands or judgments. A place of refuge. A release! How exhausting to continually perform self-sufficiency! In the hiding place, I like to think that, for both David and me, our imaginations survived and in a small way we had power. *You can't know me. I am hidden from you. Here I am me.* And yet I also recognize that protection is a defensive act, a resistance: beneath it lies fear and resentment, confusion, and anger. Once anger stirs, there's a release to a future, but also a noose: how can you not be furious at yourself for having once been so dependent?

Only here, writing this, do I begin to see the hiding place not just as protective cover but also as a formative psychology. It's possible that what David and I both learned in childhood was never to need anyone so badly that we'd feel dependent. A kind of reactionary autonomy: intimacy tied to constraint; self-preservation as a first instinct. Not long ago I found this sentence in one of my journals: *I haven't allowed myself to love deeply, heedlessly, without expectation. I don't mean that I haven't loved at all, but there's this barrier to something deeper, something bottomless and big, something that could sweep me away.* I wrote that over thirty-five years ago during a bad period, but when I read it today, I recognize myself. I learned to keep people at a distance while appearing intimate and engaged, another strategy of self-preservation. If you believe that other people can be poisonous, then you are rightly terrified of their power. It is the old story of a tentative commitment—I will only go so far.

Is it possible, I wonder, to step beyond self-protection?

THOUGH I DON'T BELIEVE that individual moments change lives as cleanly, as poetically as epiphanies in fiction, there *are* moments of pause, moments that startle one's consciousness, allowing old patterns to shift and resolve.

I think back to the walk we took on Easter Sunday, a week after David came home from the hospital. It's not the surprise of David telling a neighbor that he's a cancer survivor that stays with me, but something more intimate. That day I remember the air soft and clean, smells of freshly cut grass, trees coming to leaf, pollen blowing across the street. The sun drapes its warmth around us, the sky a painter's blue. I'm on David's right side, my arm tucked into his like a woman in a nineteenth-century novel might do as we walk in tandem. I hold him close—"The Clutch," I call it—though mostly I'm looking down, worrying about gaps in the sideway, erosion from rain and snow that might trip us. Because I'm intent on safeguarding us from danger, I'm surprised by David's voice.

"I've always wanted you to do this," he whispers, tightening his grip on my arm.

"To be your girl?"

"Yeah."

"And here I am."

Though we're making light of it, this is the moment of pause, of loosening, the moment when I see clearly what my husband is saying: he's been waiting for me to protect and claim him and publicly show that claim. Since I've spent most of my life focused on trying to claim myself, I haven't been able to see that this small but intimate act is the necessary bonding. Today, on this day of grace, we make a slow promenade arm in arm around the block, past Boo's house with the fluted white petals of a Japanese honeysuckle twining up her black lamppost, past new shoots of hostas, bright green and stalky, bursting up in clusters in the next yard. As we walk, a little piece of my armor cracks, my mind lighter, the rhythm of our steps mirroring the rhythm of our spirits.

What we have both wanted is for someone strong to love us, someone with a firm heart and a willful mind, a person who would stand up and say "mine." Today, walking arm in arm, we've become those people.

ALL LOVE STORIES ARE subjective and universal, euphoric and conflicted. There isn't one relationship I know of where trust hasn't been questioned, where generosity hasn't been thwarted, where misperception and miscommunication haven't jeopardized the story, sometimes beyond repair. Even as I write this, I know that David would tell our story differently. He'd remember separate moments and emphasize other terms of mattering. He'd put a different spin on things, find humor in odd corners, crank up the volume in others. Perhaps our story has infinite permutations. So many things could be resurrected and reimagined, so many things analyzed and questioned, and yet this—what I've told—is what matters to me.

Of course, we still have arguments, still verbally push and shove at each other so that the "we" of us catches in my throat. I can't swallow it down, can't cough it out. In such times, I'm angry at the loss of ease between us as much as the disagreement itself. I want to be done with worrying, to be free of fury. *Marriage is just hard*, I think, *who am I kidding*?

But then one of us will say, "Let's not do this," and we begin to sort it out. We do this much quicker now, not dragging out the fight, not pouting and punishing as if there must be a winner take all.

More than that, I surprise myself with where my mind wants to go. I'm sitting in David's study where we're watching a movie. When I turn to him, I notice the skin beneath his right eye sags, a tiny fold I could tighten with one finger. It gives his face a kind of bruised tenderness, the look of a man intelligent and aging. At a certain point, youth is much less interesting, less risky and moving. I look around me. David's study is cluttered with stacks and stacks of art prints, some spilling onto the floor; his comfort clothes and underwear are folded and layered on a sofa cushion. Oh, dear, he's using that cushion for a dresser again. It usually makes me sigh, but today, I don't care. I simply put one leg over his and let it dangle. What I want is to be right here in the middle of the middle of my life: a seventy-year-old woman, still writing, with a husband who makes her laugh.

Later, when I glance out the window, the sky is smoky, the light still edged with blue, the crickets gathering. Soon, it will be night.

Acknowledgments

I'd like to express my gratitude to Crux, the nonfiction series at the University of Georgia Press, and especially to Nicole Walker, nonfiction series editor; Sarah Shermyen, acquisitions editor; and Bethany Snead, acquisitions coordinator. I also want to thank the Fairhope Center for the Writing Arts and the Inaugural Writing Residency at Sun Yat-sen University, where portions of this book were written and edited.

Most importantly, my deep appreciation to David, my husband, for his enduring love and faith in me. Without his commitment to uncovering the hidden story of his past and his permission to write about our marriage, this book could not have been written. "Navigator CF (control freak!) thanks you every day of her life."

For their friendship, support, and reading of portions of this book, I want to thank Marilyn Abildskov, Linda Bauer, Kathryn Ann Ford, Robin Hemley, Laura Julier, Jody Keisner, Jay Lamar, Patrick Madden, Jim McKean, and Kris Vervaecke.

For their expertise and kindness in treating David at the University of Iowa Departments of Oncology and Plastic Surgery, I want to thank Mohammed Milhem, MBBS, and Dr. Wei Chen (now at Cleveland Clinic).

In a slightly different form:

One chapter in this book won a Pushcart Prize (*Ploughshares*).

Three chapters were named Notable Essays in *The Best American Essays* series.

One chapter won the Theodore Hoepfner Award.

Chapters were published or are forthcoming in *Colorado Review*, *Ploughshares*, *Antioch Review*, *Southern Humanities Review*, *Florida Review*, *The Sun*, *Fourth Genre*, *The Linden Review*, and *The Examined Life*.

Personal information about my husband's foster care, parenting, and childhood were provided in documents from the Commonwealth of Massachusetts Executive Office of Health and Human Services, Department of Children and Families, Boston, Mass.

Ancestry.com was also consulted.

Notes

Chapter 14

125–26 **In unhappy marriages . . . for imaginative dominance:** Phyllis Rose, *Parallel Lives: Five Victorian Marriages* (London: Chatto & Windus, The Hogarth Press, 1984), 7.

Chapter 16

140 **I read recently . . . out of old:** Jeneen Interlandi, "A Revolutionary Approach to Treating PTSD," *New York Times Magazine*, 2014, p. 12 (quoting Bessel Van der Kolk).

140 **The story of . . . impact on life:** Cathy Caruth, *Unclaimed Experience: Trauma, Narrative & History* (Baltimore: Johns Hopkins University Press, 1996), 7.

141 **Freud believed . . . past the censors:** Caruth, *Unclaimed Experience*, 97.

Chapter 17

144 **What I'm listening to . . . changes in the brain:** Jon Hamilton, "Childhood Maltreatment Can Leave Scars in the Brain," *All Things Considered*, NPR (November 4, 2013).

144 **It's been several . . . involved in processing fear:** Jon Hamilton, "Childhood Maltreatment Can Leave Scars in the Brain," *All Things Considered*, NPR (November 4, 2013).

144–45 **At home, I read . . . later in life:** Vincent J. Felitti, "Adverse Childhood Experience and Stress: Paying the Piper," *ACE Reporter* 1, no. 4 (Spring 2007): 1.

145 **From the study . . . men and women:** Vincent J. Felitti, "The ACE Study: Depression & Suicide," *ACE Reporter* 1, no. 3 (Winter 2006): 2.

145 **Experiencing any . . . chronic fatigue syndrome:** Tracie O. Afifi et al., "Child Abuse and Physical Health in Adulthood," *Health Reports* 27, no. 3:10–18. Statistics Canada.

146 ***While you were* . . . went to prison:** ACE Study Questions: "ACEs & Trauma: ACEs Score," Pinetree Institute, Pinetree Institute Learning Center, Eliot, Maine, https://pinetreeinstitute.org/aces-test/.

147 **While you were growing . . . support each other:** ACE Study Questions: "ACES & Trauma: ACES Score," Pinetree Institute, Pinetree Institute Learning Center,Eliot, Maine, https://pinetreeinstitute.org/aces-test/.

Chapter 24

193 **Each move means . . . *End of June*:** Cris Beam, *To the End of June: The Intimate Life of American Foster Care* (New York: Mariner Books, 2014), 35.

193 **Days later, I'm shocked . . . as war veterans:** Candice Plotkin, "Study Finds Foster Kids Suffer PTSD," *Harvard Crimson* April 11, 2005.

194 **very reactive to . . . with other children:** Mary Dozier et al., "Attachment Behavioral Catch-Up: The ABCs of Helping Infants in Foster Care Cope with Early Adversity," *Zero to Three*, no. 5 (2002): 10.

Chapter 26

203 **the most dramatic for those . . . at an early age:** Hope Edelman, *Motherless Mothers: How Mother Loss Shapes the Parents We Become* (New York, HarperCollins, 2006), xxvi.

Chapter 31

238 **Most children placed . . . responsive and contingent:** Mary Dozier et al., "Attachment Behavioral Catch-Up: The ABCs of Helping Infants in Foster Care Cope with Early Adversity, *Zero to Three*, no. 5 (2002): 10.

Selected Bibliography

Books

Beam, Cris. *To the End of June: The Intimate Life of American Foster Care*. New York: Mariner Books, 2014.

Caruth, Cathy. *Unclaimed Experience: Trauma, Narrative, and History*. Baltimore: Johns Hopkins University Press, 1996.

Coutts, Marion. *The Iceberg*. New York: Black Cat, 2014.

Edelman, Hope. *Motherless Mothers: How Losing a Mother Shapes the Parent You Become*. New York: Harper Perennial, 2007.

Harris, Nadine Burke. *The Deepest Well*. New York: Mariner Books, 2019.

Herman, Judith. *Trauma and Recovery*. New York: Basic Books, 1997.

Jaouad, Suleika. *Between Two Kingdoms: A Memoir of a Life Interrupted*. New York: Random House, 2021.

Rose, Phyllis. *Parallel Lives: Five Victorian Marriages*. London: Chatto & Windus, The Hogarth Press, 1984.

Van Der Kolk, Bessel. *The Body Keeps the Score*. New York: Penguin, 2014.

Articles

Afifi, Tracie O., et al. "Child Abuse and Physical Health in Adulthood." *Health Reports,* 27, no. 3 (2016): 10–18. Statistics Canada.

Belin, E., et al. "Factors in the Surgical Management of Primary Eccrine Porocarcinoma: Prognostic Histological Factors Can Guide Surgical Procedures." *British Journal of Dermatology 165* (2011): 985–989.

Berghaus, Barry J. "A New Look at Attachment Theory and Adult Attachment Behavior." *Behaviorology Today* 14, no. 12 (Fall 2011): 3–10.

Bowers, Mallory E., et al. "Intergenerational Transmission of Stress in Humans." *Neuropsychopharmacology 41* (2016): 232–244.

Conway, Martin A., et al. "The Construction of Autobiographical Memoirs in the Self-Memory System." *Psychological Review 107, no. 2* (2000): 261–288.

Dozier, Mary, et al. "Attachment and Behavioral Catch-up: The ABCs of Helping

Infants in Foster Care Cope with Early Adversity." *Zero to Three* 22, no. 5 (2002): 10
Felitti, Vincent J., and Robert F. Anda. "Adverse Childhood Experiences and Stress: Paying the Piper." *ACE Reporter* 1, no. 4 (2007): 1–4.
Felitti, Vincent J., et al. "Relationship of Childhood Abuse and Household Dysfunction to Many of the Leading Causes of Deaths in Adults." From *The Adverse Childhood Experiences Study. American Journal of Preventive Medicine* 14, no. 4 (1998): 245–258.
Gubar, Susan. "Living with Cancer: A Quilt of Poetry." *New York Times,* July 25, 2013.
Herringa, Ryan, et al. "Childhood Maltreatment Is Associated with Altered Fear Circuits and Increased Internalizing Symptoms by Late Adolescence." *PNAS* (2013): 1–3.
Holman, Dawn M., et al. (Division of Cancer Prevention and Control, Centers for Disease Control and Prevention). "The Association Between Adverse Childhood Experiences and the Risk of Cancer in Adulthood: A Systematic Review of the Literature." *Pediatrics,* supplement 1, vol. 138 (November 2016): 581–559.
Interlandi, Jeneen. "A Revolutionary Approach to Treating PTSD." *New York Times,* May 22, 2014, 1–9.
Irving, Michelle Kelly, Benoit LePage, et al. "Childhood Adversity as a Risk for Cancer: Findings from the 1958 British Birth Cohort Study." *BMC Public Health* 13 (2013): 767.
Keding, Taylor J., et al. "Abnormal Structure of Fear Circuitry in Pediatric Post-Traumatic Stress Disorder." *Neuropsychopharmacology* (2014): 1–9.
Mandel, Betty Reid. "Foster Care." *New Politics* 11, no. 1 (2013). http://newpol.org.
Plotkin, Candice. "Study Finds Foster Kids Suffer PTSD." *Harvard Crimson,* April 11, 2005, 1–6.
Robson, A., et al. "Eccrine Porocarcinoma: A Clinicopathologic Study of 69 Cases." *American Journal of Surgical Pathology* 25 (2001): 710–720.
Schorr, Nanette. "Foster Care and the Politics of Compassion." In *Family Matters: Readings on Family Lives and the Law*, ed. Martha Minow, 117–24. New Press, New York: 1993.
Shaw, M., et al. "Malignant Eccrine Poroma: A Study of Twenty-Seven Cases." *British Journal of Dermatology* 107 (1982): 675–80.

CRUX, THE GEORGIA SERIES IN LITERARY NONFICTION

Debra Monroe, *My Unsentimental Education*

Sonja Livingston, *Ladies Night at the Dreamland*

Jericho Parms, *Lost Wax: Essays*

Priscilla Long, *Fire and Stone: Where Do We Come From? What Are We? Where Are We Going?*

Sarah Gorham, *Alpine Apprentice*

Tracy Daugherty, *Let Us Build Us a City*

Brian Doyle, *Hoop: A Basketball Life in Ninety-Five Essays*

Michael Martone, *Brooding: Arias, Choruses, Lullabies, Follies, Dirges, and a Duet*

Andrew Menard, *Learning from Thoreau*

Dustin Parsons, *Exploded View: Essays on Fatherhood, with Diagrams*

Clinton Crockett Peters, *Pandora's Garden: Kudzu, Cockroaches, and Other Misfits of Ecology*

André Joseph Gallant, *A High Low Tide: The Revival of a Southern Oyster*

Justin Gardiner, *Beneath the Shadow: Legacy and Longing in the Antarctic*

Emily Arnason Casey, *Made Holy: Essays*

Sejal Shah, *This Is One Way to Dance: Essays*

Lee Gutkind, *My Last Eight Thousand Days: An American Male in His Seventies*

Cecile Pineda, *Entry without Inspection: A Writer's Life in El Norte*

Anjali Enjeti, *Southbound: Essays on Identity, Inheritance, and Social Change*

Clinton Crockett Peters, *Mountain Madness: Found and Lost in the Peaks of America and Japan*

Steve Majors, *High Yella: A Modern Family Memoir*

Julia Ridley Smith, *The Sum of Trifles*

Siân Griffiths, *The Sum of Her Parts: Essays*

Ned Stuckey-French, *One by One, the Stars: Essays*

John Griswold, *The Age of Clear Profit: Collected Essays on Home and the Narrow Road*

Debra Monroe, *It Takes a Worried Woman: Essays*

Joseph Geha, *Kitchen Arabic: How My Family Came to America and the Recipes We Brought with Us*

Lawrence Lenhart, *Backvalley Ferrets: A Rewilding of the Colorado Plateau*

Sarah Beth Childers, *Prodigals: A Sister's Memoir of Appalachia*

Jodi Varon, *Your Eyes Will Be My Window: Essays*

Sandra Gail Lambert, *My Withered Legs and Other Essays*

Brooke Champagne, *Nola Face: Memoirs of a Truth-Telling Latina in the Big Easy*

Maddie Norris, *The Wet Wound: An Elegy in Essays*

Cris Mazza, *The Decade of Letting Things Go: A Postmenopause Memoir*

Lydia Paar, *The Exit Is the Entrance: Essays on Escape*

Joe Bonomo, *Play This Book Loud: Noisy Essays*

Wes Jamison, *My Corpse Inside*

Clifford Thompson, *Jazz June: A Self-Portrait in Essays*

Ashley Anderson, *Sifting the Feminine: Essays on a Woman's Body*

Yelizaveta P. Renfro, *The Season of Birds and Stones: Essays*

Alison Kinney, *United States of Rejection: A Story of Love, Hate, and Hope*

Patricia Foster, *A Marriage in Startled Air: A Memoir*